# THE ADVOCATE'S DESKBOOK:

## THE ESSENTIALS OF TRYING A CASE

# THE ADVOCATE'S DESKBOOK:

## THE ESSENTIALS OF TRYING A CASE

# IRVING YOUNGER

 PRENTICE HALL LAW & BUSINESS

Printed in the United States of America

**Second Printing, October 1989**

**Library of Congress Cataloging-in-Publication Data**

Younger, Irving
    The advocate's deskbook.

    Includes index.
    1. Trial practice — United States.  I. Title.
KF8915.Y68 1988                     347.73'7                     88-25286
ISBN 0-13-018169-2                  347.3077

# Contents

# Foreword

Irving Younger, the master of the vivid lecture, decided several years ago to preserve his most important insights on trial practice and evidence in a form that could not only be studied at leisure but, unlike video and audio tape recordings, could be used for easy reference and, if need be, carried into court. Professor Younger completed his initial manuscript for "The Advocate's Deskbook," and the work was edited by senior editor Larry Lempert. At the time of Professor Younger's tragic death of cancer, at age 55, in March 1988, he was still in the midst of fine-tuning the manuscript in the fashion characteristic of an artist who always strove to give his public the best work possible.

After conferring with his wife, Judith Younger, herself an esteemed law professor, we at Prentice Hall Law & Business believe that publication of Irving Younger's work is a fitting memorial to the profession's most highly regarded advocacy teacher.

We fully recognize that Professor Younger would have continued to improve his prose, as he did whenever he took pen to paper; the author of a regular column on persuasive writing could do no less. Yet, the manuscript in its substantially completed form is a legacy to the Bar and aspiring lawyers.

We have made every effort to incorporate his latest thinking, as refected in his notations on the edited manuscript and, in the case of scientific evidence (Sections 6.4 and 6.5), an update that was prepared under his direction based on his lecture on the subject.

We are confident that this volume is as faithful as possible to his vision of the book. If the book falls short of the perfection Irving Younger would have wrought had he continued to refine it, nonetheless many generations of lawyers and students will be the richer, given this opportunity to partake deeply of Irving Younger's philosophy, his practical wisdom, and his colorful style.

Stephen A. Glasser
Lynn S. Glasser
Co-Publishers

# About the Author

Irving Younger, 1932-1988, was the nation's foremost speaker on advocacy, trial practice, evidence, and civil procedure. He was popular among thousands of lawyers and law students who saw or heard his lectures for his insight, the clarity of his presentation, and his marvelous, wry sense of humor.

Irving Younger was the Marvin J. Sonosky Professor of Law at the University of Minnesota Law School in Minneapolis. He had previously taught at the Cornell Law School, where he was the Samuel S. Leibowitz Professor of Trial Techniques, and at the Columbia, Georgetown, Harvard, and New York University law schools.

He had also been a practitioner and judge, as well as a teacher of the law. He practiced with New York's Paul, Weiss, Rifkind, Wharton & Garrison; served as an Assistant U.S. Attorney in the Southern District of New York; practiced law with his wife, Judith Younger, in New York; served as a judge on the Civil, Criminal, and Supreme Courts of New York City; and practiced at Washington, D.C.'s Williams & Connolly.

Professor Younger graduated from Harvard University in 1953 and the New York University School of Law in 1958. Previous writings include a book co-authored with Michael Goldsmith, *Principles of Evidence* (National Practice Institute, 1984), and his monthly column on persuasive writing for the *American Bar Association Journal*.

# CHAPTER 1

# The Craft of Advocacy

## §1.1 Trial Techniques: An Introduction

Certain of my own beliefs about the trial of a lawsuit inform everything that follows. In the interest of full disclosure, I must make those personal convictions explicit.

First, the trial of a lawsuit is an art. Like every other art, it involves a combination of two elements. Done well, it requires talent, inspiration, or whatever else we choose to call it — that God-given spark that makes Rembrandt uniquely Rembrandt. But to try a case well also demands technique. Even Rembrandt once had to learn to mix paints and hold a brush. Talent probably cannot be taught — it is too closely intertwined with every other aspect of an individual's personality — but technique is accessible to anyone. It is technique, then, that will occupy our attention here.

Neither talent nor technique alone marks the better lawyer. The masters, of course, combine both in ample measure. But among the rest of us, a lawyer with less talent than another may prove to be the more effective advocate of the two. He may prepare more carefully, conduct a more thorough factual and legal investigation, and be more sensitive to the delicate interplay of psychology in the courtroom. Thorough preparation in particular is indispensable. Nothing can ever substitute for it.

It is my second conviction that the craft of advocacy is independent of the jurisdiction, be it federal or state. The craft is likewise independent of the nature of the case, whether it be criminal, commercial, tort, domestic relations, or anything else. And the craft is independent of which side the lawyer represents. Plaintiff, prosecutor, defense — it makes no difference. The techniques are the same.

Third, I see the craft of advocacy as occupying a space between two other bodies of learning: the law of evidence on one side, and the law of procedure on the other. Despite some overlap at the margins, the craft of advocacy is independent of and distinct from these other two.

Fourth and last, the craft of advocacy can rarely offer any one correct solution to a problem. Too much depends upon imponderables: the lawyer's personality, the opponent's personality, the juxtaposition of the two; the personality and style of the judge; the feel of the courtroom; the jury in the box; the witness on the stand. No single answer can possibly make sense under all circumstances and for all lawyers. Nor can the uncertainties be charged in any way against the craft itself. A trial simply sets up too many unpredictable factors to allow for right and wrong answers.

There are, however, considered answers and unconsidered answers. A considered answer is one upon which a lawyer has brought to bear all of his experience, a sense of his own personality, and the best of his intelligence. Even a considered answer may not work, but it is the most that a lawyer owes himself. The most common mistake is to make an unconsidered decision — one that has not been thought about sufficiently or at all. Every lawyer must work the problems through and come up with his own answers. From time to time in the following pages, I will give my own answers. If they prove useful to others, so much the better. But if my answers do not suit another's personality and approach, then he must reject what I say and arrive at more appropriate solutions.

This caveat also takes a more general form. It is an error to take on a pattern of behavior that is unnatural — to adopt any personality other than one's own. In fact, it cannot be done; the mistake is to try. Jurors will quite rightly perceive the effort as an attempt to put something over on them, and they will react accordingly. It is far wiser to discover the strong points of one's own personality, and to learn to use them effectively. In short, know thyself.

At the same time, there is an important bound on the expression of one's own personality in the courtroom, a limitation that goes to the heart of advocacy. It is unprofessional for lawyers to make any direct statements before the jury that reflect their own beliefs about the cause they are advocating. The rule obviously creates some difficulty. A good advocate is precisely one who succeeds in leading the jury to share his beliefs — in particular, the belief that the client should prevail in the case. But it is not permissible to express that belief in so many words: "I think my client had the green light." Instead, one must plead the client's cause indirectly. The rule regulates the form and manner of the lawyer's advocacy; it does not prevent him from displaying indirectly a commitment to the client's cause.

The reader will note that everything in these pages presupposes a jury in the jury box. If a lawyer knows how to try a case to a jury, then he also knows how to try a case to a judge. In contrast to the complexities of a jury trial, a bench trial is easy.

The reader will also observe that these chapters include a variety of checklists. In many situations, these should eliminate the need to reinvent the wheel. On the other hand, while a checklist represents the universe of possibilities, it cannot tell you what choice to make. That necessarily requires judgment, common sense, and a familiarity with the circumstances of the case. The checklist merely helps by setting down all of the alternatives. Its utility is to free attention for the more important and creative aspects of trying the case.

## §1.2 The Function of a Trial

The function of a trial, in part, is to provide a forum in which lawyers can attempt to prove whatever facts are necessary to their case. This book will discuss the process of proof at some length. But we should note at the outset that a trial is more than an opportunity for proving facts. A trial is among the most complex of human institutions, fulfilling a variety of important purposes. It is — in some respects, at least — a disinterested search for the truth. It is a major form of popular entertainment; the trial lawyer must always bear in mind that what goes on in the courtroom is much akin to what goes on in the theater. A trial also is a kind of ritual, a way society has evolved for getting over today's crisis and on to tomorrow. And it is a civic ceremony by which government is made manifest and palpable so that the citizenry can actually see it.

These are aspects of a trial that will appeal primarily to philosophers and law professors. For the working trial lawyer, what goes on in the courtroom involves another purpose. The trial lawyer always bears in mind that a courtroom is not reality. Reality is "out there," the accident or business transaction or crime that constitutes the subject matter of the lawsuit. What the trial lawyer does in the courtroom is to build a model, more or less accurate, of the real world transaction the case is about.

The blueprint for that model is furnished by the substantive law applicable to the case. The law of evidence is the set of rules by which a lawyer builds the model.[1] It is the doctrinal foundation upon which the lawyer stands. One cannot function in the courtroom without it. Possessing it, and given a good grasp of the techniques of advocacy, a lawyer is ready to begin trying cases.

---

[1]To understand the formal rules of proof, it is important to appreciate that the word "evidence" is used in three wholly different senses by trial lawyers.

First, the word "evidence" stands for the body of rules that go under the collective name of the law of evidence, the rules that govern the process of proof in a courtroom. Second, "evidence" can refer to the proof itself, the materials upon which the rules of evidence work. Third, we speak of our proof being "received in evidence," which means that the process has taken such a turn that the evidence, in the second sense of the word, is actually before the finder of fact, the judge or jury, for its consideration. It means that the finder of fact might properly and legitimately rely upon this evidence in coming to a conclusion in the case.

Most of what this book has to say about evidence deals with the law of evidence (first meaning), the way in which the lawyer brings it about that something is put into evidence (third meaning). There is little of use to say about evidence in the second sense of the word — the stuff itself, the proof, the raw materials that the lawyer uses in the courtroom — because the content of litigation is not law, it is human nature. And so it is that the possibilities of proof are infinite.

## §1.3 What Is a Good Trial Lawyer?

The quality of the lawyer counts for more in litigation than it does in any other branch of the profession. There are lawyers whose work consists of writing registration statements to be filed with the Securities and Exchange Commission. Beyond whatever minimum level of competence it takes for the SEC to accept the registration, the quality of work hardly matters. Furthermore, many investors do not read prospectuses; lawyers write prospectuses for other lawyers. But the courtroom is different. There, the quality of counsel is all-important.

Clients may not always be rational people, but by and large their lawyers are. When the client comes to the lawyer with a dispute, and the lawyer sees only one possible resolution, usually that dispute will not go to trial. Instead there will be a settlement, or a guilty plea, or a withdrawal of the indictment, or some other resolution. Thus, when a dispute does go to trial, most often it is because there is no predetermined correct result. Everything then depends on how things work out in the courtroom.

The trial is an exquisitely subtle method of resolving disputes. Truth has some bearing on what happens in the courtroom, but there are other factors as well. Consider, for example, the exclusionary rules and the various privileges. These seek to achieve certain social objectives, but they do so at the cost of impeding our determination of the truth. Such rules exclude perfectly truthful evidence because, under some circumstances, we value other social objectives more highly than we do the truth.

Given a genuinely triable issue, the outcome cannot be determined in advance on the merits. But it can sometimes be determined on a different basis: With a good lawyer on one side and a bad lawyer on the other side, the good lawyer will always win. And that raises a potentially troubling question. Good lawyers tend to be more expensive than bad lawyers. As a result, a rich litigant should always win over a not-so-rich litigant. That would indeed be disturbing, but in the real world of litigation the problem seldom arises. It is rare, in practice, to have a good lawyer against a bad lawyer. Far more often we have bad lawyers on both sides. With the lawyers thus evenly matched, the system works.

Rarest of all is the third possibility: good lawyers on both sides, with a presiding judge who knows how to conduct a trial. A day at such a trial will be more instructive than anything I can set down in these pages. It will make you proud of your profession. And it is astonishing to watch, because it moves along faster and more quietly than anyone might think possible. There are very few objections, for reasons discussed below.[2] When a lawyer does object, the judge does not make a speech or request a sidebar conference to agonize over whether he should overrule or sustain. He simply rules and moves on. A good judge knows that to a good trial lawyer, the rhythm is more important than the ruling, and so he keeps it on the beat.

Having said that good lawyers win more cases than bad lawyers, I ought next to define what constitutes a good lawyer. But I cannot do that, and I doubt that anyone can. There is no handy recipe for becoming a good trial lawyer. Good ones are instantly recognizable, to be sure; watching a number of lawyers at work, we can all agree on who the good ones are. And yet we cannot pin down just why it is that we choose them.

Let me attempt to solve the problem indirectly, by way of a metaphor. As a boy, I spent many of my summer days in what was probably the safest and least expensive place in New York City accessible by trolley car: Yankee Stadium. Watching the games was a major part of my childhood. This interest was to serve me well, because after college I became a sports reporter covering the New York Giants baseball team for the *New York Daily Mirror*. My job was to follow the photographer around, taking notes for captions for the pictures.

At the end of the day, still full of enthusiasm from the game and too excited to go home, I sat in the corner of the city room devoted to the sports section and talked with my older and wiser colleagues. "Today I saw Willie Mays make the most incredible catch!" I would say. "He was running, and he was twenty feet from the fence, and it was too late to stop! So he turned himself into a human doughnut, and he rolled right up to the fence! And as he rolled he got his glove up between his legs and he caught

---

[2]See Chapter 14.

the ball! Willie Mays has to be the best center fielder who ever lived!"

"No," my colleagues would say. "Willie's pretty good. But the best center fielder who ever lived was Joe DiMaggio."

"You're out of your mind!" I would say. "I spent my whole childhood watching Joe DiMaggio play ball, and not once did I ever see him make the kind of catch Willie Mays makes three times a day!"

"That's right," they would say. "Joe DiMaggio never once made an incredible catch. You see, when the batter would hit the ball anywhere in the outfield, as the ball reached the peak of its trajectory and began its descent to the ground, there, standing idly under it, tapping his glove, breathing quite normally, was Joe DiMaggio. He put out his glove; the ball infallibly landed in his glove; and with an almost insolent grace he returned the ball to the infield, hence permitting the game to resume. That," said my older and wiser colleagues, "was the best center fielder who ever lived."

The more I thought about it, the more I concluded that they were right. And that image of Joe DiMaggio playing center field is the most vivid picture I can draw of what it means to be an able trial lawyer.

When DiMaggio in his prime was playing center field and the ball was hit to the outfield, we all knew what was going to happen. It was not at all like the surface excitement of wondering if Willie Mays would make the catch. Instead, DiMaggio exuded a sublime confidence. When the ball went to the outfield, even the pitcher would not bother to turn around. He was already thinking about the next batter. DiMaggio was utterly reliable. He had the trustworthiness that marks the ultimate professional.

Every good trial lawyer gets across to the jury that same quality of absolute reliability and trustworthiness. In the law, it has many facets. It means technical proficiency, professionalism, knowing the job. And most important, it means always telling the jury the truth.

Given a genuinely triable controversy with no predetermined correct result, the jury chooses, consciously or not, between the lawyers. The lawyer who strikes the jury as more trustworthy

7

is the lawyer who will win. The good lawyer is one who can communicate to the jury his or her own trustworthiness. And that is why good lawyers win more cases than bad lawyers.

# CHAPTER 2

# Facts

## §2.1 A Taxonomy of Facts

"The facts of a case": Each of us heard the phrase during the first law school class we attended. "Mr. Smith," the instructor in Torts may have said, "What were the facts in *Brown v. Kendall?*"[1] Or in Property, "Miss Jones, state the facts of *Armory v. Delamirie.*"[2] And we palpatingly did, thus commencing a progress in subtlety that marks both the development of a lawyer and the growth of the law.

"The facts were," recites Mr. Smith, "that Kendall tried to separate two fighting dogs by beating them with a stick. He raised the stick over his shoulder and struck Brown in the eye. Brown sued Kendall for the resulting damages." Says Miss Jones: "In the *Armory* case, a chimney sweep found a jewel in the dust. He took it to a jeweler to be examined, and when the jeweler refused to return it, sued for it in King's Bench."

Mr. Smith and Miss Jones know that these are the facts of the case because the opinion in the casebook says that they are. How the author of the opinion came by these facts is a question beyond the comprehension of Mr. Smith and Miss Jones on that

---

[1] 60 Mass. (6 Cush.) 292 (1850).
[2] 1 Strange 505 (K.B. 1722).

first day of law school, and understandably so. The facts, we tend to think at the beginning, are like acorns on an oak tree. When they are ripe, they drop to the ground. If you want some, just bend down and pick them up. Observe how they are arranged: Should they fall into the pattern we designate "negligence," Brown wins his suit against Kendall. If the pattern is that of one of the bundle of rights called "property," Armory prevails over Delamirie. Why, there's nothing to it but learning the patterns — that, at least, is what teachers of the law seem to have thought for a very long time.[3]

With experience and reflection comes a deeper understanding. Facts do not grow on trees, we learn. They must be investigated and proved. Sometimes the facts fall into a preexisting pattern, but sometimes a pattern is devised to fit their configuration, whatever that happens to be.. The facts, in short, are just as obscure as the law, just as malleable, just as controversial, and, in determining the outcome of a lawsuit or the elaboration of a rule, they are more important than paltry logic. This each lawyer must learn, and this teachers of the law began to learn about half a century ago.[4]

Even now, there is something of the acorn on the oak tree about the way we look at facts. "Facts are obscure, malleable, controversial, and important, of course," we say to ourselves, "but when you finally get down to it, a fact is a fact." It is a single category or class of things; as the Oxford English Dictionary tells us, facts in the context of law are the "circumstances or incidents of a case, looked at apart from their legal bearing." If this is too general, one might follow Jeremy Bentham in assigning facts to one of two categories. A fact, says Bentham, is either a state of things, that is, an existence, or a motion, that is, an event.[5]

Surely, things as interesting as facts are something more than

---

[3]*E.g.*, said Dean Christopher Columbus Langdell of Harvard in 1886: "First, that law is a science; second, that all the available materials of that science are contained in printed books." Centennial History of the Harvard Law School 1817-1917, at 231 (1918).

[4]*See, e.g,* J. Frank, Law and the Modern Mind (1930).

[5]This puts into a sentence the burden of a long section of the Rationale of Judicial Evidence. 6 Jeremy Bentham's Works 217 (Bowring ed. 1843).

merely *that*. It certainly is possible to talk about facts with greater sharpness of point and edge than do the dictionary and the philosopher. Among the host of the tribe of facts are no fewer than ten separate types.

**First.** Through the five senses of sight, hearing, touch, taste, and smell, we receive data from the world outside us. When someone takes the stand and testifies to what he saw, heard, touched, tasted, or smelled, the witness is presenting to the judge or jury a fact of the first sort: a fact that was the object of a witness's sensory perceptions. In the trial of *Brown v. Kendall,* a witness might testify that he saw two dogs fight, that Kendall stepped between them, that he raised his stick over his shoulder, and that the stick hit Brown in the eye. In the trial of *Armory v.. Delamirie,* a witness might testify that he saw the chimney sweep pick a jewel out of the gutter, that he accompanied the sweep to the jeweler, and that the sweep gave the jewel to the jeweler, who refused to give it back. Facts of the first sort were once virtually the only sort of fact likely to be encountered in litigation. Today, though, it is not uncommon to run into any of the nine other sorts.

**Second.** The fact in this category would be a fact of the first sort — the object of a witness's sensory perceptions — save that the witness's perceptions were aided or enhanced by some device in ordinary use. For example, the witness says that, through a pair of binoculars, he watched the airplane fly into the side of a distant mountain; or the witness says that, although he is appallingly nearsighted, he was able to see the stop sign some twenty-five feet away because he was wearing his eyeglasses at the time; or the witness says that, while he is hard of hearing, his hearing aid was in place and functioning that morning, and hence the witness heard what the plaintiff said to the defendant.

**Third.** The fact here would be of the first sort, save that the witness's perceptions were aided or enhanced or altogether made possible by some device or procedure not in ordinary use, but rather requiring special skill to employ. For example, the witness says that he felt the texture of the pebble on the far side of the moon, having arrived there by rocket and lunar landing module; or the witness says that he saw the material blocking the plaintiff's larynx by looking through a medical instrument introduced for the purpose into the plaintiff's mouth and down his throat; or the witness says that, by plugging into a supersensitive parabolic microphone maintained by the CIA, he heard what the party chairman said to the premier as they went through the line in the Kremlin coffee shop.

**Fourth.** This fact would be a fact of the first sort, save for the chance circumstance that no one exists or can be found who is able to take the stand and say, in effect, "I perceived it." For example, two cars moving in opposite directions collide on a two-lane highway in the middle of the night. No bystander sees the accident, and neither driver survives. It is necessary at trial for plaintiff to prove that the car driven by defendant's decedent was on the wrong side of the road.

**Fifth.** This would be a fact of the first sort, save that it is incapable of being perceived because of the prevailing limits of technology. However, the technology of the future may permit our professional posterity to overcome these limits. What is the shape and approximate size of the Loch Ness monster? Assuming that *something* is down there, those are facts capable of perception, but as yet the engineers have failed to contrive the television cameras and floodlights able to pierce the sedimentary gloom of those Scottish waters. They will before long, and then, with the aid of those devices, someone will perceive the facts in question. At that point, they will be facts of either the second or third sort, depending on the complexity of the equipment.

**Sixth.** This fact cannot belong to any of the preceding categories because science tells us that, even with advances in technology that can be reasonably expected, the fact is and will be immune to perception. For example, scientists say that it will never be possible to hear the noise at the center of the sun. Still, lawyers must once in a while try to prove this kind of fact which might be capable of deduction if not perception. Consider a case of murder by explosion. The evidence showing that the fragments of the bomb came from a closet of materials accessible to the defendant may rest upon a technique of the physics laboratory called neutron activation analysis, in which the energy of gamma rays is analyzed to determine the identity of elements in minute samples that have been bombarded with neutrons to make them radioactive. To persuade the judge to admit that evidence, the prosecutor will need to prove facts of this sixth sort.[6]

**Seventh.** This fact, by contrast with the preceding six, is not in any immediate sense a part of the physical universe either past or present. It is therefore impossible in principle to prove the fact through a witness's perceptions. But neither is the fact a fiction. The fact figures in the real universe, though it lacks tangibility. For example, in a murder trial, the defendant admits shooting the victim, but says that the revolver went off by accident. The prosecution contends that the defendant pulled the trigger intending to kill. The jury must determine the fact of *mens rea*. It is real. It exists. Yet it has no corporeal substance.[7]

**Eighth.** The fact in this category is of a very different sort, both from the preceding one and from the six before that. It is not a part of any universe, the external one of physical reality or the internal one of state of mind. Instead, it is a question of definition, a point of language. For example, a witness testifies to facts of the first sort, namely, that the defendant-driver was, at a moderate rate of speed, approaching the last car of a line of cars stopped for a red light. A youngster hiding behind a tree at the side of the road threw a handful of pebbles at the defendant's car. They landed on the roof and rear window with a noise like a burst of machine gun fire. Startled, the defendant looked around to see what was happening. He saw nothing. While seeing nothing, neither was he watching the stopped car ahead of him. Returning his head and eyes to the forward position, the defendant instantly saw that he had moved dangerously near the stopped car. He jammed on the brakes. Too late. The defendant's car rear-ended the stopped car.

From these facts of the first sort the jury must now determine a fact of the eighth sort. Do these facts having to do with the defendant-driver's conduct, all objects of perception, fit the meaning of the phrase "reasonable care in driving a car"? This is a fact, not of perception, but of definition.

---

[6]*See* United States v. Stifel, 433 F.2d 431 (6th Cir. 1970), *cert denied*, 401 U.S. 994 (1971). (See also §§6.4-6.5.)

[7]*See* United States v. Staggs, 553 F.2d 1073 (7th Cir. 1977).

**Ninth.** This sort of fact would be a fact of the eighth sort, save that the word or phrase, the meaning of which may or may not encompass the circumstances of the case, is not one in ordinary use. Rather, the word or phrase is part of the specialized vocabulary of some science or discipline other than the law. For example, a jury determining whether a certain corporation possessed monopoly power takes a phrase used and defined by the discipline of economics, and decides whether the evidence warrants a finding that the phrase is fairly to be applied to the corporation at bar. Similarly, a jury determining whether the victim of an accident suffers from "traumatic neurosis" takes the phychiatrist's definition of the phrase and decides whether the evidence brings the plaintiff within its terms.

**Tenth.** This sort of fact would be a fact of the eighth sort, save that the word or phrase comes from the jargon of the law. For example, the judge charges the jury as follows: "Members of the jury, the law defines the crime of murder in the first degree as . . . . You determine what the defendant did [facts of the first, second, and third sort] and what was in his mind [a fact of the seventh sort] and, if these facts comport with the definition I have given you, then you must find the defendant guilty of murder in the first degree.

The taxonomy's ten sorts of facts fall naturally into three groups. The first six, involving aspects of the physical universe, might be called matters of matter. The seventh sort of fact, involving aspects of the interior life, covers matters of mind. The eighth, ninth, and tenth sorts of fact, involving the inquiry into whether a certain word or phrase fits the case, are matters of term.

## §2.2 Uses for the Taxonomy of Facts

This taxonomy of the facts of a case is useful in five ways, each of which shades off into the next.

• First is deftness of analysis. The more distinctions one makes, the readier becomes one's hand to make a satisfactory picture of the tangle of fact most lawsuits present. Nuance is all, and nuance is impossible when one paints with but a single brush.

Take an easy example. A lawyer must establish that his client suffered a myocardial infarction that caused scarring to the muscles of the heart. The lawyer might say that *that* is the fact he must prove. But it is aesthetically more satisfactory to take note of the separate facts constituting his one unparticularized sack of fact, and it is possible, with the taxonomy in the previous section, to give a different name to each of them. The wavy lines on the electrocardiogram tape are a fact of the first sort (or perhaps of the second sort, if a magnifying glass is necessary to see them properly); that these lines are aptly described as those characteristic of a myocardial infarction is a fact of the ninth sort; and that someone who has suffered a myocardial infarction is left with a scar on his heart muscle is a fact of the third sort.

There is a second, more elaborate example in *David v. John Hancock Life Insurance Co.*[8] A young woman said goodnight to her mother and went out for the evening. She never returned. A week later, her body was found on the roof of a tenement building. Those are facts of the first sort. The medical examiner performed an autopsy, in the course of which he made certain observations and measurements of the internal organs. Those are facts of the third sort. On the basis of those observations and measurements, the medical examiner concluded that the young woman had died of "acute and chronic intravenous narcotism." That is a fact of the ninth sort. The young woman owned a life insurance policy providing that double the face value would be paid to the beneficiary if the woman died "solely from accidental bodily injury." The jury concluded that death was accidental within the meaning of the word as used in ordinary speech, which was the meaning it had in the policy. That is a fact of the eighth sort.

• Deftness of analysis, being a virtue in itself, is its own reward. But for the doubtful, the taxonomy has a second use. It permits a trial lawyer to prepare and prove his case with great delicacy of focus. Recognizing differences in type among a multitude of facts, the lawyer will marshal his evidence assuredly and exactly.

---

[8] 64 Misc. 2d 791, 316 N.Y.S.2d 722 (Civ. Ct. 1970). The opinion was written by the author of this text during his service as a judge of the Civil Court of the City of New York.

Juries regard this kind of precision as the seal of professional competence and salute it with favorable verdicts.

When, for example, will testimony by lay witnesses suffice and when will it not suffice, the latter contingency making it necessary for the proponent to prove the fact by expert opinion testimony?[9] For facts of the first and second sorts — the objects of sense perception assisted at most by binoculars, eyeglasses, or hearing aid — lay testimony does the job. For a fact of the third sort, special skill is needed to pilot the lunar landing module or to use the medical instrument, but that is not the same as saying that expert opinion testimony is necessary: Once the astronaut or laryngologist uses the special device or procedure, what he perceives could have been perceived by anyone, even the most inexpert. The testimony describing what was perceived is therefore lay testimony.

The fourth sort of fact is capable of being perceived, but by chance no one is available who did perceive it. Here, we start with facts of the first sort. Recall the example of the head-on collision with no survivors. Witnesses testify that, when they came on the scene, the skid-marks were thus, the debris so, etc. They perceived these things. Now, from such facts of the first sort, the jury is obliged to deduce the fact of the fourth sort — on which side of the road the cars collided — which tells us which driver crossed the line.

Whether the jury must make the deduction on its own, or whether the jury may have the assistance of expert opinion testimony, will depend upon which of two rules is preferred in the jurisdiction to determine the admissibility of an expert opinion. One rule has it that an expert's opinion is admissible only when, without it, the jury would be helpless to decide.[10] The other rule requires merely that the expert's opinion "assist the trier of fact to understand the evidence or to determine a fact in issue."[11] Apply the former and the jury in our head-on collision

---

[9]See Chapter 6.

[10]*E.g.*, Kulak v. Nationwide Mutual Ins. Co., 40 N.Y.2d 140, 351 N.E.2d 743, 386 N.Y.S.2d 87 (1976).

[11]Fed. R. Evid. 702.

case must calculate on its own, from skid-marks, debris, etc., where the impact occurred.[12] Let the latter be the law, and an expert in the reconstruction of accidents may give the jury his opinion.[13]

The fifth and sixth sorts of fact, incapable of being perceived because of the present limits of technology or the permanent bounds on the capacity of science, will almost always be proved by expert opinion testimony from a witness who possesses the requisite specialized knowledge.

The seventh sort of fact is a matter of mind. When the person whose mental state is of interest testifies to that mental state, he testifies on personal knowledge and consequently is a lay witness. This might be treated as a fact of the first sort, except that we do not "perceive" our own states of mind in the usual sense of the word "perceive." When a witness states his perceptions of another person whose mental state is of interest, we deal with facts of the first sort. From those facts the jury will be told in many cases to infer the actor's mental state. If the witness is permitted to characterize those perceptions, for example, as "crazy," we deal with a matter of term, a fact of the eighth sort. When a witness characterizes his or another's perceptions of the person whose mental state is of interest, for example, as "schizophrenic," we deal with a different matter of term, a fact of the ninth sort.

The eighth sort of fact, a matter of term involving ordinary words or phrases, a jury determines for itself. Average people, which is what jurors are, can decide without help from anyone whether the evidence before them meets a definition drawn from everyday language. The ninth sort of fact, a matter of term that is part of the vocabulary of some science or discipline other than the law, must be proved by expert opinion testimony, for only an expert will be able to define the term for the jury. The tenth sort of fact, involving legal words or phrases, the jury determines

---

[12]Stafford v. Mussus Potato Chips, Inc., 39 A.D.2d 831, 333 N.Y.S.2d 139 (1972) (mem.)

[13]Een v. Consolidated Freightways, Inc., 120 F. Supp. 289 (D.N.D. 1954).

by applying the court's definition of the word or phrase to the facts of other sorts in the case and deciding whether they fit.

• A third use of the taxonomy is that it permits one to mark out with great clarity the border between a witness's terrain and the jury's. An illustration is *Washington v. United States*,[14] decided at a time when the District of Columbia applied the *Durham* rule to determine exculpation on the ground of insanity; the rule provides that a defendant is not criminally responsible if his unlawful acts "stem from and are the product of a mental disease or defect."[15] The courts of the District had fallen into the habit of permitting psychiatrists to testify that, in their expert opinion, the defendant did have a mental disease or defect, that the unlawful act was its product, and that the defendant was consequently not guilty by reason of insanity.

In *Washington*, the court of appeals condemned that practice and laid down guidelines for psychiatric testimony in future cases. The physician is to diagnose; he is not to parrot the *Durham* rule. "The clinical diagnostic meaning of this term [mental disease or defect]," said the court, "may be different from its legal meaning."[16] The facts with respect to the defendant's overt behavior are facts of the first sort: Lay testimony suffices. That the structure of the defendant's personality is of a certain type is a matter of term, a fact of the ninth sort, and a psychiatrist gives his opinion on it. That the defense of insanity has or has not been made out is a fact of the tenth sort — does the evidence fall within a legal word or phrase as defined by the judge? This is a determination solely for the jury to make, and hence expert opinion about it is inadmissible.

• A fourth use of the taxonomy is to explain certain appellate decisions that, without the taxonomy, are confusing. The standard on review of a jury's finding is whether the verdict is contrary to the weight of the evidence. What then are we to make of *United States v. Simon*?[17] The defendant accountants were

---

[14]390 F.2d 444 (D.C. Cir. 1967).
[15]Durham v. United States, 214 F.2d 862, 876 (D.C. Cir. 1954).
[16]Washington v. United States, 390 F.2d 444, 457 (D.C. Cir. 1967).
[17]425 F.2nd 796 (2d Cir. 1969), *cert. denied*, 397 U.S. 1006 (1970).

convicted of certifying a false and misleading statement. How they had treated certain transactions was not in dispute. What was disputed was the quality of their treatment. Eight witnesses — to use Chief Judge Friendly's words, "an impressive array of leaders of the [accounting] profession"[18] — testified that the defendants' treatment was consistent with generally accepted accounting principles. The government's two experts, said the chief judge, "hardly compared with defendants' witnesses in aggregate accounting experience or professional eminence."[19] One might have expected a reversal on the ground that the verdict was contrary to the weight of the evidence, but the court of appeals unanimously affirmed.

The taxonomy of the facts of a case shows why. The entries the defendants made are facts of the first sort, and in any event were not in controversy. That the defendants' professional behavior was or was not consistent with good accounting practice is a fact of the ninth sort; hence both sides called experts in accountancy. But this fact of the ninth sort was not what the jury had to determine. The indictment did not accuse the defendants of failing to comply with generally accepted accounting principles. Had that been the charge, it is likely that the court of appeals would have reversed the conviction as contrary to the weight of the evidence. The crime alleged in the indictment was different: that the defendant had certified a false and misleading financial statement. This is a fact of the tenth sort. Do the entries on the statement make it false and misleading, as those words are defined by the judge? The jury alone decides facts of the tenth sort, which is why the disparity in the quality of the evidence adduced by the defense as against that adduced by the government was of no moment.

• Although the fifth use for the taxonomy is speculative, it is a possibility worth further consideration. Some judges and lawyers have been wondering aloud whether some cases are too complex to be tried by a jury. For example, one trial judge held that, because the evidence in a case at law was so voluminous

---

[18]*Id.* at 805.
[19]*Id.*

and the issues so tricky, trial by jury would not be allowed; a bench trial was mandatory.[20] That kind of ruling is troublesome because of constitutional jury trial guarantees, as in the seventh amendment to the U.S. Constitution and as in various state constitutions. The language of the federal guarantee is typical: "In suits at common law, . . . the right of trial by jury shall be preserved . . . ."[21]

If one asks about the scope of the guarantee, the response usually is historical, a reference to the forms of action. Since the Constitution preserves the right to trial by jury in suits at common law, those forms of action that were triable to a jury of old are triable to a jury today. A contract case was tried to a jury in the time of Henry II, so it is tried to a jury now. That the evidence is voluminous and the issues are tricky counts for nothing. A judge who rules otherwise may violate the Constitution. It is hard to see any other conclusion if one defines the constitutional guarantee of jury trial by reference to the forms of action.

Our taxonomy of the facts of a case opens up a different and perhaps more satisfactory approach to the problem. Yes, only certain types of cases were tried to a jury in the time of Henry II. But further, in that time only certain sorts of facts were determined by juries — facts of the first, second, seventh, eighth, and tenth sorts. Facts of the other sorts, which are just those sorts of facts that tend to involve voluminous evidence and tricky issues, were not determined by common law juries for the very good reason that the life of the times was not complex enough to engender such questions of fact. No jury before the last 100 years was ever called upon to consider monopoly power or neutron activation analysis. The energies of juries before the last four or five decades were devoted to such questions as "Did Kendall try to separate the two fighting dogs?" or "Did Armory find a jewel in the gutter?"

Might one not argue, in light of all this, that the constitutional guarantee of trial by jury extends only to facts of the sort decided by juries at common law, rather than to forms of action triable

---

[20]Bernstein v. Universal Pictures, Inc., 79 F.R.D. 59 (S.D.N.Y. 1978).
[21]U.S. Const. amend. VII.

to a jury? Might not one argue that this gives the constitutional guarantee of trial by jury a scope truly in accord with its historical context? Might not one argue that this permits striking a better balance between the right of trial by jury and the existence of complex litigation?

# CHAPTER 3

# Jury Selection

## §3.1 Local Custom

We begin the trial by selecting a jury. That is the customary expression for it, but to speak of selecting or picking a jury is actually quite inaccurate. No lawyer has ever selected a jury. It is chance that determines who comes to sit in the box as prospective jurors. The most that a lawyer can do is to cause certain of those prospective jurors to be sent home or sent back to serve as jurors in some other case. To put it more precisely, then, we should speak of unpicking or unselecting a jury.

A novice might go about it by asking himself, "Who would be the ideal juror for this case?" Using that profile as a standard, he measures the actual prospective jurors sitting in the jury box, looking for those who come closest to his ideal. That would be trying to pick a jury. At best it is inefficient; at worst, self-damaging.

The experienced hand, to be sure, will determine in advance the profile of the ideal juror for the case. And this lawyer, too, will use that profile as a standard. But he will not look for the best possible jurors. Instead, he will ask, "Who departs *farthest* from the ideal?"

No lawyer deals out the cards, in short. The most that a lawyer can do is to remove certain cards from the deck. That is the

the basic principle of jury selection. And there is no book in which to look up the rules of the game. A lawyer can go to the library and find out how many peremptory challenges he has, but that is relatively trivial. The real questions are more like these: In what manner do I exercise the peremptory challenges? What are the formulas expected of me? What is the choreography? Where do I stand? To whom do I talk?

That kind of information cannot be found in the library. The custom and practice in each courthouse are essentially unwritten law, just as are the idiosyncracies of the particular judge before whom the case is tried. The first point of proper preparation, therefore, is to become familiar with local custom in the courtroom. It takes time, but is vitally important. Before a lawyer picks a jury, he must find an hour or two to sit in the courtroom during another trial, ideally in the same courtroom in which the lawyer's own case will be tried, and preferably before the very judge to whom the lawyer's own case is assigned. That is the only way to see how local custom operates — where the lawyers sit and stand, to whom they speak, and all the rest.

There is no real substitute for this kind of direct observation. If the time is not available, it is possible to make up the deficiency in part by talking to senior lawyers in the office and to people around the bar association. The lawyer's grapevine in general is an insufficiently appreciated source of useful information. One way or another, a lawyer must find out what will be expected of him. It is most unsettling to be in court, in front of the judge and the prospective jury, and not know what to do.[1]

---

[1] I offer this advice from experience. The first time I picked a jury was in federal court in the Southern District of New York. I knew everything that could be looked up in the library; I understood that I had three peremptory challenges. But when the time came to exercise my peremptory challenges, I had not the slightest idea of how to do it.

The clerk of the court handed me a wooden frame with twelve little clips. In each clip was a piece of paper bearing the name of a prospective juror. The judge and the twelve prospective jurors were all staring at me. What was I supposed to do? I had neglected to observe; I had neglected to ask.

In that court, to exercise a peremptory challenge one takes the slip of paper with the name of the juror to be excused, turns it upside down, puts the paper back into its clip, and hands the frame back to the clerk — a most tactful way

## §3.2 Excusing Prospective Jurors

There are five methods for "unpicking"[2] particular prospective jurors. On the doctrinal map, the methods for excusing a juror fall somewhere in the region where the law of procedure and the craft of advocacy overlap. We take up the first four methods here, and the fifth separately.[3]

**Agreement.** First on the checklist, and so placed because it is often overlooked, is the method of excusing a juror by agreement between the parties. The lawyers simply agree to send someone home, and home he goes. This method has the advantage that excusing this juror is chargeable to the account of neither side. To excuse a prospective juror by agreement is by far the most common method in many courts.

**Challenge to the Array.** Used very rarely — perhaps once in a lawyer's career, if that — this method can always be anticipated well in advance. Anticipation is indispensable, because this method of excusing jurors requires close study of the cases.

Rather than removing a particular card from the deck of prospective jurors, this method asks for a whole new deck. Usually called a "challenge to the array" — a challenge to the entire panel — it rests upon a claim of some impropriety or deficiency in the process that summoned the people in the panel for jury duty. That impropriety, says the challenge, results in a skewed panel. The process may have favored old over young, whites over blacks, males over females, rich over poor, rural people over urban dwellers, or any other identifiable group over another.

The challenge to the array has a constitutional basis. The United States Constitution and the various state constitutions give the parties to a lawsuit the right to a jury drawn from a fair cross-section of the community. The challenge claims that this requirement has not been met. If it succeeds, the judge will send the

---

of blackballing someone. It is not to be found in the Federal Rules of Civil or of Criminal Procedure or in any other book, but it is something that every lawyer practicing in that court has to know. There are equivalent things to know in every other courtroom in the land.

[2] See §3.1.
[3] See §3.3.

entire panel home, and the process starts again with another that is properly selected.

There is case law on challenges to the array. Accordingly, a lawyer who plans to attempt this method should plan first to spend a lot of time in the library.

**Challenge for Cause.** Third on the checklist is a name that trips easily from the tongue of every lawyer, but is usually used inaccurately. It properly denotes a challenge that is, in fact, very uncommon. This is the challenge for cause — a challenge to a prospective juror based upon particular facts in that juror's background which require that the challenge be granted. Once the pertinent facts have been brought out, the trial judge has no discretion. The prospective juror may not be permitted to serve as a matter of law; if he remains, the appellate court will grant a new trial. The grounds for a challenge for cause are set out in the statutes, and they may be supplemented by case law. In every jurisdiction, for example, relationship to a party within certain degrees of consanguinity will support a challenge for cause. Nowadays, of course, in major urban areas the odds against this kind of relationship coming out of a random drawing are astronomical.

**Challenge to the Favor.** When lawyers talk about a challenge for cause, they usually mean something else. We have no fixed name for it; we might borrow one from English barristers and call it a "challenge to the favor." Like the challenge for cause, a challenge to the favor is based upon facts in the prospective juror's background. Unlike the challenge for cause, however, whether or not the juror is excused is entirely within the trial judge's discretion. An appellate court will take no interest in the ruling either way. For example:

Q. Juror No. 2, do you happen to know the defendant in this case?

A. Say, I think I do.

Q. How do you know him?

A. We were in high school together.

Q. How long ago was that?

A. Oh, it must have been thirty years.

Q. Were you particularly good friends?

A. No. I just remember he was in my class.

Q. Did you ever visit his home?

A. No.

Q. Did he ever visit your home?

A. No.

Q. Have you seen him since graduation?

A. Once, I guess. At the tenth reunion. He was there, but I don't think we said a word to each other.

The judge might rule either way, and as a practical matter, there is no appeal from that ruling.

When questioning a prospective juror to bring out this kind of fact, it is best to proceed with some delicacy. Usually the other jurors will be able to hear the exchange. To accuse a prospective juror of bias will not bring the lawyer favor in the other jurors' eyes. A better way, when possible, is to ask questions that bring out the bias by implication. Then the lawyer need not point to possible bias directly, but the facts will be before the judge nonetheless.

## §3.3 The Peremptory Challenge

The last of the five methods for excusing a juror arises in almost every jury case. Second in importance only to agreement between the parties,[4] this is the method of the peremptory challenge, in some states called a "strike." The law gives a certain number of peremptory challenges in every case. That number can be found in the jurisdiction's statutes or rules, and is generally low. In federal civil litigation, for example, the number is three.[5]

A peremptory challenge has been described as one for which the lawyer needs no reason. But the lawyer should always have

---

[4]See §3.2.
[5]28 U.S.C. §1870.

a reason, and so we need a more precise definition: A peremptory challenge is one for which the lawyer need never disclose his reason to the judge. Some recent cases have called that "never" into question;* for the moment, however, consider the definition in its absolute form. It reflects a rule that has prevailed for centuries: The judge is not empowered to second-guess the lawyer by declaring the lawyer's reason for excusing a juror to be unlawful. The peremptory challenge can be exercised for any reason whatsoever, and that reason remains private to the lawyer.

Novices will exercise peremptories by asking themselves, "Do I have a peremptory?" More experienced lawyers will ask it differently: "*How many* peremptories will I have left?" The experienced eye sees the use of peremptory challenges as a dynamic process, not a static one.

Let us start from the beginning. We have three peremptories. Sitting in the jury box are twelve people. We look over at No. 7. He makes our flesh crawl. It is safe to assume that we make his flesh crawl, too. We get rid of that juror, and we have two peremptories left. Juror No. 1 gives us goosebumps. We get rid of her as well, and then we have one peremptory remaining.

Juror No. 8 leaves us feeling vaguely uneasy. An inexperienced lawyer might say, "I always go on hunches when I pick a jury. I have a peremptory left, and I'll exercise it." But this is the last peremptory. Once we use it, there will be none left. Someone else will be called to fill the chair juror No. 8 leaves empty. We have no way of knowing who it will be. He could be worse than No. 8, the juror we now want to excuse, but we'll have no peremptories left.

That is the fun of this business. We concentrate with the zeal of a fanatic to make the most finely honed decisions that we possibly can. And then, having brought enormous intellectual energies to bear on the problem, we simply close our eyes and jump, praying that there will be water in the pool. Sometimes there is, and sometimes there is not. That is why the life expec-

---

*[*Editor's note:* On the issue of peremptory challenges alleged to be racially motivated, *see* Batson v. Kentucky, 476 U.S. 79 (1986); Griffith v. Kentucky, 107 S. Ct. 708, 93 L. Ed. 2d 649 (1987).]

tancy of trial lawyers is so much shorter than that of tax lawyers and corporate lawyers.

## §3.4 Information About Jurors

The hallmark of the able trial lawyer is the economic adaptation of means to ends. That is also the mark of an artist, of course, and the trying of a case is first of all an art. Like an artist at work, a good lawyer has specific goals in mind at every moment of the trial. There is no fumbling or treading water. No moves are wasted; everything is done to a particular purpose. That purpose guides the choice of means from moment to moment.

Having seen the five means of excusing prospective jurors,[6] we turn now to the goals of that exercise, and of jury selection generally. Some people mistake those goals. In the procedure course in the first year of law school, we all heard a teacher speak along these lines: "The purpose of jury selection," the professor said, "is to find six or twelve jurors who are fair and impartial, who can decide the case with an open mind, solely in accordance with the evidence and the law that the judge will explain to them." But the professor who says that either demonstrates ignorance of how the adversarial system works, or prefers not to burden the class with reality. Any lawyer who sets out to select a fair and impartial jury ought to turn in his ticket. The attempt shows not only an ignorance of the 800-year history of the common law, but also a failure to comprehend lawyers' obligations to themselves, the profession, and their clients.

Working within the rules, the lawyer's goal is to find six or twelve people who are *incapable* of deciding the case fairly. He is looking for people whose minds are utterly closed, people who can see the case in only one way: the lawyer's way. The ideal jury would be six or twelve clones of the client.

What the procedure teacher either did not understand or failed to mention is that when we pick a jury — more broadly,

---

[6]See §§3.2 and 3.3.

when we do any of the things that go into trying a lawsuit — we are not playing solitaire. There is a lawyer on the other side who has every reason to do what we are trying to do, but pushing in the opposite direction. That is the genius of the system, and it works. If one of the lawyers ceases to be an advocate and becomes a statesman, the system collapses.

There are three purposes to achieve in the course of jury selection. We take them up in ascending order of importance, the first below and the other two in the sections following. They cannot all be achieved simultaneously, and so it is necessary to move back and forth among them as the selection process goes on. Nor does the accomplishment of these purposes guarantee a jury that will bring in the verdict we want. The most that any trial lawyer can reasonably hope for is a lifetime batting average of .500. But unless a lawyer works to capacity all of the time, he will not achieve even that.

The lawyer's first purpose in jury selection is to gain specific facts about the prospective jurors, a necessary step in eliminating those people likely to be predisposed against the client. In procedural terms, we want to determine whether there is a challenge for cause[7] or a challenge to the favor,[8] and we need information to exercise peremptory challenges[9] intelligently. There are five ways to learn about prospective jurors. In some courts all five are available, and at least four of them in all other courts. The choice of methods in each particular instance depends upon the client's resources and the creativity and skill of the lawyer.

**Advance Investigation.** The six or twelve people called to sit in the jury box are drawn from a list of people summoned for jury duty in that week or month or term of court. That list is a public document; the clerk will provide it on payment of a nominal fee. The list enables us to investigate prospective jurors in advance, before anyone ever shows up in court. A full investigation of all the names can be expensive, and it can take time. In some jurisdictions the list may run to 500 people or more. The

---

[7]See §3.2.
[8]See *id.*
[9]See §3.3.

most costly way to do the job is to pay an investigator. Perry Mason would simply have given the list to Paul Drake; while Perry Mason's clients can afford that, some of our clients cannot. A little ingenuity can go a long way, however, and an investigator may not be necessary.

Lawyers who work for the government have access to truly extraordinary sources of information. A federal prosecutor, for example, can run a 500-name jury list through the FBI files and find information that would not have been available in any other way. But one need not work for the government. Directories in the public library — trade listings, *Who's Who*, and the like — can be very helpful. Credit information on the prospective jurors can be had for the payment of a fee. There are agencies that report on whether the juror has ever served on a jury before, and on the verdicts reached. Some judges will not permit these questions on voir dire, but the answers are available through the agencies.

One source of information that should not be overlooked, especially in a smaller town, is what newspapers used to call the "morgue" and now refer to as the library — a clipping file arranged by people's names. Ordinarily it is not open to the public. A good lawyer trying cases in a town with one newspaper probably would make it his business to be on good terms with the managing editor, so as to have access as a personal favor. In a small town the morgue will list school graduations, minor arrests, professional accomplishments, accidents, and a wealth of other helpful information.

**Jury Scientists.** There are social scientists who stand ready to assist lawyers with jury selection, usually for a hefty fee. They will take a survey and use the results to construct the profile of an ideal juror for the case, taking into account such matters as the nature of the case, community attitudes, and the like. The profile can serve as a standard for evaluating prospective jurors.

Lawyers who have used this service tend to think it is sensible. But on cross-examination, that turns out to mean that the scientists' results match the lawyers' instincts. Why, then, is it worth spending $40,000 of the client's money to learn what one already knows? The lawyers have an answer. It is very reassuring, they say, to have one's instinct confirmed scientifically.

**Jury Slip.** This method is free, and it is available in every court in the land. Most lawyers overlook its possibilities.

At the beginning of jury selection, the clerk hands the lawyers a piece of paper for each prospective juror. In the eastern part of the country it is literally a slip bearing only the name, address, and occupation of the juror. Some jurisdictions farther west give the lawyers an elaborately filled out questionnaire. Let us here take the harder case, however, and see what we can do with the minimum of information.

We can ascertain sex, race, and approximate age from a glance at the juror. Right after those on the list of priorities is ethnic background. In our own lives, of course, we try to put aside stereotypes and respond to people as individuals. But in the courtroom, we are not living our own lives. We are someone else's advocate in an exceedingly complex process. For however many days the trial takes, the greater part of the process consists of a kind of theatrical presentation. The audience for that presentation is the jury. We seek an audience that will respond to our presentation in particular ways. A person's ethnic background is one of the factors that determine his outlook on the world, and so it predetermines to some extent his response to the drama to come.

Certain questions should not be asked of the jurors directly — not because the law says such questions are improper, but because the questions will offend the juror and his fellows. If a question would not be tactful at a backyard cookout, it should not be used on voir dire. Saying, "Hi, are you Jewish?" will not get us invited back to the next cookout, and it will not speak well of us to the jury. But often such questions are unnecessary. Much of the time, the juror's ethnic background, and sometimes his religion also, can be deduced from the name on the jury slip.

After ethnic and religious background, the next item of importance is economic class. To ask people directly how much money they make is to violate the last great taboo of American life. But we need not ask. The jury slip gives that information, coded in the address. Suppose that we have a juror who is dressed ordinarily. His name is Smith; no help. But he lives at 10 East 78th Street in New York City. As good trial lawyers, we must know the neighborhoods of our city as well as the postmaster does. We know, then, that this juror lives in what is probably the most expensive district in the world. He is a wealthy man, and that may help us make a decision about him.

The last piece of information we find on even the most limited jury slip is the juror's occupation. That too gives a guide to income, and sometimes to politics. The man on East 78th Street may list his occupation as "self-employed." From that we can deduce that he pushes something for a living — possibly heroin, maybe stocks and bonds. What he sells makes little difference; standing alone, neither drugs nor securities are good or bad for our purposes. This is simply one more fact to take into account.

**Observation.** Most lawyers make no use at all of the technique of observation, yet it can produce more information than all of the others put together. It requires a special style of intellect, but one that can be practiced anywhere, not just in the courtroom. Beyond the mere act of seeing, a good observer notices details and draws conclusions from them. The authority on this point is Holmes, of course — not Oliver Wendell, but Sherlock:

> "When I hear you give your reasons," [Dr. Watson] remarked, "the thing always appears to me to be so ridiculously simply that I could easily do it myself, though at each successive instance of your reasoning I am baffled until you explain your process. And yet I believe that my eyes are as good as yours."
>
> "Quite so," [Holmes] answered, lighting a cigarette, and throwing himself down into an armchair. "You see, but you do not observe. The distinction is clear. . . ."[10]

Every human being is a walking advertisement of the inner man or woman. All we have to do is read the signs. Two examples will suffice.

In most cities jurors spend a great deal of time waiting in a large central jury room. The facility typically has all the charm

---

[10]A.C. Doyle, *A Scandal in Bohemia*, in The Complete Sherlock Holmes 162 (1892-1927).

of a big-city bus station: just benches and a clock, with no television set, no cards or checker games. There is nothing to do but
read. The summons to jury duty may in fact advise the jurors
to bring something along to pass the time. Accordingly, when
they are called from the central jury room, the jurors come into
the courtroom clutching their books and magazines and
newspapers.

The publications that jurors carry can tell us a great deal about
them. Not only must we be something of a postmaster, but
something of a librarian as well. We all know the difference between the *Wall Street Journal* and the *National Enquirer,* and we
can all draw conclusions about the people who carry them.
Another juror, let us say, is carrying a mystery novel. Those are
written to a formula; the first 199 pages make the facts seem one
way, and the 200th page shows that the facts were not that way
at all, but something entirely different. If I am defending in a
criminal case, I might want that juror, because my argument will
almost always be along the same lines: "I know it *seems* as though
my client is guilty, but it was not really that way at all."

Another juror is carrying a book called *A Distant Mirror.* Being part librarian, we recognize that as an account of life in
medieval France. Why, we wonder, does the juror enjoy it?
Perhaps it amuses him to participate with the author in piecing
together, from thousands of separate bits of information, a
coherent mosaic of what happened in that distant place and time.
If we are the prosecutor, or are representing the plaintiff in a civil
case, that juror might appeal to us, for at trial we shall be trying
to do much the same thing: to assemble, from thousands of bits
of information, a coherent picture of a past event. This juror may
be attuned to that sort of thing.

My second example is jewelry. Some people wear little of it,
but what there is can be informative — wedding ring, charm
bracelet, diamond pinkie ring, or whatever. Almost everyone
wears a watch. Especially for men, the watch can offer an extraor-
dinarily vivid insight into the wearer's personality.

Juror No. 3, we shall say, appears to be about thirty-three years
old. He is white, lives in a middle-class neighborhood, and works
as a clerk in a brokerage house. His job, we know, is to add up

figures. How, we ask ourselves, can he manage to add up figures day after day without snapping? But then we look at his watch. He is wearing the kind of watch designed for astronauts to wear when they walk the surface of Mars. One button lights up the radar screen; another button communicates with Mission Control; a third button makes the poison gas come out. And now we understand how this man can add up figures every day of his working life. In his mind, which is where it counts, he is not adding up figures at all. He is an astronaut walking the surface of Mars. This man leads a rich fantasy life. And for that very reason, if we are defending a criminal case, we want him.

Juror No. 4 is also thirty-three years old, white, middle-class, and a brokerage clerk. But his watch is different. His is the $8 kind from the drugstore with two hands on it and no other features at all. And now we know how he, too, adds up figures day after day. He likes it! He likes it because he leads no fantasy life whatsoever. He likes it so long as the numbers balance at the bottom of the page. He cannot cope with the sloppiness of the real world. The fraying at the margins of reality causes him psychological distress. This man is incapable of acknowledging doubt, even a reasonable doubt. If I am prosecuting, I shall grapple him to me with hoops of steel.

One last illustration of the method comes not from the courtroom, but from the Canon. Sherlock Holmes has just divulged to Dr. Watson that he has an older brother, a most sedentary man named Mycroft who lives at the mysterious Diogenes Club. To Watson's disbelief, Sherlock insists that Mycroft possesses even greater powers of observation and deduction than does Sherlock himself. Watson, his curiosity whetted, joins Sherlock for a stroll over to Mycroft's club. Watson then relates for us the conversation that ensues between the brothers:

> The two sat down together in the bow-window of the club. "To anyone who wishes to study mankind this is the spot," said Mycroft. "Look at the magnificent types! Look at these two men who are coming toward us, for example."
> "The billiard-marker and the other?"
> "Precisely. What do you make of the other?"

The two men had stopped opposite the window. Some chalk marks over the waistcoat pocket were the only signs of billiards which I could see in one of them. The other was a very small, dark fellow, with his hat pushed back and several packages under his arm.

"An old soldier, I perceive," said Sherlock.

"And very recently discharged," remarked the brother.

"Served in India, I see."

"And as a non-commissioned officer."

"Royal Artillery, I fancy," said Sherlock.

"And a widower."

"But with a child."

"Children, my dear boy, children."

"Come," said I, laughing, "This is a little too much."

"Surely," answered Holmes, "it is not hard to say that a man with that bearing, expression of authority, and sun-baked skin, is a soldier, is more than a private, and is not long from India."

"That he has not left the service long is shown by his still wearing his ammunition boots, as they are called," observed Mycroft.

"He has not the cavalry stride, yet he wore his hat on one side, as is shown by the lighter skin on that side of his brow. His weight is against his being a sapper. He is in the artillery."

"Then, of course, his complete mourning shows that he has lost someone very dear. The fact that he is doing his own shopping looks as though it were his wife. He has been buying things for children, you perceive. There is a rattle, which shows that one of them is very young. The wife probably died in childbed. The fact that he has a picture-book under his arm shows that there is another child to be thought of."

I began to understand what my friend meant when he said that his brother possessed even keener faculties than he did himself. . . .[11]

---

[11]A.C. Doyle, *The Greek Interpreter,* in The Complete Sherlock Holmes 437 (1892-1927).

**Questioning Jurors.** In state courts lawyers are generally permitted to question prospective jurors on voir dire. By and large lawyers like to question jurors, while judges, believing it to be a waste of time, would rather do the questioning themselves. The judges' view generally prevails in the federal courts.

Done properly, a lawyer-conducted voir dire takes little more time than a judge-conducted one and is much more flexible. But most lawyers do it ineffectively. Most use the voir dire merely to acquire trivial bits of information. For example:

Q. Sir, are you married?

A. Yes.

Q. Do you have children?

A. Yes.

Q. How many?

A. Three.

Q. How old are they?

And on it goes.

This does not tell the lawyer what he really needs to know. The lawyer's main interest is the contours of the juror's personality — the kind of soul that inhabits the body in the jury box. But we all know how to learn about someone else in a social situation, when meeting a new person, and it takes about two minutes. Our culture has a ground rule: People who have newly met take turns talking. After one or two exchanges we may not know how many children the other person has, but we do have a sense of who he is. That is just what we want on voir dire — to hear the juror talking for a minute or so. The technique, then, is to ask open-ended questions, questions that cannot be answered in a monosyllable. But the choice of question needs a little thought.

Q. Sir, I see from the jury slip that you are a garbage collector.

A. That's right.

We see him bristle. He is ready to be insulted about being a garbage collector.

Q. Well, sir, would you please explain to everyone here your views on capital punishment?

Why isn't this a good open-ended question? Certainly, the juror has views on capital punishment — everyone does — and his views are worth exactly as much as the lawyer's. But now he is thinking, "You're humiliating me because I'm a garbage collector. You think I don't know anything about capital punishment. All right, I'll get even." And he will get even, if we give him the chance — just as soon as the jury retires. Now we have to get rid of him, and that will cost us a peremptory challenge.

It would serve us better to try it this way:

Q. Sir, I see from the jury slip that you are a garbage collector.
A. That's right.
Q. Isn't that interesting. I once read that garbage collecting is the most dangerous kind of municipal work — that more garbage collectors are injured on the job than policemen and firemen put together. Is that right, sir?
A. Yeah. Yeah, as a matter of fact, it's true. Sometimes we get hurt pretty bad.

We have turned him around.

Q. Why is it dangerous, sir? How do you protect yourself?

Almost always, people will talk freely about the details of their job. After listening to this man for thirty seconds, we may decide that with his sixth-grade education, he is the smartest person in the room, has the most forceful personality, and will probably dominate the jury deliberation. Isn't that more important to know than the number of children he has?

## §3.5 Informing Jurors

The second purpose of jury selection is the reverse of the first. We turn now from gathering information about prospective jurors[12] to communicating information *to* the jurors.

From the simplest trial to the most complex — from a two-hour rear-end fender-bender to an antitrust case that brings a verdict in the billions — every trial involves an enormously complicated mass of information for the jury to absorb. The jury has to be taught. The lawyer is the teacher, and the jurors are his students. To the extent that the lawyer is successful in teaching the jury, he is on the way to winning the case.

We want to begin teaching the jury at the earliest possible moment. In most state courts, that will be on voir dire. In a federal-style jury selection, where the lawyers cannot talk to the jurors directly, the same issue arises later in the context of the opening statement.

Let us assume that we have a state-style voir dire, so that we are permitted to speak to the jurors. There are then two ways of communicating facts.

The first method stems from a rule that is unwritten but widely honored: The lawyer may make a brief preliminary statement before beginning to question prospective jurors. This is not the opening statement; it is part of jury selection. It is important to prepare the preliminary statement in advance. A lawyer who is not prepared will have to forgo the preliminary statement or extemporize it. Forgoing the statement gives up a chance to teach the jury. Extemporizing will never do much good, and at worst can do actual damage. If you prepare the preliminary statement by asking yourself what you want the jury to learn first about the case, it will come out well. Tell the jury who you are, who your client is, and what, in a nutshell, the case is about. Then launch into your questioning of the prospective jurors.

The second method is a technique of questioning jurors. Except for the brief preliminary statement, we are not supposed to make declarative statements on voir dire. But the structure of

---

[12]See §3.4.

the English language makes it possible to turn any declarative sentence into a question. And so we ask questions not to obtain answers, but to communicate facts in the asking. It is important always to have a specific purpose for the communication, and always to observe the limits on this sort of questioning the judge may impose.

"Hello. My name is Irving Younger." That is declarative and not permissible. But we can start off this way instead:

Q. Did you know that my name is Irving Younger?

A. Well, no, I didn't.

Q. Did you know that I am going to call a witness named John Q. Bystander, who will tell us that he saw this accident?

A. No, I didn't know that.

Q. He is also going to tell us that he served a term in the state penitentiary for burglary; did you know that?

A. No — no, I didn't.

The point is not that the prospective juror didn't know my name, but that after I ask him the question he does. We have no interest in the juror's answer, though we would if we were concerned with the first purpose of jury selection — acquiring information about the jurors. Our interest lies in asking the question, because in asking it we teach the juror something about this case.

We have a special reason for asking the last question, a reason discussed in the next section.

## §3.6 Instilling Confidence and Trust

The last purpose of jury selection is more important than the preceding two.[13] It is also more subtle and elusive; it has to do with instilling confidence in jurors the way Joe DiMaggio did in

---

[13]See §§3.4 and 3.5.

ballpark spectators.[14] A lawyer must convey an impression of trustworthiness through every part of the trial. Nonetheless, people's first impressions tend to be lasting ones. It is easier to make the right impression at the outset than to repair a bad first impression later on. From the very beginning of the trial, then, we must give the jury a sense of being in good hands. Our first chance of doing so comes on voir dire.

This section discusses ways to promote a feeling of trust in the context of jury selection. We assume a state-style voir dire in which we can convey information to the jurors by asking questions.[15] The same principles apply also in the federal courts, where the judge conducts the voir dire, except that there we must wait until the opening statement. Although perhaps less effective due to the delay, that is an easier situation to handle. In the opening statement we can say what we want outright, without having to frame each point as a question.

Whether we apply it to voir dire or to the opening statement, the Joe DiMaggio analogy is especially helpful with regard to three distinct issues. We take them up in turn.

**Lucidity.** DiMaggio had a wonderfully clean line, one that a ballet dancer would admire. He did a very difficult thing elegantly. It was a pleasure just to watch him move. To the lawyer, the analogue of the athlete's elegant line is lucidity. It is not enough that the jury hear; they must also understand.

The jury consists of people who lack a legal education. The lawyers' only advantage over them lies in technical sophistication: The lawyers know a lot of fancy words that the jury does not. Collectively, the jurors are as smart as the lawyers, and sometimes smarter. If the jury is to understand us, however, we must abandon the fancy words and reacquire the knack of speaking plain English.

All lawyers spent three years in school practicing distortions of the language: "motor vehicle" for car; "instrument" for paper; and a thousand other examples. But only lawyers talk that way. Words such as "vehicle" and "instrument," even "subsequent"

---

[14]This comparison was developed in §1.3.
[15]See §3.5.

and "prior to," are not part of everyone's spoken vocabulary. Such words confuse the jury. While the jurors are busy being confused, they will not be listening. They will not be available to be persuaded.

As a rule of thumb, everything that we tell the jury should be comprehensible to a twelve-year-old child. Important as it is, however, comprehensibility is only one of the reasons for speaking plain English. We shall come to the other reason below, in connection with the opening statement.[16]

**Maintaining Interest.** A trial has a great deal in common with the theater. A courtroom is an artificial space, just as the theater is. The jury sits in the jury box much as an audience sits in their seats. We work in the well of the court as an actor does on the stage. There are dialogue, props, and costumes. When actors in the theater are successful, the audience experiences an aesthetic effect. A successful lawyer causes the jury to experience an aesthetic effect, but of a particular kind: the effect of persuasion.

Any actor can tell us that the first requirement of achieving an aesthetic effect is to hold the audience's interest. Our audience in the jury box cannot walk out on us — the bailiff will prevent that — but they can still take a walk mentally. They can even fall asleep. If we bore a jury, we are well on our way to losing. We cannot possibly persuade a bored jury, or even impress them with our trustworthiness. We have, in short, a professional obligation to be interesting.

Most of us are inherently dull people. There are a few people endowed with that special quality that makes them interesting just by being themselves. Cary Grant and Katharine Hepburn come to mind; both could have an enormous impact on people just by walking into a room. But most of us are neither Cary Grant nor Katharine Hepburn, and must come to terms with what nature has given us.

Here is a dull lawyer conducting a voir dire. Let us concede that he needs every bit of the information. This is how he goes about acquiring it:

---

[16]See §5.3.

Q. Juror No. 1, what is your name?
A. Smith.
Q. Mr. Smith, are you married?
A. Yes.
Q. Do you have children?
A. Yes.
Q. How many?
A. Four.

Two hours later, he is still at it. "What does your wife's second cousin do for a living?" The other jurors are counting the ceiling tiles.

If we do only one thing, no matter how well we do it, it becomes boring. The secret of maintaining interest is variety. One way of achieving variety is to bounce at random among the jurors.

Q. Juror No. 1, what is your name?
A. Smith.
Q. Are you married, Mr. Smith?
A. Yes.
Q. Juror No. 4, do you have a license to drive a car?
A. Yes.
Q. Juror No. 7, have you ever been on a jury before?
A. No, I haven't.

By the third bounce, each juror realizes that he may be next. The jurors straighten up and listen carefully. They don't want to flub a question directed at them. They are playing the game with us, and, as anyone knows who has every played a game, you must trust your teammates. It may be happening beneath the level of consciousness, but the jurors are beginning to trust us.

Another source of variety is to mix the first method with occasional questions to the entire panel. It sounds like this:

Q. Juror No. 1, what is your name?
A. Smith.

43

Q. Mr. Smith, are you married?

A. Yes.

Q. Juror No. 4, do you have a license to drive a car?

A. Yes.

Q. Has anyone on this panel ever served on a jury before?

The idea is to keep it unpredictable.

**Special Problems in the Case.** Every case has its problems. The really perfect case does not come to trial, because the opponent confronted with that case will settle. But the Joe DiMaggio image of reliability and trustworthiness gives us a way of handling almost any kind of trial problem. We must look at the problem not from the viewpoint of the judge or the appellate court, but as the jury will see it. We must then find a way of saying to the jury, "There may be a problem here, but I will not try to fool you about it. You can trust me." That does not make the problem go away, but it is enormously helpful in keeping the jury on our side, and hence in minimizing the harm the problem may cause.

Almost always, the best way of gaining the jurors' confidence is simply to tell them about the problem. If there is something to be said by way of amelioration, say it; if there is not, say nothing. Either way, we lay the problem on the table.

The earlier, the better. A federal court will not give us an opportunity until the opening statement. In a state court, the first chance will come on voir dire, although we might occasionally choose to delay until the opening statement. But that is the latest by which the jury should know about every problem that we have in the case.

Suppose that we have a simple intersection collision case. The issue is which driver had the green light. John Q. Bystander, who saw the accident, is willing to testify that our client had the green light. But there is a problem: Bystander once served two years for burglary. Under the rules of evidence in our state, the other side can bring that out.[17]

A beginner faced with this situation will want to put his head in the sand and forget about it. Today is only Monday; he will

---

[17]See §15.4.

not have to call the witness until Thursday. Maybe the world will come to an end before Thursday. But Thursday will arrive right on schedule. And when it does, the opposing lawyer will leap to his feet on cross-examination, screaming.

Q. IS IT NOT A FACT, MR. BYSTANDER, THAT YOU SERVED A TERM IN THE STATE PENITENTIARY FOR BURGLARY?

A. Yes, that's right.

"My God!" The jurors recoil in horror. "He put a felon in our midst!" And they will be angry with us for doing it.

This is how we can defuse the problem on voir dire:

Q. Ladies and gentlemen, did you know that I am going to call a witness named John Q. Bystander, who will tell us that he saw this accident?

Now they know.

Q. He is also going to tell us that he served a term in the state penitentiary for burglary; did you know that?

Now they know that, too. And on Thursday, when the other lawyer bellows the impeaching question, the jury's reaction will be, "What's the big deal? We've known that for three days." Not only does the mere passage of time soften their disapproval, but our early and frank disclosure will help to convince the jury that we can be trusted.

Some lawyers ask a third question, but I advise against it:

Q. Will Mr. Bystander's burglary conviction affect the way in which you consider his testimony?

Of course it will; that is why we are bringing it out early. The question is disingenuous and better omitted.

The same technique will work if it is the client himself who has an unfortunate event in his past:

Q. You will hear that my client, John Smith, was convicted fifteen years ago of income tax evasion. Now, you understand, don't you, that this happened years ago, and has nothing to do with who went through the red light?

Depending on the nature of the problem, this kind of question may be appropriate:

Q. My client, John Smith, will tell you that he has been in a few accidents before. You understand, don't you, that we are here to decide only about this one accident — and that his earlier accidents don't say anything about what happened this time?

A second kind of problem arises from having to read to the jury at length from documents. It is a civil case, let us say. We have deposed the key witness for forty days and forty nights. There are 25,000 pages of transcript, every word of it vital to the case. The witness dies on the eve of trial, and now we have to put those 25,000 pages before the jury. Or, what is even worse, the case might involve a corporate trust indenture — seventeen pages of print so small that only an insect can read it. But we must recite the whole thing out loud to the jury. After five minutes, the jury is angry with us for subjecting them to such incomprehensible nonsense. After ten minutes they are still angry, but they have also fallen asleep.

We can deal with this problem on voir dire or in the opening statement. If it were the opening statement, it would go like this:

Ladies and gentlemen, there is something I want you to know. On Thursday, I think it will be, I shall be putting into evidence a piece of paper that lawyers call a corporate trust indenture. We'll explain to you later what that is. For now, I just want to say that when the piece of paper goes into evidence, I have to read it to you. That's what the rules of this court say. And so I will read it to you. But I want to tell you right now, it is going to be the most boring thing you have ever heard. There is nothing I can do about that. It just has to be that way.

When Thursday comes, we fish out the magnifying glass and start to read from the corporate trust indenture. And the jurors say to themselves, "Here it comes. Hey, he told us it would be boring. Let's go to sleep." Nothing can possibly stop them from going to sleep. But now they go to sleep confident that they are in good hands, knowing that we will awaken them at the proper time.

A last example. Let us suppose that the other side is planning to call a sympathetic witness. That could be someone who is very young, very old, injured, handicapped — anything that might elicit the jury's sympathy. This too is a problem. Telling the jury about it in advance will help the jury to hear that witness's testimony more objectively. And again, it conveys the message that we are a person who can be trusted.

These are only illustrations. The same principle applies, in very much the same way, to any special problem that we can foresee. It includes, as well, problems that are common to every case. For example, every juror has learned a lot about courtroom procedure by watching television. The jurors know, among other things, that the lawyer for the good guy hardly ever makes an objection, while the lawyer for the bad guy objects on every question. Perry Mason hardly ever objects; Hamilton Burger never lets up. The jurors have learned, therefore, that objections are the bad guy's way of thwarting justice. Every time we object, we are setting ourselves up on the wrong side. Accordingly:

Q. From time to time, ladies and gentlemen, when the defendant's lawyer asks a question, you will hear me object. Do you understand that I don't do that to get in his way? Do you understand that I have a professional obligation to my client to make those objections?

We can handle any foreseeable problem this way. And after thorough preparation, we should be able to foresee all of the problems. None should come as a surprise.

## §3.7 Factors in Jury Selection

A lawyer's decision about a prospective juror typically turns on certain of the juror's characteristics. These come in two main categories: personal qualities of a general nature; and specific items in the juror's background that are connected, in one way or another, with issues in the case. In most kinds of cases, it is worth considering the dozen characteristics listed below. They are the basis for most peremptory challenges;[18] less often, they will support a challenge for cause[19] or a challenge to the favor.[20] Not all of the characteristics will apply in every case, and special circumstances will often suggest others. In this instance, no single checklist can stand in for experience and common sense.

Most kinds of information could tilt the decision about a juror either way, depending upon the nature of the case and on which side we represent. There are exceptions; a juror who shows signs of illness, for example, is a candidate for rejection by either side. Few of the other factors offer hard and fast rules in either direction. At best, the information is merely raw material for formulating hunches.

These are the twelve characteristics most often useful in deciding whom to eliminate.

**1. The degree to which the juror is acquainted with the lawyers, the parties, the witnesses, the controversy, and the physical location involved.** Familiarity with the location is more important than it might seem. If one juror has personal knowledge of the intersection, the bank branch, or whatever it may be, that juror's views will carry disproportionate weight in the jury room.

**2. Juror's occupation.**

**3. Spouse's occupation.** A formula for handling this item can help to avoid offending fellow jurors. If the juror is male, the questioning should go like this:

---

[18]See §3.3.
[19]See §3.2.
[20]See *id.*

Q. Mr. Smith, are you married?

A. Yes, I am.

The very next question should be:

Q. What kind of work does your wife do?

A. Oh, she doesn't work. She just stays at home and takes care of the house and the seven kids.

This way he has said it, not you.

**4. Health considerations.** It is important to watch for indications of less than perfect health: sallow complexion, bloodshot eyes, nasal congestion, shifting in the seat from physical discomfort, and any other such signs. Even a short trial can be unduly protracted for a juror suffering an ulcer flare-up or a sinusitis attack. An emotionally demanding case will be especially tough on a juror who is not feeling well. A slightly ill juror may be able to sit without trouble through a half-day child-beating case or statutory rape case, and he will vote his conscience in the jury room, but, owing to reduced vitality, he may not take an active part in the discussion. He is a vote but not a voice, and that will affect the group dynamics.

**5. The juror's membership in a group or organization likely to have specific prejudices, in cases where those prejudices could affect the juror's reactions.** This item is largely a matter of common sense, coupled with knowledge of the community. Suppose that our client is obviously of Greek ancestry, and that one of the jurors is just as obviously of Turkish ancestry. In view of the long-standing hostility between those two groups, it might be a wise precaution to eliminate the juror. Or, if the juror is seventy-five-year-old Mr. Weinberg with numbers tattooed on his forearm and the client is a German of about the same age, Mr. Weinberg should probably be sent home.

The matter of black-white relations is extremely complicated, and it also changes abruptly from one community to the next. Local conditions and prejudices are therefore important, but not always obvious in their effects. In some parts of the country, criminal lawyers defending a black client prefer to exclude blacks from the jury. They reason that most victims of black crime are themselves black, and that a black juror may see himself and his family as among the potential victims. In consequence, the reasoning goes, black juries may be tough on a black defendant, while liberal whites might be more inclined to exert themselves to find a reasonable doubt. In civil cases also, some plaintiffs' lawyers representing a black client prefer an upper-middle-class white jury that may be influenced by racial guilt.

A strong imbalance of races on the jury can sometimes be troublesome. Suppose that there are two black panel members, and that for reasons having nothing to do with race, we wish to exercise a peremptory challenge against one. The remaining black juror, then, will go into the jury room with five or eleven white jurors. If he feels that we have put him on the spot, or if his race becomes important in the minds of the other jurors, it could affect the group dynamics and hence the outcome.

This kind of stereotyping is risky, however. It can too easily blind us to characteristics of the jurors that are more important in the case. Very often it will just be wrong. Moreover, whatever truth the stereotypes do have varies widely with geography. Simple rules are not possible, and in the end a lawyer has to make his decision according to the case, the client, and the particular panel.

**6. What the juror might have heard or read about the case.**

**7. Whether the juror has formed an opinion.**

**8. Whether the juror has had previous experience in legal controversies that might influence the deliberations.** The problem here is the juror who says in the jury room, "Listen, I was on a jury a year ago, in a drug case just like this one, and we put that guy away with a lot less evidence than this." Not only is that an influence on other jurors, but the juror in question may want to vote against the defendant simply to vindicate his vote in the earlier case. A related problem is the experienced juror who thinks he learned some law during the last trial, and attempts to impose it on his fellow jurors — even though it has nothing to do with the case.

**9. Whether the juror has had education or experience in some line of work or learning that is involved in the case.** This too will amplify his voice in the jury room.

**10. Whether the juror is accustomed to thinking in terms of large amounts of money.** If the case involves potentially large damages, this factor is important. Even an award that is small under the circumstances can look unimaginably large to a juror who is himself poor. In contrast, a middle-class accounting clerk who deals with large quantities of other people's money every day may be better able to put the amount in perspective.

**11. Whether the juror is likely to lead or follow the panel; whether he will compromise easily; how he is likely to influence other jury members.**

**12. Whether we have offended the jury with an unsuccessful effort to have the juror disqualified for cause.**

# CHAPTER 4

# From Jury Selection to Opening Statement

After the jury has been selected, the next event for the jurors will be the opening statements. Before that, however, the lawyers have to attend to five preliminary matters. Some of these may be handled before jury selection and some after, but they all must be taken care of before the opening statements.

## §4.1 Marked Pleadings

The lawyers in all civil actions should prepare marked pleadings and submit them at the final pretrial meeting with the judge. Depending upon the calendar system in the particular court, that meeting will be either before or just after the jury is selected. Most courts, by local rule, require marked pleadings of the plaintiff, yet a large majority of lawyers have never heard of them. Neither have most judges, and so the rule goes largely ignored. Whether required or not, however, marked pleadings can smooth the way for either party. Their preparation takes very little time and money; submit them as a matter of course.

The marked pleadings always include the complaint and the answer. Also included, if they exist in the case, are the reply and a bill of particulars. The answers to interrogatories, if they are not too voluminous, may also be part of the package.

To mark the pleadings, we make extra copies and proceed as follows. The complaint consists of numbered allegations. The responses to those allegations are in the answer. On a copy of the complaint, in the left-hand margin, we simply abbreviate in a bold hand the response to each allegation: *A* for "admitted"; *D* for "denied"; and *DKI* for "lack of knowledge or information." A counterclaim is functionally a complaint, to which the plaintiff makes answer in the reply, and so we mark the allegations of the counterclaim, if any, in the same manner.

We then assemble the pleadings, in this order from the top: complaint, answer, reply, bill of particulars, and answers to interrogatories. We staple the whole thing into a litigation back and take it to the final pretrial meeting with the judge.

A judge who knows about the rule will turn to us, as plaintiff's counsel, and ask for the marked pleadings. And instead of answering, "Marked pleadings? What are those?" we can say, "Of course, Your Honor," and pass them over. As defense counsel, we are not required to prepare marked pleadings, but we will have done so anyway. Then, if plaintiff's counsel says, "What? Marked pleadings?" we pull them out and say, "Permit me, Your Honor."

If we are plaintiff's counsel before a judge who does not know about the rule, we wait for an appropriate moment to say, "Judge, allow me to submit the marked pleadings." Seeing them for the first time, the judge observes that they are extremely useful. They are extra copies that he can write on, and they give him a quick view of the case. He may find them so useful that he requires them in all future cases.

## §4.2 Trial Memorandum*

Whether the case is civil or criminal, state or federal, simple or complex, always give the judge a trial memorandum. If you represent the plaintiff, give it to the judge a day or two before the trial starts; if you represent the defendant, give it just before

---

*Reprinted with permission from the September 1986 ABA Journal: The Lawyer's Magazine, a publication of the American Bar Association.

you begin to present your evidence. The memorandum should accompany any requests to charge or marked pleadings that you submit, and should be furnished even though there may already be an order regulating the trial.

The purpose of the trial memorandum is to give the judge a bird's-eye view of what is about to happen. Do not use the trial memorandum to argue or persuade. The trial memorandum merely orients, which is why it should be succinct. A few pages will almost always suffice. Ten pages are almost always too many.

You will sometimes be tempted not to submit a trial memorandum. Perhaps you are in municipal court on a matter involving only $200. Or it is a magistrate's court case and the worst your client faces is a $500 fine. Resist the temptation. Give the judge a trial memorandum, even if the case does not absolutely warrant it. If the client cannot pay for the time you put into the trial memorandum, absorb the cost yourself. It is a worthwhile investment in your reputation.

Here is an outline of the sort of trial memorandum that will be useful to a judge. It can be adapted to virtually any kind of case.

Begin with a short paragraph telling the judge how the case arose. For example: "On Nov. 30, 1982, at about noon, at the corner of Main and Market streets in this city, a Plymouth driven by William Smith collided with a Buick driven by Richard Jones."

Continue with another short paragraph stating your position in the case. For example: "The collision occurred because Jones went through a red light."

Next, list your witnesses in the order in which you plan to call them and give the gist of their testimony. For example:

Smith will call the following witnesses:
- Philip Brown, who will testify that he saw Jones go through the red light.
- William Smith, the plaintiff, who will testify that he was driving through the intersection with the green light in his favor when his car was struck by Jones's car. Smith will also describe the injuries he sustained.

And so forth.

In the next section, identify any out-of-the-ordinary evidentiary problems you anticipate, state your position on each, and cite the leading authority supporting your position. For example: "We expect plaintiff Smith to testify that, immediately before the impact, his wife, who was a passenger in their car, cried out, 'My God, he went through the light!' Defendant will object to this as hearsay. It is hearsay, but it is admissible as an excited utterance. [Citation]."

Do not talk about the run-of-the-mill evidentiary points here. The judge has no need to know in advance that you may object should your opponent ask a leading question on direct.

Now comes a section in which you do for out-of-the-ordinary nonevidentiary problems what you have just done for evidentiary problems. For example: "At the close of plaintiff's case, we expect that defendant will move to dismiss on the ground of the statute of limitations. The motion should be denied because the statute was tolled until Dec. 20, 1985, by the plaintiff's infancy. [Citation]." Limit this section to matters on which the judge will probably have to rule from the bench.

In the final paragraph of the trial memorandum, tell the judge exactly what relief you seek. For example: "Plaintiff will ask the jury for a verdict against Jones in the amount of $10,000."

When you hand your trial memorandum to the judge, you will simultaneously serve it on your opponent. Because whatever you have revealed in the trial memorandum now becomes public knowledge, you must think about that special delight of all trial lawyers, the surprise witness. If you reveal the surprise witness's name and testimony in your trial memorandum, the witness is a surprise no longer. If you omit him from the trial memorandum, you have been less than candid with the court.

You might end the witness section of your trial memorandum with a sentence something like this: "In addition to these witnesses, the plaintiff will call another witness whose identity we prefer not to disclose," perhaps adding a sentence to summarize the surprise witness's testimony.

Should you follow this course, your opponent will immediately move to compel you to reveal the identity of your surprise witness and for leave to take his deposition. You will respond that the time for discovery has long since passed, and the judge will rule in accordance with all the circumstances. The lesson here is that there is no single assured way to handle surprise witnesses.

You may not win more cases by submitting a trial memorandum, but submitting a trial memorandum in every case is the lawyerly thing to do. That is justification enough.

## §4.3 Clean-Up Motions

In every civil lawsuit, a considerable period of time passes between the pleading and discovery stages and the trial. What was true at the time of the pleadings or discovery may not still be true at the time of trial. The clean-up motions correct the record. They are made on the record but not on papers. There is no particular custom dictating which side handles them. We will have consulted with the opponent, and the motions will usually be on consent.

Here is an example. The jury is not present, but the court reporter is taking it down:

> Your Honor, you will have observed from the marked pleadings I submitted yesterday that the caption of this case is *John Smith, an infant, by his mother Mary Smith v. Defendant*. At the time that this lawsuit was commenced, Your Honor, John Smith was indeed an infant, and his mother sued under the statute as next friend. But that was some time ago, and John Smith is no longer an infant. That being so, Your Honor, might the caption be amended to read, *John Smith v. Defendant*, dropping any reference to his mother? I believe that this is on consent.

"Granted," says the judge, and it is done. A second example:

> If Your Honor will refer to the marked pleadings handed up yesterday — at the bottom of the package you will see the bill of particulars, which says that the medical

expenses incurred by the plaintiff in this case are $30,000. That was correct as of the time of the bill of particulars. But that was five years ago, and since then the plaintiff has incurred another $20,000 of expense. Counsel has the bills and canceled checks. I believe it is on consent, Your Honor, that Paragraph 3 of the bill of particulars be deemed amended to read not $30,000, but $50,000.

## §4.4 Requests to Charge

The requests to charge are a document in which we ask the judge to say certain things to the jury in his charge at the close of the case. Typically it is submitted early in the trial. It is the device by which the lawyers participate in framing the legal issues in the case.

Suppose, for example, that we represent the plaintiff in a product liability case. We have four possible theories available: negligence; breach of express warranty; breach of implied warranty under the Uniform Commercial Code; and strict liability in tort. From the plaintiff's point of view, the most favorable is strict liability. But the question of strict liability on the facts of this case has never been decided in our state. And so we submit a request to charge: "Will Your Honor charge the jury as follows, . . ." There we quote from the Restatement on strict liability, along with a few citations to cases from other states. Now the question of strict liability is a legal issue in the case, and whichever side loses can appeal it.

This kind of case is the exception. Very few cases in actual practice are legally controversial; most turn on facts, not law. But legal issues are only one aspect of the request to charge. There is a second aspect that is of enormous utility to lawyers trying cases of the more usual kind, those that turn purely on the evidence. This second aspect is useful primarily in connection with the summation or final statement, and will be discussed in that chapter.[1]

---

[1]See Chapter 17.

## §4.5 Motion *in Limine*

Translated from the Latin, the motion *in limine* means "the motion at the doorstep." Usually made orally, though on the record, it is a request for a ruling in advance, before the trial begins. Typically it concerns some problem of evidence. We are in court without the jury:

The Court: Any motion *in limine?*

Counsel: Yes, Your Honor. Has Your Honor had a chance to read the trial memorandum I submitted late yesterday?

The Court: Yes, I have.

Counsel: Your Honor will recall that I am going to call a witness who will be asked the question, "What color was the traffic light?" His answer will be, "I didn't see it, but my wife cried out, 'My God, the light is red!' " Now, Your Honor, I am offering that to prove the truth of what it asserts. We concede that it is hearsay, and I know that my opponent will object on the ground of hearsay. But I urge that it is admissible as an excited utterance. May we have Your Honor's ruling?

We want the ruling now because we will soon be opening to the jury. If the judge is going to overrule the objection and allow the testimony, we want to tell the jury about it. But we also want to avoid misleading the jury, under the Joe DiMaggio principle.[2] If the motion will be sustained, we do not want to mention it to the jury at all.

The judge can answer in three ways, each in two steps. First, the judge can grant the motion *in limine* for a ruling in advance, and sustain the hearsay objection. Second, he can grant the motion *in limine*, and overrule the objection. Third, the judge can say this: "Whether I rule in advance is within my discretion. I choose not to. I prefer to wait until the situation is before me, and then I will rule. Therefore, I deny your motion *in limine.*" The judge need not rule in advance unless he wants to, and his decision to rule or not in advance is, as a practical matter, unreviewable.

---

[2] See §§1.3, 3.6.

# CHAPTER 5

# The Opening Statement

## §5.1 Importance of the Opening Statement

Some lawyers fail to appreciate the importance of the opening statement. They open pro forma, with less psychic energy than they bring to bear later in the proceedings. The opening statement is difficult to do well, as we shall see. Yet it is of enormous consequence: It offers a magnificent opportunity for advocacy. With only slight exaggeration, we can say that the case is won or lost on the opening statement.

In one study, social scientists sought to determine the importance of the opening statement. Interviewing jurors after the verdict was returned, they asked each juror what his verdict would have been immediately after the opening statements: before any evidence, before the summations, and before the judge's charge. The researchers compared these hypothetical verdicts with the actual verdicts in the same cases and found a correlation of about eighty percent. One can always quibble with the design of such a study, but the basic result is correct in that it is in accord with the experience and intuition of trial lawyers. If, four times out of five, a jury inclined to decide the case our way after the opening statements will decide the case our way in the end, then those are very good odds indeed.[1]

---

[1] *See generally* Hans & Bidmar, Judging the Jury (1986); Kalven, The American Jury (1971).

Everyday psychology supports the social scientists' result. It is always hard to get someone whose mind is already made up to change his mind, much harder than it is to persuade someone with an open mind. At the end of the opening statements, the jurors cannot help but make up their minds, albeit tentatively. If that tentative decision is against us, then our chances of persuading the jury to change it are slim.

From the importance of the opening statement we can deduce two practical corollaries. First, the opening statement should never be waived, even if we have little to say. The temptation to waive it is greatest in a criminal case when there is, in fact, nothing to say for the defendant. Vibrating as we do to the special obligations of an advocate, we must do the best we can. There is a formula for the situation. Easy to recognize, it echoes every day through the courtrooms of the land. We speak of the importance of the jury system in American justice, and the heavy weight of responsibility that the jury before us has shouldered. We find a place for the line, "I envy you your privilege of serving on an American jury." And on it goes.

The second suggestion concerning opening statements is more controversial; not all trial lawyers will agree with it. Ordinarily defense counsel in either a civil or a criminal case opens immediately after the plaintiff or prosecutor. Depending on the local practice, however, the judge may allow the defendant to defer his opening statement until later in the trial, just before the defense puts in its side of the case. The lawyer, however, should resist reserving the opening statement. There are two reasons, both of which follow from the principle of testing everything we do from the jury's point of view.

Lawyers know that a trial is something other than a search for truth. They know, for example, that the law of evidence frequently serves to keep out truthful evidence. But the jury thinks differently. Being unsophisticated in the ways of the law, the jury tends to regard the trial as indeed a search for truth. To the jurors' ears, then, a reserved opening statement lacks something in sincerity. They suspect us of adapting the opening statement, not to the truth, but to whatever evidence the plaintiff or prosecutor has offered against us. That suspicion is rather astute of the jurors:

Defendants reserve their opening for precisely that reason. To the jury, however, the truth is the same this week as next week and has nothing to do with the other side's evidence. Being inconsistent with the search for truth, a reserved opening will not sit well with the jury. It will incline them to distrust us, and that puts us on the way to defeat.

The second reason not to reserve the opening statement follows from the analogy between the courtroom and the theater.[2] The jury is our audience when we try a case. An important part of playing to any audience, whether from the stage or from the well of the court, is to fullfill its expectations. That is why we must become familiar with what the jury expects of us. To determine their expectations, we look to the same sources of information that the jurors use. Their learning comes not from law school, nor from any substantial exposure to real trials, but from movies and television programs about lawyers. For that reason, advocates should see all of the trial movies as they come out, and also the classics of the genre on television. We will learn a great deal about how jurors *think* that lawyers ought to try a case — and it can be a mistake to do anything very different. If we depart from what the jurors expect, they will decide we do not know our business. That will incline them to distrust us, which puts us at a disadvantage.

In the movies, the defense lawyer always opens right after the prosecution. That, then, is what an able defense lawyer does — after all, there is no better lawyer in the jurors' eyes than Jimmy Stewart or Spencer Tracy. In order to keep the jury's confidence, we are well advised to do it the same way.

## §5.2 Preparation

Appellate opinions tell us the purpose of the opening statement: to outline for the jury the nature of the case and our own position in the case. Trial judges sometimes put it more plainly,

---

[2]See §3.6.

saying that the opening statement outlines for the jury what we intend to prove.

As these definitions indicate, the opening statement is not an occasion to argue the case. If we do argue, the other side will make an objection, and the judge will sustain it. Some judges will not wait to hear an objection, but will interrupt on their own when the lawyer argues in making the opening statement.

One way of arguing is to do so overtly:

> Ladies and gentlemen, I am going to call a witness named John Smith. Mr. Smith will tell you that when the cars collided, my client was driving his car, a fifteen-year-old Volkswagen, at thirty miles per hour. The other side will call Mr. Jones, who will tell you that my client's car — an old, beat-up VW, remember — was traveling at 110 miles per hour. Now, between those two witnesses, which is more likely to be telling the truth?

The other way to argue is by tone of voice. We are arguing if we yell, or if we cry, or if we merely raise our voice sufficiently.

An objection at that early stage of the trial does not help us get off on the right foot with the jury, particularly if the judge sustains it. It is even worse if the judge interrupts unprompted. But at the same time, we want to persuade the jury to decide the case our way. The problem, then, is to persuade the jury, but without appearing to argue. It is not easy to do, and it will not work every time. But when the gods are kind, it is possible to deliver an opening statement that will never once elicit an objection, yet will leave the jury eager to decide the case as we want them to.

Once again, the most important goal — especially early in the trial — is to develop the jury's confidence in us. We began that process in the context of jury selection,[3] and now continue it here.

---

[3]See *id.*

**Planning.** First, the opening statement must be carefully prepared. To extemporize it is always a mistake. The opening statement is far too valuable an opportunity for us to take a chance on winging it.

**Rehearsal.** Second, the opening statement must be rehearsed out loud. Every beginning actor knows a fact that has escaped many lawyers: Words that read perfectly well on paper may be hard to deliver orally. Writing and speech are fundamentally different. The same words that flow beautifully on the page may cause the tongue to stumble and confuse the ear. The sources of the problem are complicated, having to do with the physiology of speech and the rhythms of the language. It is a common problem on the stage, and because of its importance, actors and playwrights have developed a simple way of coping with it. Their method can serve lawyers as well.

Suppose that we are involved in the production of a new play. On the first day of rehearsal, the stage is bare. The actors merely sit on chairs with the scripts in their hands, and they read the play through, out loud. If an actor has trouble with a speech — it looks fine on paper, but the actor finds it hard to say the words — he looks up at the director, who turns to the playwright and says, "This is a terrific scene. It's going to bring the house down. But it needs work. It doesn't speak."

In Hamlet's phrase, the words must fall trippingly from the tongue. Pick up any play by Oscar Wilde or George Bernard Shaw, two modern masters of spoken dialogue. Their sentences are easy to say. They flow naturally because they are perfectly congruent with the native rhythms of English. Then, for contrast, read from an appellate opinion selected at random. Appellate opinions are not meant to be read aloud; and indeed, to speak them is sometimes all but impossible.

Jurors must listen to the opening statement, as they would listen to a speech in a play. Accordingly, we must deliver the opening statement with the same regard for the flow of language that a director requires of an actor on the stage. It is very unsettling, when opening before the jury, to hit a rough spot, a passage that "doesn't speak." We have to stop and work it out right there, in front of the jury box. That conveys to the jury a quality of amateurism inconsistent with the Joe DiMaggio principle.[4] It erodes the jury's confidence in us.

The solution, then, is to rehearse the opening statement aloud. The rehearsal can be before a moot jury of people in the office, or in front of someone at home, or into a mirror or tape recorder. Where and to whom the rehearsal is made do not matter, but it must be done. There is no other way to make sure that the words will work aloud as well as they do on paper.

**No Notes.** The third point of advice: Deliver the opening statement without notes. If names, dates, or numbers are important, they can go on a three-by-five card, but nothing more.

Our purpose is to deliver an opening statement that persuades the jury, not one that reads perfectly in the record. Many young lawyers seem to think that we persuade with intellect and the products of thought — ideas and argument. These are not entirely unimportant, but neither are they high on the list. Most of all, we persuade with our own appearance, stance, and tone of voice. These communicate to the jury our degree of commitment to the cause. The most persuasive part of a person is the face; the most persuasive part of the face the eyes. If we work from notes, then for some fraction of the time our eyes will have to be on the paper. Every second that we are not looking at the jury is a lost opportunity for persuasion. We must let the jury see our eyes throughout the opening statement.

In Cicero's time, oratory was not mere speech-making, but was closer to what lawyers do today in courtrooms, in the legislature, and before administrative committees. The title of Cicero's book on the subject, *De Oratore,* would best be translated as "About Litigation." Written around 55 B.C. for Cicero's brother, the book takes the form of an old hand talking to young lawyers. There is a passage in Book II saying much what I say here. More important than your ideas, writes Cicero, is you yourself. The most important part of you is your face; and the most important part of your face is your eyes. Therefore, he says, in order to persuade, we must look at the listener when we speak.

---

[4]See §1.3.

Apart from this, there are other reasons for not using notes during the opening statement. Everything we do in the courtroom is part of a performance. The jury expects us to know our lines. If we are to communicate trustworthiness, we must meet that expectation. At the other extreme, an opening statement that appears to have been prepared too carefully in advance sounds contrived and hence untrustworthy. The goal, then, is a natural delivery that conceals the high degree of preparation. The use of notes detracts from that image.

**Plain English.** Fourth, speak plain English. The point has already come up in the context of jury selection,[5] where we were concerned with promoting the jury's understanding. In the opening statement, another reason comes into play together with lucidity, which of course remains just as important.

Our goal is to establish trustworthiness. That will be an uphill task from the beginning, because we are talking to a jury of lay people. They know that I am a lawyer. They believe, therefore, that I am an untrustworthy rapscallion. This unsavory perception of lawyers is not merely a post-Watergate phenomenon. Indeed, that the public at large has always held lawyers in low esteem is no small part of our history. It is an element of the Western intellectual tradition that we find reflected in the works of authors from Shakespeare to Carl Sandburg.

Whenever I use fancy language to the jury, I am saying, "Never forget it! I'm a lawyer!" Every time I do that, I diminish their trust in me. One way to put across the notion that I am a lawyer by the merest accident of fate, really an honest person through and through, is to speak plain English. Let the other side use the lawyerisms and tar himself with the malodorous reputation of the legal profession.[6]

---

[5] See §3.6.

[6] We can take this point a little further. Ordinarily, attacking the other lawyer is unwise, but occasionally it becomes necessary. He has been pushing us around, and now we have to hit back. But we do not call him a liar, or a scorpion, or a moral serpent. There is a much better way: We call him a lawyer.

This tactic is not routine; we do it only when absolutely necessary. In our summation, we might say:

**Sequence; Exposition.** The fifth suggestion, like the others, follows from the need to establish the jury's trust. We want to convey the same kind of professional competence that Joe DiMaggio displayed; we want to make something that is really quite difficult look easy. To do that, we must put across to the jury a sense of control. That is why we never ask the clerk in front of the jury, "How do I do this?" We never say to the judge in open court, "Your Honor, I guess I'm confused here." The jury may sympathize with our problems, but they will conclude that we are professionally incapable, and hence untrustworthy.

The point has special importance for the opening statement. Here we must convey our mastery of the case. All of the facts, no matter how complex, must seem to be in the palm of our hand. To communicate this sense of control early in the trial, we must give the opening statement a principle of organization. The opening statement is a literary genre — a humble one, to be sure, but it must have a literary form nonetheless. The jury may not be aware of the form as such, but they will respond to it by sensing that we are in control of the case.

The form we need is not complicated. Nor is it a new idea. It goes back at least as far as Aristotle, who said in the *Poetics* that a Greek tragedy should have a beginning, a middle, and an end. And that is what an opening statement should have — a beginning, a middle, and an end.

---

Ladies and gentlemen, we have arrived at the summations, the final stage of the case. And a remarkable thing has happened. Do you remember the opening statements three days ago? I know you remember, because I saw you paying close attention. And I saw you note the amazing thing that Mr. Smith said to us then. As a matter of fact, I wrote it down. Here it is, in his exact words. I know that you remember his saying that.

Mr. Smith said — yes, you said it, Mr. Smith — he said, "I am going to prove to you that the light was red." Here we are, now, at the end of the case. You have heard all of the witnesses. You have seen all of the exhibits. You have every bit of proof that either side has. And is there one syllable to show you that the light was red? Not one! And that's the kind of case he's put in. No evidence. No proof. All lawyer talk!

The beginning of the opening statement is especially important. Every case involves an enormous amount of information for the jury to absorb. The jury has not been through the pleadings and discovery; they have not lived the case as the lawyers have. At the trial, they hear it all for the first time. In order to understand the line of the case as it develops, the jury needs a fair amount of information quite early. They must know the who, what, where, when, and why. That is the office of the beginning of the opening statement: to give the jury the preliminary information they need in such a way that they can understand and absorb the rest of the case.

Playwrights have the same problem. In order to follow the unfolding of the plot, the audience must have certain information at the outset. The part of a play that provides this information is called the exposition, and it must come at the beginning. Take, for example, any of the Kaufman and Hart comedies of the 1930s. Typically, the curtain comes up on a middle-class living room. The telephone rings. Enter the maid. She answers the telephone. We hear only her side of the conversation, but by the time she hangs up, we know where we are, who the main characters are, and what the problem is.

For a harder case, recall the opening pages of *Hamlet*. Consider it from the point of view of the audience in the Globe Theater on opening night — opening afternoon, it would have been in those days. Not having studied the play in high school, the audience knows nothing about it. And the dramatic situation is complicated, to put it mildly. The play is set in Denmark. The old king is dead under suspicious circumstances. The new king is the dead king's brother, and he's actually had the temerity to marry his brother's widow. Young Hamlet, the dead king's son, is some sort of lunatic who has come home from school to attend his father's funeral and his mother's wedding. What is more, there are reports of a ghost walking around in the towers, apparently the ghost of the old king. And on top of all that, it appears that Norway, seeing an opportunity for political aggrandizement, is raising an army, perhaps with the intention of invading Denmark.

In print it runs only a couple of pages, and it takes about three minutes on the stage. In those three minutes the audience has heard patches of supreme poetry and some very funny material. And when it is over, they know everything they need in order to follow the play. None of us can deliver an exposition in an opening statement equivalent to the one in *Hamlet*. But we can certainly try for the quality of a Kaufman and Hart exposition.

## §5.3 Delivery

We have seen that there are two things to be accomplished in the opening statement.[7] First, we must continue the process, begun during jury selection, of convincing the jury that we are trustworthy. Second, we must deliver the information that the jury needs in order to understand the case, and in such a way that the information sinks in.

Some lawyers deliver their opening statement timidly, in a soft voice, seemingly afraid to impose themselves on the jury. None of us wants to appear pushy, of course. In our society, an excess of self-assertion is considered gross. Polite behavior calls for modesty and self-effacement. That is how we were brought up; and indeed, modesty is a great virtue. But in front of the jury, a certain display of confidence is needed. We have a job to do, a performance to put on. Confidence on our part is especially important at the beginning, for from the very start, we want to assure the jury that they are in good hands. We know our business, the message says, and they can trust us.

Here is one way to begin. Individual styles will vary, of course; still, the underlying principles may be useful. To help expose those principles, there are annotations along the way.

**Introductions.** Typically, we might say:

Good afternoon, ladies and gentlemen. You know, we actually met yesterday, when you were selected as the jury in this case; so I remember you, but you may not remember me. Let me reintroduce myself. My name is . . .

---

[7]See §5.2.

This is ten seconds of empty talk, with no demands whatsoever on the jury's intelligence. It is to establish ourselves. "This is me," it says. "Look at me; listen to my voice. Apart from you, I am the most important person in this courtroom for the next three days. Make sure you know who I am."

> My name is _____. Now, I'm a lawyer here in town . . .

We'll try to get across the idea that we are a lawyer only by accident.[8] In the meantime, though, the fact that we are a lawyer is no secret to anyone. We might as well put it on the table. But notice that I call myself a lawyer. I will call the other side an attorney. The word "lawyer" ends with "-er," like baker, butcher, and carpenter. It helps to connote an honest man or woman doing an honest day's work. To the jury, "attorney" is a fancy word. An "attorney" is a pettifogger and not to be trusted.

> I'm a lawyer here in town, and as lawyers do, I talk for people.

Talk for people; not "represent clients." That is too fancy, and the jury may not be sure what it means. Let the other side represent clients. We just talk for people. Anyone can understand that.

> I talk for people. And today the man I talk for is sitting right there. His name is Jack Smith, and I'd like you to meet him.

Nine times out of ten, physically introduce your client. When the client is a corporation, introduce whoever is sitting with you as though he were the client. Even in criminal defense work, the client is usually presentable, or can be cleaned up sufficiently to look presentable. (There is, however, that one case in ten where to see the client is to know that he is guilty. Such clients are better left unintroduced.)

---

[8]See *id.*

I'd like you to meet him. Jack, would you stand, please?

If he looks younger than you, call him by his first name; otherwise, he is "Mr. Smith."

The client has been prepared to give a slight nod of his head at this point. And the six or twelve people in the jury box nod back. Their mothers taught them to do that. By nodding back to him, they have acknowledged the existence of another human being. They have embraced him as a fellow mortal. That makes it a little harder to decide against him.

Be seated, Jack. Thank you.

Do nothing unthinkingly; but sometimes, if opposing counsel hasn't yet spoken, you might turn and introduce him. It puts across the idea that you are in charge; and it has the added effect, as we shall see, of rendering him helpless before the jury. He will not be helpless in the corridor later on, however, and he may then choose to express himself in strong terms. It is well to have some kind of response ready.

This is how it works. Notice again that opposing counsel is always an "attorney."

Now, ladies and gentlemen, I'd like you to meet the attorney for the defendant. He's one of the finest attorneys in this city, and it is a privilege to be trying a case against him. Robert Smith. Bob, would you stand, please?

He must stand. He has no choice.

Ladies and gentlemen, this is Bob Smith. Thank you, Bob; be seated.

I have sometimes introduced the other client in a civil case. About half the time I have introduced the court reporter, but only with his permission. When asked, his answer is usually, "Sure, why not? That's great. Nobody ever introduces me." And again, we become the master of ceremonies introducing the jury to another neutral person in the trial.

> Ladies and gentlemen, this lady is Mrs. Smith. She is the best court reporter in this courthouse. And believe it or not, on that little machine she is taking down every word I'm saying. She will take down every word that's said in the course of this trial. She can't stand up and say hello right now, because she's busy taking all this down, but I'd like you to meet her. Ladies and gentlemen, Mrs. Smith.

They nod, and Mrs. Smith nods, and everyone feels warm and friendly. It is a fine way to start a trial.[9]

**Narrative.** With the introductions over, we come to the second part of the opening statement. Again, the problem of the opening statement is to persuade the jury without ever once invoking the objection that we are arguing.[10] The preceding section posed several specific suggestions involving preparation, rehearsal, working without notes, using plain English, putting matters in sequence, and providing an exposition. Here, through an analogy, a more general principle will be assembled from those bits of advice.

We can agree that the purpose of a trial is to resolve a dispute. Underlying every trial, then, is a dispute, a dispute arising from some aspect of human affairs. One synonym for dispute is conflict.

We can also agree that conflict forms the basis for every work of narrative literature — conflict generated by people living and

---

[9]Only once did I think I might get away with taking this a step farther. His Honor had not so much as told the jurors his name. When I had finished introducing the court reporter, the moment seemed right.

> Ladies and gentlemen, best of all, I'd like you to meet the jurist who will preside over this trial. It is an honor to be working before him. There is not a lawyer in this city who would not want to be here right now, trying a case before Judge Smith. Ladies and gentlemen, Judge Smith.

I had established myself in that courtroom. I had become the man in charge; people did what I told them to. And that is exactly what I wanted of the jury: I wanted them to do what I told them to do — to decide the case my way. They were well along to being conditioned in that direction.

[10]See §5.2.

working together. Without that conflict, a written work may be a prose sketch or an essay, but it is not a story.

If a dispute underlies every trial; if conflict underlies every kind of narrative; and if conflict means the same thing as dispute, then within every lawsuit, regardless of the jurisdiction and the nature of the case, there lies a story. The story is always about human beings engaged in some aspect of human life. The story sometimes lies right at the surface, as in a child custody dispute: two parents in conflict over which of them shall care for a child they both love. We all respond to that story. But there is also a story in a major antitrust case between the government and a multinational corporation. That kind of story is harder to bring out, of course. Finding it is a challenge to the skill and creativity of the lawyer.

Because we cannot make up the story at will, our task as a lawyer is harder than that of a novelist or short story writer. We must piece the story together from the evidence. And having done so, we tell it to the jury in the opening statement. We are merely telling the jury what we are going to prove, but in an artful way. And never once will the judge sustain the objection that we are arguing.

There is no better vehicle for persuading a jury than a story. It is in the nature of the human nervous system that a story properly told can make the audience feel exactly as the story-teller wants. If Mark Twain wants us to laugh, we laugh. If Chekhov wants us to cry, we cry. If Tolstoy wants us to experience a religious conversion, that happens too.

We have now finished with the introductions. We are ready to proceed with the next part of the opening statement. It is, let us say, an intersection collision case. We might then continue as follows:

> Ladies and gentlemen, if you had been standing near the corner of Main and Market Streets here in town, at about 10 a.m. on May 18 last year, you would have seen a young man come out of a house that's right there on the corner. Parked in front of the house was a yellow Plymouth. He got behind the wheel and he started the car. He moved

away from the curb, and in just a couple of seconds he came to the intersection of Main and Market. Now, the light was green in his favor. He put on his right turn signal, and he began to make a right turn.

It is simple enough. But the jury is leaning forward attentively. What happened next? What happened when he made the right turn?

A story engages the jury's attention by making them eager for each next development. That is the nature of narrative. In a book about the novel as a literary form, E.M. Forster could as well have been talking about the opening statement when he said, "*Qua* story, it can have only one merit: that of making the audience want to know what happens next. And conversely it can have only one fault: that of making the audience not want to know what happens next."[11]

What we tell the jury in the opening statement, however, is only the first part of the story. The body of the story is the trial itself. And with its verdict, the jury will determine the story's outcome. The art of the opening statement is to tell the story in such a way that the jury wants the story to end with the verdict we want them to render. We try to tell them a story in which that verdict is the only possible happy ending.

**Other Matters.** Because the overriding goal is to make ourselves trustworthy in the eyes of the jury, it is important in the course of the narrative not to relate facts that we do not expect to prove. We cannot get away with it. The jury will remember; they will lose trust in us; and we're on our way to losing. Sometimes the law makes it uncertain whether we'll be able to prove a particular point. In that event, the motion in limine may help resolve the question.[12]

If they are to follow the trial easily, the jury needs certain other information to go along with the story. It is most important that they have the cast of characters straight: who the parties are, which lawyer represents whom, and what each side contends.

---

[11]E.M. Forster, Aspects of the Novel 35 (Pelican ed. 1962).
[12]See §4.5.

Often this information can be woven into the narrative itself:

> The young man who got behind the wheel of the yellow
> Plymouth that morning was Jack Smith. You've met Jack;
> he's sitting right over here. And you know that Jack is the
> man I talk for. Now, one of the questions in this case is
> about the traffic light on that corner of Main and Market
> Streets — whether Jack had the green light that morning,
> when he made his right turn onto Main Street. Tomor-
> row Jack will take the witness stand. He will take an oath
> to tell the truth, and then he will tell you himself that the
> light was green. And a man named Mr. Bystander was
> there, standing on that very corner. Mr. Bystander saw
> what happened. He too will swear to tell the truth, and
> he will tell you that the light was green.

Like any good story, the opening statement should be no
longer than necessary. A short opening is easier for the jury to
understand and to remember. Just as important, brevity helps
to convey a sense of control over the case,[13] and that in turn helps
to build the jury's confidence in us.

This does not mean, however, that the opening statement
should be rushed. To the contrary, careful pacing will help the
jury to absorb what we tell them. Silence, the best attention-
getting device of all, can be an especially potent tool. Deliberate
pauses at the appropriate points will focus the jury's thoughts
on what we have just said and on what will come next.

It also fosters brevity to have a definite conclusion to the opening statement. This is Aristotle's end, which follows the beginning and the middle. Some lawyers deliver the beginning and
the middle of the opening perfectly well, but then, unable to stop,
go into a cycle of repeating themselves. They cannot find a point
at which to break off and sit down. Planning ahead for the conclusion will solve the problem and get us off our feet.

The opening statement must give the jury enough information to orient them to the case, but it should not convey a great

---

[13]See §5.2.

deal more than that. The other side is listening, too, hoping to use whatever it learns from our opening. The ideal opening statement, then, will give the jury everything that they need, and will also leave the other side a little in the dark.

In a multiparty case, each party delivers its own opening statement. Most judges will allow the lawyers on each side to determine their own sequence of opening statements. If we are on the side with multiple parties, it is best to deliver our opening statement first. This allows us to make the earliest impression on the jury, and first impressions tend to be the strongest ones. It is a matter for negotiation with the other lawyers.

If there are problems in the case that we have not yet told the jury about, it is time to face up to them in the opening statement.[14]

## §5.4 The Opponent's Opening

There are only two things of any importance to be said about the opponent's opening statement. By their nature, neither can take the form of a hard and fast rule.

**Objections.** It is my own inclination not to object during the other side's opening, even when opposing counsel does something that he clearly should not. As always, we must consider the situation from the jury's point of view. In our efforts to gain their trust, we try to meet their expectations of the way a trial lawyer should behave. And the jury's expectations, we have seen, tend mostly to come from movies and television programs about trials.[15] These have taught the jury to expect objections during the interrogation of a witness. But in the opening statements and summations, the jury expects to hear a smooth, uninterrupted flow. That is how it goes in the movies. If we interrupt, the jury is likely to think that we are not playing the game as it is supposed to be played, that we are hitting below the belt. Mistaken though it is, the impression can nonetheless interfere with our primary goal of convincing the jury that we are trustworthy.

---

[14]See §3.6.
[15]See §5.1.

Another reason, too, suggests that we should not object: There is simply not much to object to. The opening statement offers only two major grounds for objection. One is that the opponent is arguing. But if the opponent's arguing becomes excessive, the judge will interrupt, and our image with the jury remains intact. In the jury's eyes, the interruption will also seem to be a rebuke to the opponent if it comes from the judge. Of course, some judges do not interrupt unless asked to. Hence the importance of knowing your judge and the impossibility of laying down hard-and-fast rules. The second ground appears when the opponent says something in his opening statement that we know he will not be able to prove. But instead of objecting, it is far more effective to let him say it and later on, in summation, to remind the jury of the discrepancy.[16]

**Motion for Judgment on the Opening Statement.** A motion infrequently made but permissible anywhere is the motion for judgment on the opening statement. It is part of the unwritten law of procedure, nowhere codified although it is authorized by a 1934 Supreme Court decision.[17]

The other side has just opened. We ask for a sidebar conference, or we go into the robing room. What happens next takes place out of the jury's hearing, although it is on the record. We move as follows:

> Your Honor, Mr. Smith has just finished his opening statement. We all know the purpose of the opening statement — to outline for the jury what we intend to prove. For purposes of my present application, I will concede that Mr. Smith is going to prove everything he has said in his opening statement. But even having proved everything in his opening statement, he still will not have a case. You will just have to dismiss at the end of the trial. In order that we all save time, Your Honor, I move for dismissal now.

---

[16]See §5.2 n. 6.

[17]Best v. District of Columbia, 291 U.S. 411, 415 (1934) ("There is no question as to the power of the trial court to direct a verdict for the defendant upon the opening statement of plaintiff's counsel where that statement establishes that the plaintiff has no right to recovery.")

There are scattered cases in which the motion has been granted. They are rare, to be sure, and frequently reversed on appeal.[18] Once in recent years the dismissal stood — in an unappealed case, and then only as to certain defendants.[19] It is safe to assume that the judge is more likely to respond to the motion along these lines:

> All right, counselor — very clever. The day is long past when we decide cases because a lawyer misspeaks or leaves something out by accident. If I dismiss, it will be because of a genuine failure of proof, not because some lawyer made a mistake. Sit down. Your motion is denied.

There are instances in which we might want to consider making the motion nonetheless. As a rule, it is best if we leave our opponent alone and the opponent leaves us alone. Once in a while, though, we have an opponent who goes over the line too often or too far. In response to unnecessarily rough play from the other side, one might be tempted to make the motion.

The judge will deny it. But we may cause the other lawyer, although only momentarily, to worry, "My God! I make a speech and the judge throws out the case! How will I ever explain it to the client?" In response to sudden stress like that, the sympathetic nervous system turns on the adrenaline very fast, but the effects of that effort are felt for hours. Our opponent may be off balance for the rest of the day.

This use of the motion raises a troubling ethical question. True, the question seems less troubling when the other lawyer has misbehaved, and we are simply evening the score. But some lawyers will be tempted to make the motion under other circumstances, simply to throw the opponent off stride and keep him from concentrating. This offends some people's sense of fair play. If done routinely, moreover, it loses its effect. Opponents

---

[18]*See, e.g.,* Oliver v. S. Ry. Co., 475 F.2d 895 (D.C. Cir. 1972) (reversing dismissal on opening statement); Hentz v. CBI-Fairmac Corp., 445 A.2d 1004 (D.C. 1982) (same).

[19]Thomas v. Am. Cytoscope Makers, Inc., 414 F. Supp. 255 (E.D. Pa. 1976).

will come to expect the motion, and so its shock value will fade. And someone who uses the motion too often may gain an unsavory reputation in the profession.

Questions of this sort never have simple right or wrong answers. We all agree that the client is entitled to zealous representation, but each of us must find for ourselves the margin at which zeal turns into foul play. Wherever we put the margin, there are bound to be marginal cases.

# CHAPTER 6

# Judicial Notice

## §6.1 Well-Known Facts

Ironically, we begin our discussion of the law of evidence with a set of rules that permit the lawyer to avoid altogether the rest of the law of evidence. These rules are a shortcut, a way of enabling facts to be deemed proved even though no one has done anything formally to prove them. We call this shortcut "judicial notice." There are many aspects and many categories of judicial notice.

We begin with a category represented by *Varcoe v. Lee*,[1] an old California case that arose after a motorist struck and killed a five-year-old girl playing in the street in San Francisco. As all trial lawyers must do very early in their preparation, the lawyer who brought the lawsuit against the motorist should have drawn up a blueprint, a schematic representation for the model of reality that he was going to prove in the courtroom. In *Varcoe v. Lee*, the blueprint would have been that for the ordinary common law negligence case, except for the special feature that this was a wrongful death. The blueprint would read something like this: (1) there was an accident; (2) the accident was the result of . . . (here the lawyer notes his theory of causation); (3) defendant was

---

[1]180 Cal. 338, 181 P. 223 (1919).

negligent; and (4) damages resulted. Precedent provided that in a wrongful death case, the plaintiff need not be concerned with proving lack of contributory negligence on the part of the deceased.

Let us focus on the third element: the defendant's negligence. Hypothetically, there are several possibilities: that the defendant was drunk when he drove down the street and hit the little girl; that he was looking in one direction and driving in another; or perhaps that he was busy talking to a companion in the car with him. None of these, however, is supported by the evidence in the case.

The theory of negligence in *Varcoe v. Lee* was more subtle. Broken down into its components, the third element of the blueprint would have said that the defendant's negligence was to be established as follows: (3-A) The defendant was driving at thirty miles per hour. That standing alone, of course, does not constitute negligence. But (3-B) he was driving thirty miles per hour at an intersection of Mission Street, which is a business district in San Francisco. And (3-C) the local statute says that the speed limit in a business district is fifteen miles per hour. Thus, the plaintiff's way of persuading the judge and jurors that the defendant was negligent was to argue a violation of the statute. Having violated the statutory limit of fifteen miles per hour in a business district, the defendant was negligent per se.

In the days when this case came along, before the First World War, the intersection where the accident took place was something like the intersection of Fifth Avenue and 42nd Street in New York City, the very heart of the commercial and shopping district. It would seem, on the face of it, that the plaintiff should have had no difficulty whatsoever in proving that Mission Street was a business district, and therefore subject to the fifteen-mile-per-hour speed limit in the statute.

But the plaintiff did not prove that. Perhaps, through carelessness or inadvertence, the plaintiff's lawyer failed to do what all trial lawyers must do as a matter of practice in every single case: prepare the blueprint, jot it down on a piece of paper, and make sure that they know exactly the model they are going to build in the courtroom, exactly what they must prove — item by item.

The plaintiff made his mistake in connection with the third and crucial element of the case, negligence. He did introduce evidence — plenty of it — to show that the defendant was traveling at thirty miles per hour. And the judge was aware that the statute restricts speed in a business district to fifteen miles per hour. But the plaintiff failed to prove that the site of the accident was a business district, which it undoubtedly was. He adduced not a shred of evidence to show the nature of the intersection.

On that state of the record the plaintiff rested. Defense counsel should then have leapt to his feet and said, "I move to dismiss because the plaintiff has not built the model that the law requires him to build." That is the idea; in more familiar language, it would have come out like this: "I move to dismiss because the plaintiff has failed to prove a prima facie case." But defense counsel did not do that. He, too, was careless, inadvertent, and ill-prepared.

With respect to the crucial element — the nature of the intersection as a business district — the judge's charge to the jury amounted to this: "Ladies and gentlemen of the jury, there is evidence that the defendant was going thirty miles an hour. I tell you that the applicable statute limits speed to fifteen miles an hour, and I instruct you as a matter of law that where somebody violates a statute in circumstances such as this, it is negligence — negligence per se. The question that remains is whether Mission Street is a business district. I tell you that, of course, it is."[2]

On went the judge to other things. The jury brought in a verdict for the plaintiff.

Defense counsel argued on appeal that what the judge did was tantamount to a directed verdict, and noted that a directed verdict is permissible only when the evidence is so overwhelming that no juror could reasonably find to the contrary. Here the evidence was hardly overwhelming. Indeed, it was nonexistent.

Agreed, said the Supreme Court of California; but it still found no error in the case. It is true, said the court that the nature of that intersection as a business district is a fact that was not proved. But we will deem it proved nonetheless.

---

[2]*Id.* at 341, 181 P. at 224.

To put it in lawyer's language, a fact of the sort involved here is appropriate for judicial notice. It is a fact that will be deemed proved by a shortcut, without formal invocation of the rules of evidence. Note that judicial notice connotes absolutely nothing about the judge's personal knowledge of the fact in question. Whether or not the judge actually knew the fact before a lawyer brought it to his attention in the courtroom is entirely beside the point.

Observe also that in *Varcoe v. Lee* it was the Supreme Court of California, not the trial court, that took judicial notice. That is the general doctrine, followed virtually everywhere: An appellate court may take judicial notice whenever it would have been proper for the trial court to have done so. Even though the trial court did not take judicial notice, an appellate court still may. And, through taking judicial notice, an appellate court can save a verdict, as occurred in this case.

If a trial court takes judicial notice under inappropriate circumstances, we may have reversible error. It is never error, however, for the trial court to decline to take judicial notice. The trial court can always choose to insist on formal proof, though it will rarely do so when judicial notice is appropriate.

We have judicial notice because one of the great interests valued by common law judges and lawyers is efficiency. The preference is to do things at minimal cost and with minimal expenditure of time. When it would be a pointless waste of time to prove facts that everybody knows, we do not require lawyers to prove them.

If someone trying a case wanted to prove that Minneapolis is in the state of Minnesota, he could certainly prove it using the formal modes of proof. He could call an expert witness, some geographer who had devoted his life to the study of which American cities are in which states, and ask the witness's expert opinion on the question. But that is the kind of thing that gives law and lawyers a bad name. When something is virtually self-evident, it is absurd to bother with formal modes of proof.

*Varcoe v. Lee* is a classic case because it lays down the prerequisites that must be met before the fact will be judicially noticed. For facts of the kind that *Varcoe v. Lee* typifies, such as the nature of an intersection, there are three such prerequisites.

- The fact, by its nature, must not be subject to rational dispute;
- The fact must be common knowledge, in the sense that "everybody knows it"; and
- The fact must be common knowledge in the locality where the court sits.

If a fact meets these three tests, then judicial notice will be proper, and the fact will be deemed proved even though no one has proved it. While the category of such appropriate facts is probably without limit, examples certainly include the overt facts of history — that there were two world wars and that Franklin Delano Roosevelt was elected president in 1932; and facts of geography, such as the fact that the city of Minneapolis is in the state of Minnesota.

The shortcut of judicial notice is available at the option of the proponent, the lawyer who seeks to prove the fact. He need not invoke judicial notice unless he wishes to. In its place, he can always resort to the formal modes of proof. But almost always, a lawyer will want to take advantage of judicial notice simply because it is economical, and it makes for a tighter presentation in court.

How would it go in practice? Suppose that *Varcoe v. Lee* were retried with the lawyers now enlightened by the appellate court's opinion. The plaintiff's lawyer, the proponent of the fact that Mission Street is a business district, would stand up at whatever moment seemed artistically apt and would say to the court, "Your Honor, I ask you to take judicial notice of the fact that Mission Street is in a business district."

His Honor would look over to defense counsel and say, "What's your position?"

Defense counsel might say, "I concede the fact." Judicial notice is then irrelevant. Alternatively, defense counsel might say, "I concede that judicial notice is proper." Or defense counsel might say, "I dispute it. I don't think judicial notice should be taken."

His Honor then turns back to the proponent and says, "Why should I take judicial notice?" The answer is not, "Your Honor, you know it's true!" That invokes the judge's personal knowledge, which has nothing to do with judicial notice. The lawyer-like answer is something along these lines: "Well, Your Honor, that fact is indisputable by its nature. It is common knowledge where this court sits. Therefore, judicial notice is proper."

With facts of the kind in *Varcoe v. Lee*, the gain in efficiency brought about by judicial notice is clear enough. But the very next case to come along will raise the question of efficiency in very different circumstances. Accordingly, we must complicate our understanding of judicial notice.

## §6.2 Court Records

Your case is on trial. A year before the trial, a motion for summary judgment was made and denied. In connection with that motion, your adversary put in an affidavit in which he admitted a certain fact. Now you wish to prove that admission. You may, of course, do it by invoking the formal modes of proof, but that might be a waste of time.

Suppose it were possible to stand up and say to the court, "Your Honor, there was a motion for summary judgment in this case last year."

"I'm aware of that," says the judge.

"At that time, Your Honor, certain affidavits were submitted in connection with that motion."

"So you tell me," says the judge.

"The file of this case, Your Honor, contains those affidavits, and I believe that the file is before you at this very moment."

"It is," says the judge.

"Would Your Honor look into that file, and perhaps find there the affidavit dated thus-and-so, submitted by my adversary." The judge does so, and tells you that he has the affidavit in his hand. That affidavit contains the admission you now wish to prove.

Using the formal modes of proof, you might have to call the clerk of the court to identify the file; and there are various other possibilities. But that is absurd. The judge can simply say, "Here is the affidavit. It is in the court file. It is in evidence." Even though no one has done anything formally to put it in evidence, efficiency requires this, and it can be done.

We call the procedure judicial notice because that is the name generically attached to the shortcut. But note that it is not the type of judicial notice we encountered in *Varcoe v. Lee*.[3] The fact that the affidavit is part of the file in this case may well be indisputable by its nature, but it is hardly common knowledge in the locality.

We have, then, a second category in our developing survey of the structure of the law of judicial notice. First category: *Varcoe v. Lee*. Second category: court records. A court will, when the circumstances are appealing, take judicial notice of the contents of the file of the records of the court.

Common sense is always in order. In the example above, we were asking the judge to take judicial notice of a paper that was filed at an earlier stage of this very case. Probably every judge in the land will take judicial notice under such circumstances. Now change the circumstances. Suppose you were to say, "Your Honor, I ask you to take judicial notice of a court record."

"Glad to do so," says the judge. "What record?"

"Well, Your Honor, we're trying this case here, in New York City, and the record of which I ask you to take judicial notice is an affidavit filed in connection with a motion for summary judgment made in the United States District Court for the District of Alaska."

That is a different court, a different jurisdiction, and 5,000 miles away. Most probably, the judge will not take judicial notice. He does not have the file in front of him. The very reason for taking judicial notice, efficiency, is inapplicable here. This does not mean that you are prevented from proving the affidavit. You simply may not invoke the shortcut. Instead, you will have to go about using the formal modes of proof. You will have to subpoena the file from the clerk of the District Court in Alaska and put the paper into evidence in accordance with the rules we shall explore below.[4]

---

[3] 180 Cal. 338, 181 P. 223 (1919). See §6.1.
[4] See §§7.3-7.5.

## §6.3 Facts in Reference Works

A good example of a third category of judicial notice can be drawn from a trial that took place in 1857. The jurisdiction was Illinois, the circuit court of Cass County. While no perfect stenographic transcript exists, there are enough contemporaneous records to reconstruct the circumstances.

It was a murder case, *People of the State of Illinois v. Armstrong.*[5] The theory of the prosecution was that the defendant, Armstrong, had engaged in a drunken brawl with another man, in the course of which Armstrong pulled out a revolver. It was not loaded, so he could not fire it. But he used it as a blackjack. He brought it down on the victim's head, cracked his skull, and killed him. Armstrong was indicted for murder.

He had no money, and in those days there was no public defender or legal aid society. Armstrong turned to his mother, Hannah, but she had no money either. Hannah, however, had known a rather prominent lawyer when he was a young man, before he became a lawyer. As of 1857, when the trial took place, he was probably the leading lawyer in the entire Midwest, and certainly in Illinois. He had argued more cases in the Illinois Supreme Court than any other lawyer of his time (a record that stood until just a few years ago).

The letter that Hannah Armstrong wrote to the lawyer still exists. It runs something like this: "You may remember me from the old days. My son is in trouble. Will you represent him? But I can't pay you."

The response of the lawyer, Abraham Lincoln, also exists. He wrote back, in part, "[T]he gratitude for your long continued kindness to me in adverse circumstances prompts me to offer my humble services gratuitously. . . . It will afford me an opportunity to requite in a small degree, the favors I received at your hand, and that of your late lamented husband, when your roof afforded me a grateful shelter, without money and without price."[6]

The prosecution's case rested chiefly upon the testimony of an eyewitness who took the stand and said under direct

---

[5]Cass County Circuit Court (1858).
[6]A. Woldman, Lawyer Lincoln 111-12 (1936).

examination, in effect, "I was there. I saw the whole thing. I saw Armstrong hit the victim over the head and kill him." Anyone who has tried criminal cases knows that dramatic moment in the courtroom when the prosecution's eyewitness points the finger at your client and says, "*He* killed the victim!"[7]

Abraham Lincoln cross-examined in a manner that we could use today as a textbook illustration of good cross-examination.[8]

Q. Did you actually see the fight?

A. Yes.

Q. And you stood very near to them?

A. No, it was one hundred and fifty feet or more.

Q. In the open field?

---

[7]Those who defend criminal cases know that the defense lawyer, during that kind of testimony, must distract the jury. Not every kind of distraction is permissible, of course. It is not fair to go into a juggling act, or to pretend a fit and collapse on the courtroom floor. But certain things can be done. One of them is simply to freeze. There is nothing that attracts the attention of judge and jury so infallibly as silence and lack of motion.

At the time of the Armstrong case, Lincoln was so famous a trial lawyer that people would come from miles around to watch him try a case. There is a letter written by a young lawyer who came to watch this great master. He wrote the letter home after sitting through one session of the trial — the session of the cross-examination set forth below — and in the letter he described Lincoln's demeanor in the courtroom. His description indicates that Abraham Lincoln knew exactly what any modern lawyer knows about how to handle himself in a courtroom.

The young lawyer wrote that during the direct testimony of the eyewitness, "Lincoln sat with his head thrown back, his steady gaze apparently fixed upon one spot of the blank ceiling, entirely oblivious to what was happening around him, and without a single variation of feature or noticeable movement of any muscle of his face." A. Woldman, Lawyer Lincoln 113 (1936). Remember that Lincoln was very tall, six feet three or so at a time when the average height of men was no more than about five feet five. He was very thin, and he was stretched out so that his body made a straight line from his shoes to the top of his head, sideways to the jury, at an angle of 45 degrees. No doubt all twelve men in that jury box were saying to themselves, "What is he looking at on the ceiling?" And while they were wondering that, they were not listening to the direct testimony.

[8]The examination is reconstructed from A. Woldman, Lawyer Lincoln 113 (1936); E. Hertz, Lincoln Talks 24.25 (1939).

A. No, in the timber.

Q. What kind of timber?

A. Beech timber.

Q. Leaves on it are rather thick in August?

A. It looks like it.

Q. What time did all this occur?

A. Eleven o'clock at night.

Q. Did you have a candle there?

A. No, what would I want a candle for?

Q. How could you see from a distance of one hundred and fifty feet or more, without a candle, at eleven o'clock at night?

That is the famous question. It sounds like a question that the cross-examiner should not ask. It argues with the witness; and you don't know what the answer is going to be; and it is not a leading question; and you are going to be devastated. The answer came, and it was devastating.

A. The moon was shining real bright.

The harpoon goes in, and Lincoln seems to make it worse. He pushes the harpoon in even deeper.

Q. Full moon?

A. Yes, a full moon.

It looks as though Armstrong is on his way to the gallows, except that Lincoln is not without resource. He reaches into his back pocket, and he takes out that famous blue-covered almanac, and he says to the judge something like, "Would Your Honor take judicial notice of the page of the almanac that I now show you?" The page was the astronomical table that showed the state of the moon for the day on which the murder is supposed to have occurred. The judge said, "I will take judicial notice of it. It is in evidence." Lincoln put that astronomical table in front of the witness, and the cross-examination concluded as follows.

Q. Does not the almanac say that on August 29 the moon was barely past the first quarter instead of being full?

(No answer from the witness.)

Q. Does not the almanac also say that the moon had disappeared by eleven o'clock?

(No answer from the witness.)

Q. Is it not a fact that it was too dark to see anything from fifty feet, let alone one hundred and fifty feet?

(No answer from the witness.)

And the jury acquitted Armstrong.

Let us be technicians for a moment. How did it come about that the judge accepted the astronomical table in evidence? In saying, "Will Your Honor take judicial notice?" Lincoln asked the judge to deem the almanac to be in evidence, even though he had not used the formal modes of proof. The almanac, however, does not fit *Varcoe v. Lee*. While the state of the moon on a given evening is certainly indisputable by its nature, it is hardly common knowledge in the area, not many months later. Nor, obviously, is an almanac a court record.[9] Yet the judge took judicial notice of it in 1857 for Abraham Lincoln, and he would take judicial notice of it for you today.

We have before us, then, a third category of judicial notice. Almanac-type facts — the sorts of things one can look up in an almanac, an encyclopedia, or the like — are judicially noticeable. The reason, still, is efficiency. It would be absurd to require proof of such facts as the day of the week on which a given date fell. It is extraordinary how often we must do that, and an almanac, with its perpetual calendar, will give the answer. Another example is an overt fact of history that is not common knowledge. That FDR was elected to the presidency in 1932 is common knowledge, and so it does not fall in this category. But suppose that someone needed to prove the date on which Hitler's army invaded the Soviet Union in World War II. That is not common knowledge, but it can be looked up. And so a court will take judicial notice of it.

---

[9]See §6.2.

## §6.4 Scientific Basis

The aspect of judicial notice we discuss next is growing fast in importance. It may be an overstatement, but not much of one, to say that every busy trial lawyer in this latter part of the twentieth century, at one point or another in his career, will need to deal with the issues that concern us here: those that arise whenever a trial lawyer uses some scientific or technical device in litigation.

We will use "device" to mean a machine, a process, a test — any of the products of science and technology that turn out to have utility in litigation. Science and technology are constantly providing new ones. Examples include the tests for alcohol content in the bloodstream used by the police on the highways; the blood-grouping tests so important in paternity cases; and the various biological tests useful in the prosecution of sex crimes.

The best way to see the pattern that develops in the cases is to follow a technical device from its first use in litigation. Radar makes a good example beause it is suitably complex. Radar is also relatively recent. Though commonplace in litigation today, it first came to be used in litigation during the lifetimes of most of us.

Radar was invented in England, in the Cavendish Laboratories of Cambridge University in the latter part of the 1930s. By then it was perfectly obvious that there would be a war between England and Germany, so the work was kept secret; radar devices were made and installed all along the English Channel. When Germany had occupied all of Western Europe, it was Hitler's intention to knock England out of the war so that he could turn his efforts entirely against Russia. The method he chose was to bomb London into submission. That was the Battle of Britain. England's resources consisted of a bunch of nineteen- and twenty-year-old kids in Hurricanes and Spitfires held together with Scotch tape and safety pins. Yet those kids and those planes managed to defeat the massed might of Germany and the Luftwaffe. All through the Battle of Britain, we now know, Hermann Goering, the commanding officer of the Luftwaffe, kept asking, "Why is it that when we put 500 bombers in the air for England, no matter when we take off or from whatever direction we come, the Hurricanes and the Spitfires are already in the air waiting for us, always in the right place?" I suppose they told him at Nuremburg, "Why, Goering, it's because the English had radar." And so radar saved Western civilization.

In 1945 the war ended, and radar was put to other uses. There must have been a lawyer who came out of World War II and found a job as an assistant district attorney. He went to work with all the pent-up energy and frustration of having lived through the war. But when he opened the file on his first case, to his disappointment it was only a speeding case. "Well," he said, "maybe it's not murder or kidnapping, but I will put the defendant away!" And then he read the file. "Radar," it said. Remember, this was in 1945 or 1946. He read that, and he said to himself what Hermann Goering said: "What is radar?" He was about to try the first case in the history of the world in which radar would be used.

**Three prerequisites.** Whatever we say about radar in 1946 will be true tomorrow in connection with some new technical device yet to come along. What must a lawyer prove in a case using some scientific or technical device for the first time? Let us stay with our speeding case. The lawyer needs a blueprint of the model he is going to build in the courtroom. This one, a four-element model, is as good as any: (1) The defendant (2) drove a car (3) at eighty miles per hour (4) in an area where the speed limit was (let us say) fifty-five miles per hour. Now, to the proof.

*First element:* that it was the defendant. No difficulty; the policeman will testify, "That's the man I saw."

*Second element:* that the defendant was driving a car. Again, no difficulty; the policeman will say, "I saw the defendant behind the wheel of a car."

*Fourth element,* that the defendant was in a fifty-five-mile-an-hour zone. This is a matter of law, and the judge will be informed of it in whatever way is appropriate.

It is the third element of the blueprint that engages us. We must take that third element and break it down in detail. To show that the defendant was driving at eighty miles per hour, we must prove three subsidiary propositions. There is no way to look these up in the law library; they come from common sense and from the lawyer's analytical powers.

*Subelement 3-A:* The pointer or pen on the radar device must have read eighty miles per hour. This question of the "reading" applies, with appropriate variations, to any technical device.

*Subelement 3-B:* The device must have been in good working order. This means that it was wound up, adjusted, calibrated, oiled, fed, in a good mood — whatever it takes for that device. And it means that the person using the device knew what he was about.

*Subelement 3-C:* This item has engendered a good deal of litigation. It says that the device must operate in accordance with the rules of nature, that it rests upon the laws of the universe, that it has a scientific basis. Only then can we be confident that when the pointer read "80," subject to the margin of error inherent in every machine, the defendant was in fact going eighty miles per hour.

To illustrate the point, let us change the facts a little. Here is the same case, except that our technical device is no longer radar. "Your Honor, I have a technical device, not newly invented, but one I propose to use here for the first time. It is a Ouija board, Your Honor. I close my eyes and the pointer moves. First it moves to the number '8,' and then it moves to the number '0.' This shows that the defendant was going eighty miles per hour." The Ouija board indeed gives a reading of "80." We can also assume it to be in good working order, and properly used on this occasion. But the judge will not permit the evidence to come in. The third element, that the device rests upon the laws of nature, is missing.

Many judges regard the lie detector, or polygraph, as not very different from a Ouija board. In most jurisdictions, evidence from the polygraph is inadmissible. It is a technical device; it produces a certain reading; it is properly used. Yet in most jurisdictions, the judges have not been persuaded that it rests upon the laws of nature.

Returning to that first radar case, the lawyer must prove that the device does rest upon the laws of nature. To prove it, he will call a scientist or an engineer, someone who is familiar with the principles of radar, and he will question him as an expert witness in accordance with the rules that pertain to expert witnesses.[10] The expert will tell the judge about the laws of nature on which radar rests. If the judge considers the scientific basis proved, he will permit the reading of the defendant's speed to go into evidence.

**The Role of Judicial Notice.** If a scientific or technical device is useful in one lawsuit, however, it will be useful in others. It will not be offered just once, but again and again as other lawyers try suits involving the same device. Each time, the proponent of the evidence will need to prove, using the formal modes of proof, that the device rests upon the laws of nature.

After enough instances of this, with no specific number for "enough," it will typically be an appellate court that writes an opinion along these lines: "We have now seen enough records to persuade us that it cannot any longer be doubted that this device rests upon the laws of nature. Accordingly, the proponent of the evidence will no longer be obliged to prove that it rests upon the laws of nature. From now on, judicial notice will be appropriate." Or, as the Supreme Court of Missouri put it in the case of radar particularly, "We think it is now time for the courts . . . to recognize by judicial knowledge . . . that a radar speedmeter is a device which, within a reasonable engineering tolerance, and when properly functioning and properly operated, accurately measures speed in terms of miles per hour."[11]

Observe that judicial notice is never appropriate as to sub-element 3-A, that the device registered "80"; or as to 3-B, that it was in good working order and properly used on the occasion. But 3-C, that the device rests upon the laws of nature, will be proper for judicial notice. Today, in no jurisdiction in the United States is there much doubt that the scientific basis of radar will be judicially noticed.[12]

---

[10]See Chapter 13.

[11]State v. Graham, 322 S.W.2d 188, 195 (Mo. 1959).

[12]Other devices that have been used often enough to show this pattern of cases are blood-grouping tests, and the tests used by police to determine alcohol content in a motorist's bloodstream. The scientific basis for these too will be judicially noticed. Another example is perhaps the very first technical device ever to be used in litigation: the fingerprint. Its scientific basis is the

**An Addendum.** The man chiefly responsible for inventing radar was physicist Sir Robert Watson-Watt of Cambridge University, England. In 1965, while Sir Robert was traveling about the United States lecturing, he was arrested in a Southern state for speeding through a radar trap. That led to his spending a few hours in jail, where he wrote this poem:

Pity Sir Robert Watson-Watt,
Strange victim of this radar plot,
And thus, with others I can mention,
The victim of his own invention.
His magical, all-seeing eye
Enabled cloud-bound planes to fly
And bites, no doubt with legal wit,
The hand that once created it.

In due course Sir Robert pleaded guilty to the charge, and was permitted to go on his way.

## §6.5 The *Frye* Rule and Its Deficiencies*

Some scientific and technical devices of fairly recent origin, although used frequently in litigation, have not yet reached the point of judicial notice. For these, the proponent still must prove formally that the device has a scientific basis. One example of such a device is voiceprint analysis, an electronic device which, according to its proponents, permits identification with the same certainty as a fingerprint. There has been much litigation on it, with the cases splitting roughly half and half. Some judges are persuaded that voiceprint analysis rests upon the laws of nature; others are not.

---

uniqueness of the human fingerprint. Without that precondition, the identity of the fingerprint has no probative value. But the uniqueness of the human fingerprint need not be proved, for judges are persuaded that it cannot be disputed. Because we have had enough experience with it, it will be judicially noticed.

*[Editor's note: This section combines portions of Professor Younger's original manuscript with an edited transcript (not reviewed by him) of a talk he gave on the *Frye* rule.

How is a judge to be persuaded that a device has a scientific basis — that it operates like radar, not like a Ouija board? Radar once again makes a good example, because its basic operation is easy to understand. Most of us are familiar with the general principles. Certain waves are transmitted out and bounce back. From the time they take to bounce back, and from their frequency on rearrival, it is possible to figure the distance and speed of the object from which they bounced.

That level of explanation, however, is not enough to establish a scientific basis. It takes a degree in physics to understand a textbook that actually sets forth the scientific basis of radar. The exposition involves calculus of a rather complicated kind, and it requires a detailed comprehension of the nature of electromagnetic radiation and the Doppler effect.

*State v. Graham*,[13] the case in which the Missouri Supreme Court held that judicial notice would be appropriate for the scientific basis of radar, sets forth some of the technical detail. It also provides a rare example of deliberate judicial humor. In the text, the opinion says, "This court yields to no group in its collective ignorance of science in general, but, *if we understand* the subject, . . . ."[14] At that point the court copies some intricate physics out of a textbook. It also adds a splendid footnote that says, "If this explanation is not clear, we refer to . . . ."[15] There the court reprints an utterly incomprehensible formula for the Doppler effect.

Except for an occasional individual who happens to have the background, judges cannot become expert enough in physics actually to understand the scientific basis of radar. The same is true for tests of alcohol content in the bloodstream, the voiceprint, and all the rest. Each requires specialized qualifications that almost no judge will have, and almost no lawyer. How, then, is the judge to decide whether the device rests on the laws of nature?

**The Nose-Counting Rule.** The rule that had apparently been settled, until recent years, is commonly called the *"Frye* rule," after an old federal case of that name.[16] The rule recognizes that

---

[13]322 S.W.2d 188 (Mo. 1959).
[14]*Id.* at 196 (emphasis in original).
[15]*Id.* at 196 n.18.
[16]Frye v. United States, 293 F. 1013 (D.C. Cir. 1923).

the judge is not a scientist, and cannot be made into a scientist. But judges are very good at counting noses. And so the test: Is the judge persuaded that, among the scientists concerned, the scientific basis of the device is generally accepted?[17]

In applying the *Frye* test, the evidence to be put before the judge on radar (for example) is not the actual scientific basis of radar — not the calculus and the wave mechanics and all the rest of it. Rather, the evidence is more like this: "Mr. Professor of Physics, can you tell the court whether or not all professors of physics are in general agreement that this device does rest upon the laws of nature?" The witness replies, "Yes, I can tell the court, and my answer is that all professors of physics are in agreement." That, the judge can understand. In the case of the voiceprint, the proponent will call physicists who say, "Well, people I know are in agreement that this thing does rest upon the laws of nature." The opponent will call other physicists, who say, "I don't accept it; and I know other people who don't accept it; and at this moment in the development of physics we don't know who's right. We're in disagreement."

**Deficiencies of the Rule.** At first glance the *Frye* rule is rather appealing, but upon analysis, it has three deficiencies of enormous practical significance. The first deficiency is that the *Frye* test is indeterminate. It does not give a reliable result, because the test will permit the court to come out any way it wants. The *Frye* test simply tells the judge to determine whether among the scientists concerned there is general agreement that the evidence is scientifically valid. The judge determines who the scientists concerned are and, by making that determination, the judge decides the outcome. Do you want polygraph results to be admissible? Easy. Simply define the community of scientists concerned as the community of polygraph operators. Obviously, among polygraph operators there will be unanimity of view that the polygraph rests upon the laws of nature. However, if you define the scientific community concerned as university professors of psychology, you get the opposite outcome, because there will be unanimity or near unanimity of view that the polygraph does not rest upon the laws of nature.

---

[17]*Id.* at 1014.

The second deficiency is that the *Frye* test is an abdication of judicial responsibility. The test simply permits the judge to determine whether the scientists concerned are in general agreement that a particular device or process is or is not scientifically valid. The scientists are, in effect, deciding an issue of the admissibility of evidence, and that is a judicial responsibility. In other words, under the *Frye* test, the court has simply passed to the scientific community the responsibility of making a decision that is a judicial responsibility.

An example of these two deficiencies at work is *Dowd v. Calabrese,* decided in 1984.[18] In the *Dowd* case, a lawyer tried to persuade a judge to receive in evidence certain polygraph results. First, the reading was to the effect that the subject was or was not telling the truth. Second, it was agreed that the device was in good working order and properly used. As to the third prerequisite, the lawyer offered in evidence the results of a poll taken of polygraph operators on the question of scientific validity of the polygraph.[19] The judge, however, refused to allow the polygraph reading into evidence.

First, the judge noted that defining the community of scientists concerned is the key to the problem. The judge is the one who defines it, and the judge in the *Dowd* case refused to define the community of scientists concerned as the community of polygraph operators. Second, the judge stated that it would be improper for a proponent to satisfy the requirements of *Frye* by taking a poll. The proponent, rather, would have to call to the stand a scientist from the relevant community, have him testify to scientific validity, and have him exposed to cross-examination.

The third problem — the final and perhaps most important problem — is that the *Frye* test simply breaks down when the scientific device or process is new. When there has not been enough time for the scientific community to learn about a device, there cannot be general agreement in the scientific community about its scientific validity. An example of the breakdown of the

---

[18]585 F. Supp. 430 (D.D.C. 1984).
[19]The three prerequisites for admitting scientific evidence are discussed in §6.4.

*Frye* test when applied to a newly created scientific device or process is the *Coppolino* case.[20]

Dr. Coppolino was indicted for murdering his wife. The theory of the murder was that the doctor murdered his wife by injecting her with poison. The prosecution's main witness was Milton Helburn, regarded as the founder of modern forensic pathology; at the time, he was the head of the New York City medical examiner's office, then regarded as the leading center for pathological work.

Dr. Helburn performed an autopsy on the body of Mrs. Coppolino and discovered that there was nothing unusual about the corpse, except that there was a puncture wound from a pinprick on her left buttock as well as discolored tissue surrounding the buttocks.

Dr. Helburn reasoned that, assuming Mrs. Coppolino was murdered, she was murdered by an injection of poison that left no symptoms in the body. What kind of poison? There is only one kind: silksino caleen chloride. When injected into the body, silksino caleen chloride causes instant death, and it also immediately breaks down into two separate chemicals that are found naturally in the body, call them A and B.

What Dr. Helburn had to do, therefore, was to ascertain the amounts of chemical A and chemical B normally found in the body, and then find that Mrs. Coppolino's body had amounts of chemical A and chemical B in excess of the normal amount. Thus, by circumstantial evidence, Dr. Helburn sought to show that Mrs. Coppolino's body was injected with silksino caleen chloride, and that Dr. Coppolino did it.

A quantitative analysis was needed to determine the amount of chemical A and chemical B in Mrs. Coppolino's body, but Dr. Helburn could not do this. The prosecution turned to one of the leading biochemists of the time, Dr. Umberger. Dr. Umberger said that biochemistry had not yet invented a quantitative analysis to determine the amounts of chemical A and chemical B, but Dr. Umberger went on to invent the analysis. At the conclusion of

---

[20]Coppolino v. State, 223 So.2d 68 (Fla. App. 1968), *appeal dismissed mem.*, 234 So.2d 120 (Fla.), *cert. denied*, 399 U.S. 927.

the analysis, Dr. Umberger found that the amounts of chemical A and chemical B in Mrs. Coppolino's body were far in excess of the normal amounts.

The question was whether the evidence would be admissible. First, was there a reading? Yes, the reading was that there were excess amounts of chemical A and chemical B in Mrs. Coppolino's body. Second, was the scientific device in good working order and properly used? Yes, the testing glassware was clean and the testing reagents were fresh. And third, was the process, the quantitative analysis to determine amounts of chemical A and chemical B, scientifically valid?

Under the *Frye* test, as we have seen, the inquiry to satisfy this third prerequisite is whether among the scientists concerned there is general agreement as to the scientific validity of the process. Was there general agreement among the biochemists? No. No other biochemists had heard of the process, the quantitative analysis to determine the amounts of chemical A and chemical B. There could not be any general agreement about scientific validity. The process was too new. The judge, however, allowed Dr. Umberger to testify to his findings and the process by which he came to them.

On appeal, the appellate court affirmed the lower court's ruling on the admissibility of the scientific evidence. The appellate court simply said that, in a case such as this, the admissibility of evidence is within the sound discretion of the trial judge. The significance of the *Coppolino* case is that it is the first case in which a court departs from the *Frye* test. It is the first judicial acknowledgement that the *Frye* test is deficient.

**Alternatives to the Rule.** Courts have now begun to consider replacing the *Frye* test. *United States v. Lopez*[21] is a leading example. After the defendant set off an electronic weapons detector at an airport, he was searched and found to be carrying narcotics. Those detectors operate by monitoring the natural magnetic field of the earth. Certain metals, including steel, distort the magnetic field. When the machine detects such a distortion, it is because a certain amount of steel is passing through, and the machine

---

[21]328 F. Supp. 1077 (E.D.N.Y. 1971).

sounds an alarm. At the time *Lopez* was decided, no court had taken judicial notice of whether the electronic weapons detector has a scientific basis.

Under the *Frye* rule, the *Lopez* court would have asked whether all physicists were in general agreement that the electronic weapons detector rests upon the laws of nature. But it did not ask that. Instead, the court described for itself how the device works. In support of that description it cited several highly technical papers in engineering and physics journals. The opinion then went on to say:

> Though these scientific principles are not matters of common knowledge they may be readily and accurately determined, are verifiable to almost a certainty and are not disputed. The literature was placed in the Court file, notice was given to the parties that the Court intended to rely upon it, and there was no objection by either party.
>
> Under these circumstances the Court takes judicial notice of the scientific principles utilized in the design of the Friskem unit. It finds that such a machine, if properly constructed and operated, can perform in the manner described to the Court by testimony and manuals.[22]

In addition to the technical articles, the court also heard and relied on expert testimony. But in the end, it came to its own conclusion as to scientific basis, rather than simply yielding to the majority vote of the scientists or technicians concerned.

There is yet another alternative. Consider the scientific devices and processes we have discussed. The thought is that scientific evidence is different in nature from any other kind of evidence and therefore requires special rules to determine its admissibility. The special rules are summarized as the three prerequisites of the *Frye* test. This approach considers scientific evidence as separate, as an entity unto itself. This approach is the scientific evidence *vel non* approach.

------

[22]*Id.* at 1085. The evidence taken from the defendant was ultimately suppressed, but on other grounds. *Id.* at 1101-02.

An alternative approach is to consider scientific evidence not as a separate kind of evidence with separate rules but, rather, as a kind of evidence obtained in certain ways. In short, this alternative focuses on the means by which the evidence is obtained and not the end, the scientific evidence itself. There are two means, two ways, to present scientific evidence. Scientific evidence can be offered by way of a document, or it can be offered through an expert witness, the scientist.

Consider scientific evidence offered by way of a document. Usually, the offer is made in connection with large-scale tort litigation. The government will conduct an investigation of the accident and produce a two-part report. The first part details the investigation. The second part gives the conclusions of the investigation: The skywalk collapsed because . . .; the engine fell off the DC-10 because . . . .

The report is obviously hearsay. It is an out-of-court statement offered to prove nothing but the truth of what it asserts. Under Rule 802 of the Federal Rules of Evidence, hearsay is not admissible. There is, however, an exception for government reports. Rule 803(8)(C) states that government reports are admissible as an exception to the rule against hearsay insofar as the report sets forth "factual findings." Are the conclusions, the second part of the government report, factual findings?

The most important case construing the phrase "factual findings" is *Complaint of American Export Lines, Inc.*[23] The case holds that conclusions in a government report were not factual findings under Rule 803(8)(C). The court refers to the conclusions in the government report as "evaluative." Concluding that Congress did not intend to permit evaluative findings into evidence under Rule 803(8)(C), the court finds the report's conclusions inadmissible.

Another important case is *Ellis v. International Playtex Inc.*,[24] a toxic shock syndrome case. The plaintiff is a woman who has sued a tampon manufacturer, claiming that it manufactured the tampon that caused her to suffer toxic shock syndrome. The plaintiff has a report from the Centers for Disease Control, an official

---

[23]73 F.R.D. 454 (S.D.N.Y. 1977).
[24]745 F.2d 292 (4th Cir. 1984).

agency of the U.S. government and the world's leading center for epidemiological research. The Centers for Disease Control conducted an investigation of toxic shock syndrome and concluded in its report that the likeliest explanation for toxic shock syndrome is the use of the manufacturer's kind of tampon. The trial court follows *American Export,* excludes the conclusion in the report as an "evaluative finding," and the case is dismissed. The case is then appealed and the Fourth Circuit reverses.

The Fourth Circuit holds that the report is admissible. The court says, first, that the agency is the world's leading center for epidemiological research. Second, if the Centers for Disease Control were willing to publish the report, it is extremely reliable. Third, it is therefore not unfair to allow the report into evidence and shift the burden to the defendant to cause the scientist to come to court and respond to questions concerning the report. Of course, an important question remains after *Ellis*: What is to be done when the investigative agency is not as reliable as the Centers for Disease Control?

The second means for putting scientific evidence into evidence is the expert witness. There are well-settled rules for determining when an expert may testify.[25] Under Rule 702 of the Federal Rules of Evidence, an expert witness may testify to his opinion if it will assist the jury. The judge therefore does not have to analyze the admissibility of the evidence under *Frye,* but simply has to ascertain whether the expert's testimony will assist the jury.

The next question is, upon what may the expert witness rely to form his opinion? The common law rule is that the expert can rely on whatever he wishes so long as everything upon which he relies is in evidence. In other words, the expert's opinion may not go beyond the record. Under Rule 703 of the Federal Rules of Evidence, however, the expert may go beyond the record. The expert may rely on evidence not in evidence to form his opinion, but only if it is "reasonable" for the expert to rely on the nonrecord information.

How do the federal courts construe the word "reasonable"? It involves a two-step process. First, is it customary in the

---

[25]See Chapter 13.

expert's field to rely on such information? Second, assuming it is, is the judge prepared to say it is reasonable?[26]

## §6.6 Federal Rule of Evidence 201

The kinds of judicial notice we have looked at so far fall into four categories. First, the type of fact in *Varcoe v. Lee*:[27] indisputable by its nature, and common knowledge in the area where the court sits. Second, judicial notice of court records.[28] Third, judicial notice of almanac-type facts.[29] And fourth, the application of judicial notice to the scientific basis of scientific devices.[30] Bear these four categories in mind. They help in recognizing issues, and can make it possible to take advantage of judicial notice when the possibilities might otherwise be overlooked.

The Federal Rules of Evidence, the most recent attempt to codify and rationalize this mish-mash of rules, try to deal with the four categories that I have discussed in Rule 201. The federal rule, however, does not spell out the four categories. Rather, it reads this way: "A judicially noticed fact must be one not subject to reasonable dispute in that it is either (1) generally known

---

[26]*See* In re Swine Flu Immunization Product Liability Litigation (Bean v. United States), 533 F. Supp. 567 (D. Colo. 1980), in which expert opinion based on tests on the effect of the swine flu vaccine was held to be admissible. The court said:

> Dr. Lewis . . . based his opinion upon tests conducted by laboratory personnel under his supervision. It is beyond question that physicians regularly base opinions on laboratory findings. Therefore, Dr. Lewis may base his opinion on the results of those tests.
> . . . [T]he fact that the results are preliminary, and may not generally be accepted by the medical community, goes to the weight we give to Dr. Lewis's testimony, not to its admissibility.
> . . . The testimony of Dr. Lewis is admissible in evidence in this case. It is useful for a better understanding of the medical issues inherent in the litigation."

533 F. Supp. at 578-79.
[27]180 Cal. 338, 181 P. 223 (1919). See §6.1.
[28]See §6.2.
[29]See §6.3.
[30]See §6.4.

within the territorial jurisdiction of the trial court or (2) capable of accurate and ready determination by resort to sources whose accuracy cannot reasonably be questioned."[31] The last few words refer, of course, to sources such as almanacs and encyclopedias. In its terms, Rule 201 does not apply to judicial notice of the scientific basis of technical devices, and to that extent it can be criticized as deficient.

## §6.7 Legislative Facts

Some years ago Professor Kenneth Davis, well known for his scholarship in administrative law, did some work on judicial notice, which is very important in administrative litigation. Professor Davis did not do literally what I describe here, but it added up to much the same thing. He and his research assistants pulled off the shelves of the law library every single case in which a court took judicial notice of a fact. The cases made a very big pile. Professor Davis then took from that pile all of the cases involving the four categories of judicial notice discussed so far in this chapter: facts that are indisputable by their nature and common knowledge in the area where the court sits; court records; almanac-type facts; and scientific basis. With these he made four little piles. But the big pile was still very big. The four categories do not account for every situation in which a court will take judicial notice.

Professor Davis pointed out that the cases representing the four categories are related, in that they all involve judicial notice of a common kind of fact. In each of those cases, the judicially noticed fact is of no particular significance to the law, except insofar as the fact figures in deciding that particular case. That Mission Street is in a business district has no legal significance apart from its significance in arriving at a decision in *Varcoe v. Lee*.[32] That the moon was in a particular phase on August 29, 1857, is of no

---

[31]Fed. R. Evid. 201(b).
[32]180 Cal. 338, 181 P. 223 (1919). See §6.1.

particular significance in the law, except insofar as it figured in Armstrong's trial.[33] And so on down the line.

Professor Davis came up with a generic name to describe the kind of fact that is significant only in the particular case. He called it "adjudicative fact." We can see now that judicial notice of adjudicative fact has been our subject in the previous sections. Judges and lawyers use the phrase; indeed, Federal Rule of Evidence 201 is titled, "Judicial Notice of Adjudicative Facts."[34] Despite some deficiencies in draftsmanship, the rule is intended to convey all four categories.

The remainder of Professor Davis's cases, although speaking in terms of judicial notice and deeming facts proved without formal proof, involve matters other than adjudicative fact. These facts, like adjudicative facts, are important in the particular lawsuit, but also have significance for the law beyond the particular lawsuit. These facts bear upon the process of understanding or creating the law. They illuminate, for example, the legislative intention in passing a statute. They shed light on the reasons why a particular rule of the common law should now be rejected and replaced by a different rule. They tell something about what the founders intended when they adopted provisions of the Constitution. Professor Davis called these facts "legislative facts." The term goes beyond the legislative process, however. It refers to facts generally relevant to the process of formulating the law, and is relevant to the workings of the common law as well.

Peculiarly in the United States, by contrast with every other nation, most great issues of a social, political, or economic nature are ultimately decided by lawsuits. We dispose of virtually every issue of the day by having lawyers argue it and judges decide it as though it were strictly a legal question. As long ago as 1835, Alexis de Tocqueville pointed out, "Scarcely any question arises in the United States which does not become, sooner or later, a subject of judicial debate . . . ."[35] That is why, he told us, lawyers

---

[33]People of the State of Illinois v. Armstrong, Cass County Circuit Court (1858). See §6.3.

[34]See §6.6.

[35]1 A. de Toqueville, Democracy in America 284 (rev. ed. 1900).

are the aristocracy of America — the elite, the practitioners of power.[36] Issues that in other countries at other times have been decided by people shooting at each other in the streets, in the United States are settled by having lawyers submit briefs and make oral arguments so that judges may decide.

With all due deference to the nine justices of the Supreme Court, they cannot know more than anyone else about the morality of abortion. Nothing in legal training illuminates the difficulties of the question; nothing in the citators or the digests helps. Nevertheless, in America questions about abortion are decided by courts. And so it becomes absolutely necessary for lawyers in such cases to have a mechanism for bringing to the court's attention whatever the court should know to help it decide.

The classic starting point for tracing the development of the doctrine of legislative facts is *Muller v. Oregon*,[37] which goes back to 1908, the heyday of substantive due process. The state of Oregon had enacted a statute that limited the number of hours women could work. Today the statute would be regarded as a violation of the equal protection clause, but in those days it was seen as extremely liberal. If women were not protected, then sweatshop employers would have them working seventy and eighty hours a week, which was not good for families or for the women themselves.

Oregon's statute was attacked immediately on the grounds of what we understand today as substantive due process, because it interfered with a woman's freedom to contract. When the case reached the U.S. Supreme Court, the state of Oregon, rather than rely on its attorney general, retained Louis D. Brandeis, then in private practice in Boston. As an associate on the case, Brandeis employed another young Boston lawyer named Felix Frankfurter.

The two of them wrote the brief, the first "Brandeis brief." It ran to fifty pages and contained two points. The first point, taking up about a page and a half, argued a rule of law: The Constitution requires only that the legislature act reasonably in enacting a statute. The second point in the brief was that it was

---

[36]*Id.* at 277-85.
[37]208 U.S. 412 (1908).

reasonable for the Oregon legislature to limit the number of hours women could work. That point took up many pages — reports of commissioners of hygiene, and studies by psychologists and sociologists from all over the world on the impact upon women and families of women working long hours.

The Court was impressed by that brief. Its opinion acknowledges, in effect, that while one need not be persuaded by Brandeis's collection of reports, the Court was persuaded that a reasonable person could be persuaded by them. Thus, it was rational to conclude that there ought to be a limit on the number of hours women could work; and therefore the statute was constitutional.

That was the beginning of the doctrine that Professor Davis later called "judicial notice of legislative fact." Of those many pages of material in Brandeis's brief, which Felix Frankfurter had found in the Harvard University library, none of the authors had testified. None of the reports had been formally offered in evidence. None had been subject to the crucible of cross-examination. How, then, do we account for the Supreme Court's deciding the case on the basis of those reports? They were in evidence, for all practical purposes, though no one had put them in evidence. There must have been a shortcut: judicial notice. This was not judicial notice of adjudicative fact, because these facts have significance to the law beyond this particular controversy between Muller and Oregon. They shed light on how to give meaning to a provision of the Constitution. *Muller v. Oregon*, in short, teaches that a court may take judicial notice of such legislative facts.

What are the limits? Consider *Brown v. Board of Education*,[38] the school desegregation landmark. Some experts testified on each side; but there was also a mass of literature written by people who did not testify, including those who could not have testified because they were dead. Most of that literature worked against Brown, that is, against the position maintained by Thurgood Marshall, who argued the case before the Court. Most of the

---

[38]347 U.S. 483 (1954).

material claimed that a separate school system was in fact not bad for children, so long as it was actually equal.

In oral argument, Thurgood Marshall tried to make the point that the Court should not read that material — that doing so would be unfair because none of the material had been subject to cross-examination. He argued that judicial notice should not extend that far. Sitting on the panel was Felix Frankfurter, who had collaborated on the very first of such briefs.

There is a colloquy famous among evidence teachers in which Marshall said, in effect, "Your Honor, I don't think it's fair for you to go to the library and read this stuff."

From the bench, Frankfurter replied, "[I]n these matters this Court takes judicial notice of accredited writings, and it does not have to call the writers as witnesses. . . . It is better to have witnesses, but I did not know that we could not read the works of competent writers."[39] After two or three more attempts to press the matter Marshall backed off, because he saw that he would only alienate Frankfurter.

That five-minute segment of oral argument in *Brown v. Board of Education* raises the question of how far it is proper to go with judicial notice of legislative fact. We can assume it is legitimte to submit a Brandeis brief, with background materials bearing on some question of statutory construction or constitutional interpretation; and let us say it is also legitimate, as *Brown v. Board of Education* suggests, to tell the court that there are books in the library it might read on the subject. But suppose that a judge who presides over a bench trial says, when the trial is over, "I'll reserve decision." He goes home and thinks it over, but still cannot make up his mind. He says to himself, "Well, my next door neighbor, Charlie, is a pretty wise fellow. I'll ask him." And he does; he knocks on Charlie's door and says, "Charlie, let me tell you about this case. How do you think it ought to be decided?"

We can agree that the judge may not do that. Counsel are not informed that he is doing it; it goes beyond the record; there is no way for counsel to cross-examine Charlie. If the judge can

---

[39] 49 Landmark Briefs and Arguments of the Supreme Court of the United States: Constitutional Law 341 (P. Kurland & G. Casper eds. 1975).

go to the library but cannot go to Charlie next door, it is hard to draw the line.

Given the extraordinary nature of litigation in the United States, a judge must have some freedom to study authorities beyond what appears in the record. Yet every time a judge does go to the library, he undercuts the adversarial nature of a common law trial. The more nearly we approach the situation in which the judge consults neighbor Charlie, the more nearly we come to pulling the props right out from under the common law judge and the common law trial. We cannot draw the line, although it is a terribly important matter.

In the abortion decision, *Doe v. Bolton*,[40] Chief Justice Warren E. Burger said in a concurring opinion, "I am somewhat troubled that the Court has taken notice of various scientific and medical data in reaching its conclusion; however, I do not believe that the Court has exceeded the scope of judicial notice accepted in other contexts."[41] Burger did not dissent, but he did raise the warning.

When the drafters of the Federal Rules of Evidence came to write Article II on judicial notice, they wrote Rule 201, headed "Judicial Notice of Adjudicative Facts." But there is no Rule 202 entitled, "Judicial Notice of Legislative Facts." The drafters did not know how to write that rule. We are simply not far enough along in the development of this doctrine to articulate the dividing line between what is permissible and what is not. For now the issue remains one for case-by-case determination.

## §6.8 Foreign Law

Alongside judicial notice of adjudicative fact and of legislative fact is a third category, judicial notice of law. How does one account for the presence in the courtroom of matters of law? Sometimes it is simply a question of accounting for the judge's

---

[40]410 U.S. 179 (1973). The case is a companion to the better-known Roe v. Wade, 410 U.S. 113 (1973).

[41]*Id.* at 208.

knowledge of the law; for example, as in *Varcoe v. Lee*,[42] that the speed limit in a business district was fifteen miles per hour. But sometimes, the problem is more elaborate. A case may cut across political dividing lines, as in a multistate torts case. An international transaction may touch upon several nations.

These cases lead to problems in conflicts of law, including choice of law and all the rest. A lawyer may be trying a case in a court of State *A*, and under the applicable conflict-of-laws principles, the rule to be applied to the case derives from the laws of State *B*. Sometimes the lawyer may use judicial notice to bring to the judge's attention, in State *A*, the rule of law in State *B*, under the label "judicial notice of law." In a handful of jurisdictions, this is regarded as a problem in the law of evidence; in most, it is considered part of the law of procedure, and is left to the rules of procedure.

The federal jurisdiction is one of the majority that treats judicial notice of law as a matter of procedure, not of evidence. To find the rules that apply in a federal court, we look not to the Federal Rules of Evidence, but to the Federal Rules of Civil Procedure[43] or the Federal Rules of Criminal Procedure,[44] as appropriate.

---

[42]180 Cal. 338, 181 P. 223 (1919). See §6.1.
[43]Fed. R. Civ. P. 44.1.
[44]Fed. R. Crim. P. 26.1.

# CHAPTER 7

# Types of Evidence

## §7.1 Real Evidence

Every item of evidence will fall into one of four categories: real, demonstrative, documentary, or testimonial. These categories are convenient to bear in mind, because they can serve as a kind of checklist. They help to enhance the efficiency of a lawyer's performance in the courtroom by triggering reactions to issues and objections that otherwise might be missed.

This chapter takes up the first three categories. Discussion of the fourth begins in the chapter following.

Real evidence is exactly what its name says. This kind of evidence is not someone's recollection; it is not an account of what happened; it is not a reconstruction of the transaction at issue. This kind of evidence is a piece of reality itself, the real thing. For example, the bullet that killed the victim is real evidence. To be admitted as real evidence, the bullet must be the very one dug out of the victim. A different bullet, even though identical in all respects, would not be real evidence in the case.

Real evidence is very dramatic, and it affords many opportunities for persuasion. But insofar as doctrine is concerned, all of the cases on real evidence, thousands of them, can be summarized in a single sentence. The sentence is simply this:

Real evidence is admissible if the proponent proves it to be the real thing.

Every rule of evidence has an exception, and this rule has one too. Put succinctly, the exception is this: Real evidence is admissible, once it is proved to be the real thing, unless its emotional impact will outweight any probative value it may have.[1] A lawyer called upon to invoke the exception would put it something as follows: "Your Honor, this is unduly inflammatory. It will so upset and distress the jury that the defendant can no longer receive a fair trial."[2]

**Impact of Real Evidence.** In recent years the work of Melvin Belli and others has attracted considerable interest to the use of real evidence. It has also brought into print a small library of materials on the subject. The sense of this literature, and the party line among trial lawyers generally, is that real evidence has enormous impact on the jury. That is beyond question. The literature and the party line go on to say that because it has such an enormous impact on the jury, real evidence should be used as often as possible. The latter proposition, however, goes too far. To understand why, we need to understand why real evidence has the impact that it does.

We return once again to the analogy between the courtroom and the theater.[3] Consider the state of mind of an audience waiting for the curtain to go up. The audience knows that they will see mere playacting. They will hear actors reciting memorized lines, perhaps written centuries earlier, while stepping through carefully choreographed moves. And yet, understanding full well that it is not the real thing, each of us in the audience is prepared to accept what we see as reality. Coleridge called this disposition the "willing suspension of disbelief." We suspend our faculty of disbelief for the duration of the play, even though we know with our intellect that what we see is simply not so.

---

[1] Speaking plainly, real evidence is inadmissible if it will make the jury vomit.

[2] *See* Fed. R. Evid. 403 ("evidence may be excluded if its probative value is substantially outweighed by the danger of unfair prejudice").

[3] See §3.6.

Once in a while, however, something goes wrong on stage. The script might call for a fist-fight, let us say. There is a whole technology of stage fighting to make the action look real, even though it is not. But in this performance, there is an accident; by mistake, one actor actually slugs the other. This sort of thing happens far more often than audiences know. We are rarely aware of it because a professional actor prides himself on the ability to cover such mishaps. As a matter of craftsmanship, no actor wants the audience to know that something has gone amiss. The audience has suspended disbelief because they know that what they see is playacting. When suddenly it is not playacting, when it becomes real, there is a jolt. The audience does not know how to respond. The abrupt injection of reality tears the convention on which the audience has agreed to rely, and that has a tremendous impact.

The use of real evidence in the courtroom deliberately tears the same convention. It is not, like the rest of the evidence, *about* something; it is the thing itself. Again, the playacting suddenly becomes reality. It shakes the jury, and they do not know how to respond. That is why real evidence has such a great impact.

Prosecutor: Doctor, did you carry out an autopsy on the body of the victim of this homocide?

Witness: I did.

Q. Did you find a cause for his death?

A. Yes.

Q. What is that cause?

A. A bullet that I found in his brain.

Q. Doctor, I hand you this object, which has been marked "People's Exhibit 1" for identification. Do you recognize it?

A. Yes, I recognize it.

Q. What is it, Doctor?

A. That is the bullet I found in the brain of the victim.

Q. How do you recognize it?

A. Why, I scratched my initials on it, and the date. There they are.

115

Prosecutor: Your Honor, I offer it in evidence.

The Court: Received.

Prosecutor: And now, Your Honor, may I pass it among
the jurors?

But the jurors will not touch it! They recoil in horror. They are
afraid that the bullet is still sticky with the brain tissue of the
human being whose death it caused. It is a juju object, the metal
slug that caused a fellow human being to die. And that is precisely
why the prosecutor puts it in evidence.[4]

Used once, real evidence is a hand grenade going off in the
courtroom. The second time, and maybe the third time, the hand
grenade goes off. But the fourth time, one of the jurors thinks,
"Wait a minute. This is being done to us deliberately. We are being manipulated. This is showmanship." Of course it is; but it
must be showmanship that conceals showmanship. If one juror
decides that we are putting on a show, then the jury will not trust
us. In consequence, we will lose the case.[5]

Real evidence works by tearing convention — but once the
convention is gone, once the jurors have seen through the showmanship, real evidence works against us. Precisely because it has
such an impact, real evidence should be used sparingly — just
a very few times in the course of the trial, as the high points.
Ideally, we would end with real evidence.

**Introducing the Real Thing.** In order to introduce real
evidence, we must first satisfy a bit of doctrine. We must prove
that the item is in fact real evidence — that it is the same item

---

[4]Once, when I was serving as assigned defense counsel in a narcotics case,
the prosecution had fifty pounds of pharmaceutically pure heroin. This particular batch came from a chemical factory in a then-unfriendly nation. It was
deliberately sold to the defendants at a very low price, in order to move it into
this country and thereby subvert the social fabric of the United States. Diluted
down to street strength, fifty pounds of pharmaceutically pure heroin is enormously valuable. You can buy an air force with it.

At trial, the government walked in with the fifty pounds of pure heroin
sealed up in heavy plastic — and they piled it into the jury box. The jurors
went right up against the back wall. They were afraid to touch the stuff — afraid
that they would be instantly addicted.

[5]See §3.6.

that formed a part of the transaction that is the subject matter of the lawsuit. We must prove that the item is the real thing.

Putting in real evidence is the kind of thing that a trial lawyer should be able to do with square corners, like a center fielder handles a routine fly ball or a surgeon sews up an incision so as to leave an almost invisible scar. This mechanical skill calls for no special creative genius; it is simply something that we must know how to do. Without that skill, we will probably manage to get the item into evidence, but we will not impress the jury with the kind of professionalism that leads them to trust us.

There are three ways of proving that an item is the real thing. The three ways correspond to three distinct categories of real evidence. To get the item in smoothly and cleanly, we must determine in advance the category into which the real evidence falls. We then use the appropriate method of proof, and stop. A lawyer who uses two or all three of these methods together will look like an amateur.

**Unique Objects.** The rarest category consists of items that are by their nature unique. There is only one of each such item in the world. To get it in, we need only call a witness to say, "Yes, that's the ---," whatever the object may be.

Here is an example from a real case. I was then in the U.S. attorney's office, the prosecutor in charge of interstate transportation of stolen property. In this case the stolen property was a painting by Degas. It was huge, the size of a blackboard, and hideously ugly. Degas made it ugly on purpose. It was painted late in his life, when Degas was short of money. A banker named Augustine offered a large sum for a picture of his wife, his two children, and the dog. Degas hated himself for taking the money, and he let his feelings come out in the picture.

The FBI recovered the picture in Texas and brought it back to New York. Before trial I asked a colleague, a skilled amateur carpenter, to build a huge stand. We put the stand, with the picture on it, across from the jury box. With my own three dollars I bought a king-sized bedsheet, and we used that to cover the picture.

After a few days of trial we had proved everything about the theft and transportation, but the picture itself was not yet in evidence. The judge asked at one point, "Younger, why do you have that bedsheet covering the picture?"

"Well, Your Honor," I answered, "it's not in evidence yet, so the jury can't look at it."

"Oh," he said. "Right." And so the jury sat through three days of trial staring at the bedsheet. By the end, their curiosity was overwhelming. They could not contain themselves.

I saved the unveiling for the last witness. Other witnesses had already supplied testimony on the questioned relevance, so it was just a matter of getting the picture in. This was the testimony, almost verbatim.

Q. What is your name, sir?

A. Theodore Rousseau.

Q. What is your occupation, Mr. Rousseau?

A. I am the curator of modern European painting at the Metropolitan Museum of Art.

Q. Mr. Rousseau, would you step down from the witness stand — with Your Honor's permission — and go over to whatever it is that is behind that bedsheet.

A. Yes, sir.

Q. Mr. Rousseau, without removing the bedsheet, please look under it. Now, resume your place on the witness stand. Mr. Rousseau, did you recognize what is under the bedsheet?

A. Yes, I did.

Q. What is it?

A. Degas's painting of the Augustine family.

The painting is unique, of course. It is not a reproduction, and there can be only one original of a painting.

Mr. Younger: Your Honor, I offer it in evidence as Government Exhibit 10.

The Court: Received.

Mr. Younger: Now that it is in evidence, Your Honor, may I remove the covering?

The Court: Please

From the jury box: "Ugh! That's ugly!"

Mr. Younger: Your Honor, the government rests.

**Objects Made Unique.** It is relatively unusual to introduce in evidence an object that is by its nature unique. More often we deal with an object that is commonplace in itself, but which has become unique because the witness on the stand did something to make it unique. Typically he put his initials on it, or marked it in some other way. All we need to do, then, is to establish what was done to the object to make it unique.

Suppose, for example, that we have an assault case. The weapon was a beer bottle. A policeman is on the stand.

Q. Officer, when you made the arrest, did you remove something from the defendant's hand?

A. Yes.

Q. What did you remove?

A. A Schlitz beer bottle.

Q. I hand you what has been marked "Commonwealth Exhibit 1" for identification. What is it?

A. That's the beer bottle I removed from the defendant's hand.

A beer bottle is not unique. There are millions of Schlitz bottles and they all look the same. We need the next question:

Q. How do you know that this is the same beer bottle you took out of the defendant's hand?

A. Because, when I took it away from him, I wrote my initials and the date on the label. There they are. You can see them.

Prosecutor: Your Honor, I offer it in evidence.

**Chain of Custody.** The third kind of object is not by its nature unique, nor did the witness do anything to it to make it unique. Nonetheless, we must prove it to be the same object that figured in the transaction that is the subject matter of the lawsuit. If the object is neither unique nor made unique, the only way of proving it to be the same object is to trace the object through time, from then to now. The process is called establishing the chain of custody, or the chain of possession.

Q. Officer, did you remove a beer bottle from the defendant's hand?

A. Yes.

Q. What did you do with it?

A. I took it back to the station house.

Q. What did you do with it there?

A. I put it in my desk, in the lower left drawer.

Q. Do you share that desk with anyone?

A. No.

Q. Does the desk have a lock and key?

A. Yes.

Q. What did you do that night?

A. I locked the lower left-hand drawer.

Q. Did you open that drawer at any time from that night up until this morning?

A. No, sir.

Q. To your knowledge, did anyone else open the drawer?

A. No.

Q. Did you open it this morning?

A. Yes.

Q. When you opened it, what did you see?

A. The beer bottle.

Q. What did you do with it?

A. I brought it to court.

Q. You mean, it's here in court now?

A. Yes, sir.

Q. Where?

A. In my briefcase.

Q. Where is your briefcase?

A. Right here on the floor, next to my foot.

Q. Open it. Reach in, and take out whatever you feel. What is that?

A. This is the bottle I took from the defendant's hand that night in the bar, six months ago.

Prosecutor: Your Honor, I offer it in evidence.

## §7.2 Demonstrative Evidence

The second of the four categories of evidence is demonstrative evidence: evidence which is not the real thing, but which graphically demonstrates, represents, or explains the real thing. It is hard to define beyond that, but there are many illustrations. A map, for example, is demonstrative evidence. So are a model, a diagram, and a photograph.

Because a picture is worth a thousand words, trial lawyers use demonstrative evidence frequently. Accordingly, as with real evidence, there are many reported cases on demonstrative evidence. And again, they all boil down to one proposition, the sum total of what the law of evidence has to say on demonstrative evidence:

If the proponent proves that, with accuracy sufficient for the purposes, the item does accurately demonstrate what it purports to demonstrate, then the evidence will be admitted.

The same exception holds as for real evidence. If it is unduly inflammatory, then it is not admissible.

Cases involving demonstrative evidence most often turn on whether the evidence is in fact sufficiently accurate for the proponent's purposes. One example will suffice.[6] In the town of Oyster Bay, on the north shore of Long Island in New York, teenagers walking home from a double date, the plaintiff among

---

[6]Uss v. Town of Oyster Bay, 37 N.Y.2d 639, 339 N.E.2d 147, 376 N.Y.S.2d 449 (1975).

them, apparently fell into some sort of horseplay. One of them hit the pole that supported a street sign, whereupon the street sign itself fell off, according to the plaintiff, and struck the plaintiff on the head. His father, immediately alert to the possibility of a lawsuit, ran out and took custody of the street sign, which in due course was offered in evidence. This street sign, being the object itself, was real evidence, and came in as such.

Counsel for the defendant town lugged into the courtroom something different: a life-size model of a street sign pole. This was not real evidence; it was not the same pole that had held the sign that fell off. It was only a model, some four feet shorter than the real pole, and set in a movable concrete block rather than in a street. With the jury watching, counsel for the defendant put the real street sign up on his model pole and proceeded to reenact the event. That is, he hit the pole with his hand. This time, of course, the sign did not fall off.

Plaintiff objected that, because of the differences between the model pole and the real pole, the demonstration was no good. In the terms we use here, he argued that the evidence was not sufficiently accurate for the purposes. The New York Court of Appeals held that the trial judge could have forbidden the demonstration, but did not have to, the matter being within his discretion. And besides, said the court of appeals, plaintiff had all the opportunity in the world to convince the jury through cross-examination that the differences between the model pole and the real pole were so great that the courtroom demonstration did not deserve much weight. The jury not having been convinced, the court of appeals affirmed the verdict for the defendant.

## §7.3 Documentary Evidence

The third category, after real evidence and demonstrative evidence, is documentary evidence. Instantly recognizable, this is simply evidence in the form of documents.

Documentary evidence can present four evidentiary issues. Not all four issues need arise in every instance, but they may. A lawyer would be wise to memorize the four as a checklist and always to call the checklist into play:

- Parol evidence rule
- Best evidence rule
- Authentication
- Rule against hearsay.

The parol evidence rule is a rule of contract law. If people have a written contract, and one of them also claims a previous oral agreement that bears on the subject matter of the contract, the parol evidence rule bars evidence of the oral agreement. Another version of the rule applies to wills. There is much more to say about the parol evidence rule and its exceptions, but this — being a book about trying cases and not about the law of contracts — is not the place to say it. Any lawyer handling a case involving a written contract or a will has to be thoroughly familiar with the parol evidence rule in his or her jurisdiction.

The second and third items on the checklist, the best evidence rule and authentication, take up the two sections following. The last item, the rule against hearsay, brings us to the largest topic in all of the law of evidence and is left for another work.[7]

## §7.4 Best Evidence Rule

The best evidence rule, despite its name, does not tell us that some evidence is better than other evidence. It has nothing to do with a hierarchy of probative value. It is, rather, a mechanical rule that should long since have been rejected as an anachronism. Yet it has survived and has been incorporated, albeit in modified form, into the Federal Rules of Evidence.[8]

To understand the best evidence rule, it is well to keep in mind the kind of situation that impelled the judges of England to invent the rule some three centuries ago. Felix Frankfurter once remarked that the most important event in the history of the common law was the invention of the steam engine. With the industrial revolution that resulted came all sorts of changes in

---

[7]*See* Younger, Hearsay: A Practical Guide Through the Thicket (1988).
[8]Fed. R. Evid. Art. X.

society. These in turn produced concomitant changes in the nature of litigation. Before the industrial revolution, litigation tended to be one on one, brought by plaintiffs who said, "I was injured through the tortious conduct of the defendant." With the industrial revolution, economic activity became complicated, and so civil lawsuits tended to become more complicated also. As soon as something like the lawsuit of today developed, there arose the phenomenon to which the best evidence rule is addressed: In most cases, no human being has personal knowledge of each aspect of the transactions at issue.

Suppose we are in England, in the first third of the nineteenth century. The industrial revolution is roughly 100 years old, and commercial life has become quite complicated. Tomorrow morning in court, there is to be tried the case of *Somebody v. Ebenezer Scrooge*, a case arising out of the conduct of the business of Scrooge & Marley. It is not likely that Scrooge, or Marley, or Bob Cratchit, or any one human being has personal knowledge of all the events involved in the lawsuit. That information rests in the business records of Scrooge & Marley.

Scrooge knows that, in order to prove his case for the defense, he must put his records into evidence the next morning. So, as he leaves for the day, he turns to Bob Cratchit, who is sitting on his tall stool, and he says to him, "Bob, I'll need the records in court tomorrow. But we're going to need the original records here in the office. Make me a copy." Scrooge leaves. Bob Cratchit stays behind, sitting on his tall stool, and he makes a copy — not with a Xerox machine, which will not be invented for another 150 years, but by hand.

Hand-made copies raise two problems. One is the possibility of fraud. The other possibility is human error. Consider it. There sits Bob Cratchit, tired, uncomfortable, cold because Scrooge will not let him put more coal on the fire, thinking about poor Tiny Tim and no money for doctors, no money even for a Christmas turkey. And besides, it is boring to write out copies of documents by hand. The chances are good that he will make a mistake.

The judges of England are alert to the possibilities. The judges of England, being members of the landed aristocracy, also bear a considerable hostility toward the growing influence of the merchant class, to which Scrooge belongs, and have little sympathy for the practical needs of a commercial establishment such as Scrooge & Marley.

The next morning, Scrooge walks into court. He hands the documents to the judge, and he says, "Your Honor, I put into evidence my books and records."

The judge says, "Now, wait a while. What actually are these?"

Scrooges replies, "Well, these are copies of my books and records written out by my clerk, Bob Cratchit."

The judge's response? "I will not receive these copies, because the possibility of fraud is always with us. And, more important, there is the possibility of human error. If you want to put your books and records into evidence, bring your books and records. Do not bring copies."

That is the best evidence rule. As it applied to the case involving Ebenezer Scrooge two centuries ago, it will apply tomorrow in the federal courts and in any state court. When you put a document into evidence — or, what is the same thing, when you seek to prove the content of a document — you must produce the original. A copy is not the original. Even a photographically exact copy made with today's equipment will not do. It must be the original.

Three examples will help to illustrate how the rule operates. Suppose you have a witness on the stand.

Q. Sir, on that date, were you living in an apartment?
A. Yes.
Q. And what rent did you pay?

Opposing counsel objects. "Best evidence rule, Your Honor. The best evidence of the rent is the lease."

Wrong. The objection should be overruled. The best evidence rule does not, as opposing counsel thinks, enact a hierarchy of probative value, in which the lease is more probative or reliable than the witness's recollection of the rent. The best evidence rule is properly invoked, however, when the questions take this form:

Q. Sir, on that date, were you living in an apartment?

A. Yes.

Q. Did you have a written lease?

A. Yes.

Q. What did the lease say your rent was to be?

Again, opposing counsel objects. "Best evidence rule, Your Honnor." This time the objection is sustained, because we are trying to prove the content of the document without producing the original.

Here is a third example.

Q. Sir, on that date, were you living in an apartment?

A. Yes.

Q. Did you have a written lease?

A. Yes.

Q. I hand you Plaintiff's Exhibit 1 for identification. Is that the lease?

A. Yes.

Q. Thank you. Your Honor, I offer it in evidence.

Assume it is a photocopy. "Objection, Your Honor. Best evidence rule." Sustained, because a copy is not the original.

Again, every rule of evidence has at least one exception. The exception to the best evidence rule is this: When a lawyer puts a document into evidence — or, what is the same thing, when he seeks to prove the content of a document — he must produce the original, unless he cannot. The exception lies in the last three words: unless he cannot. Whether the original has been lost, destroyed, or merely misfiled does not matter. When the original cannot be produced for one reason or another, after the exercise of reasonable diligence, the proponent may prove the content by secondary evidence, that is, by evidence other than the original.

The best evidence rule, as stated earlier, is an anachronism. Fraud is always a possibility, to be sure. But with the development of mechanical and photographic copiers, the possibility of human error has vanished. One might think, then, that the law would have rejected the best evidence rule, but it has not. We still have the best evidence rule, even in the Federal Rules of Evidence: "To prove the content of a writing, recording, or photograph, the original writing, recording, or photograph is required, except as otherwise provided . . . ."[9]

We also have the exceptions: The original is not required if it has been (1) lost or destroyed; or (2) is not obtainable by judicial process; or (3) is in the opponent's possession; or (4) is not closely related to a controlling issue.[10]

The Federal Rules of Evidence do, however, add to the best evidence rule a wrinkle that does much to bring the rule into conformity with the achievements of modern technology: "A duplicate is admissible to the same extent as an original unless (1) a genuine question is raised as to the authenticity of the original or (2) in the circumstances it would be unfair to admit the duplicate in lieu of the original."[11]

In short, a photocopy will be treated as the original, unless the adversary can show some reason why it ought not to be. The showing might be, for example, that there are marginal notations on the original that do not show up clearly on the copy, or that there is reason to suspect chicanery in preparation of the copy. This accommodation between the claims of tradition and the achievements of modern technology seems, in all, to be a sensible one.

## §7.5 Authentication

The third item on the checklist for documentary evidence, after the parol evidence rule and the best evidence rule, is authentication. Not only documents but any tangible objects introduced in evidence need to be authenticated.

Suppose that a policeman is on the stand in an accident case. The questioning goes something like this:

---

[9]Fed. R. Evid. 1002.
[10]Fed. R. Evid. 1004.
[11]Fed. R. Evid. 1003.

Q. Officer, did you investigate the accident?

A. I certainly did.

Q. And in the course of your investigation, did you look for skid marks?

A. I did.

Q. Did you find them?

A. Yes.

Q. Did you measure them?

A. Certainly.

Q. How long were they?

A. Counselor, I don't remember. That was five years ago. I've investigated a thousand accidents since then. I can't possibly remember the details of that investigation.

When a witness cannot remember, there are four possible ways of dealing with the situation. The first three are ways to help him remember, and we shall come to those in due course.[12] For now, let us suppose that we try those, and that none of them works. The witness still cannot remember. But the evidence we need does exist nonetheless. As policemen do generally, our policeman has a memo book. He had his memo book when he investigated the accident, and in it, at the time, he wrote down the length of the skid marks. As a substitute for the witness's absent memory, then, we wish to offer the memo book in evidence.

Q. Officer, I hand you Plaintiff's Exhibit 1 for identification. Do you recognize it?

A. Yes.

Q. What is it?

A. It's my memo book.

Assuming that this is the original memo book, not a copy, we have no problem with the best evidence rule. And if the

---

[12]See §§11.5-11.7.

policeman says, "Yes, this is my memo book," then we have no problem with authentication, either. The policeman has authenticated the memo book by telling us that this is indeed the memo book in which he wrote down the length of the skid marks.

"Authentication" is a term of art, a fancy word that lawyers use for a very ordinary sort of difficulty. To a layman it is often no difficulty at all. Suppose that your client bought a bottle of soft drink. For reasons that will presently become clear, and without meaning to cast aspersions upon the product, we shall say it was a bottle of Coca-Cola. He took it home and drank it down to the very bottom of the bottle. There, at the bottom of the bottle, he discovered one of three things: a cigar stub, or a partially decomposed mouse, or a severed human thumb.[13]

As a result of finding the cigar stub, the mouse, or the thumb, your client, in the language of the pleadings, is rendered sick, sore, lame, and disabled. You bring an action against the Coca-Cola Co. Plaintiff's Exhibit 1 is the bottle of Coca-Cola. But it is necessary to show the connection between the defendant Coca-Cola Co., and the Coca-Cola bottle.

Now, the Coca-Cola bottle may well be the most widely recognized object on the face of the earth. There is nowhere in the United States, and there are few places elsewhere in the world, where people will not recognize that object to be a Coca-Cola bottle. You offer it in evidence, assuming that the judge, like everyone in the world, will recognize this to be a Coca-Cola bottle, and so will permit it to be received in evidence against the defendant, the Coca-Cola Co.

But the judge says, "How do I know it's a Coca-Cola bottle?"

"Look at it, Your Honor," you say.

The judge says, "How do I know? Maybe it's a fake. Maybe it's a substitute. Maybe it's an unfair competitor who's using the same bottle."

---

[13]Judging by the reported cases, these appear to be the foremost possibilities for unpleasant surprises at the bottom of soft-drink bottles. The thumb is particularly intriguing, because no one ever comes forward to claim it. I do not know how it happens that someone can lose a thumb in the soft-drink machinery and say nothing about it.

In order to satisfy the judge, we would now have to call the appropriate person from the Coca-Cola Co. to look at the bottle and say, "Yes, that is a bottle my company makes." That authenticates the bottle.

Suppose, now, that you want to offer the *Wall Street Journal* in evidence. Everyone recognizes the masthead. But beyond your telling him that everyone recognizes it, how does the judge know that this is the *Wall Street Journal*? That is the problem of authentication, of proving that something is what it purports to be.

Any tangible object must be authenticated. And every jurisdiction has a bundle of rules dealing with authentication.

A good place to start, because in most other jurisdictions you will find much the same thing, is Article IX of the Federal Rules of Evidence. Things are not quite as absurd as this discussion makes them seem, because in the Federal Rules, certain kinds of objects are deemed to be self-authenticating. The proponent need not put in any evidence to authenticate those.[14] The *Wall Street Journal*, for example is in this category.[15] Another way to satisfy the authentication requirement under the Federal Rules is by "[a]ppearance, contents, . . . or other distinctive characteristics, taken in conjuction with circumstances."[16] Thus, for all practical purposes, the Coca-Cola bottle too is self-authenticating.

The policeman's memo book, however, is not self-authenticating. The policeman must tell us that it is what it purports to be.[17] Likewise, suppose we hand a witness her apartment lease, assuming it to be the original so that the best evidence rule does not apply.

> Q. I hand you this document, Plaintiff's Exhibit 1, for identification. What is it?
>
> A. It is my lease. I see my signature on it. I recognize it.

---

[14]Fed. R. Evid. 902.

[15]Fed. R. Evid. 902(6) ("Printed materials purporting to be newspapers or periodicals").

[16]Fed. R. Evid. 901(b)(4).

[17]Fed. R. Evid. 901(b)(1) ("Testimony that a matter is what it is claimed to be").

She is authenticating the document. Every document, every tangible object that is not self-authenticating under the rules of the jurisdiction, must be authenticated before it will be received in evidence.

## §7.6 Computer Printouts

Suppose that the case of Scrooge & Marley[18] were to come to trial, not early in the nineteenth century, but today. As he did then, Scrooge would need to offer his business records in evidence. Bob Cratchit, of course, would be spared the need to spend the night before trial on his tall stool, copying out Scrooge's business records by hand. But the chances are that he would not use a photocopy machine either, not unless Scrooge & Marley were a very small concern. Few businesses keep their records in ledger books any more. Most likely, the evidence that Scrooge presents in court would take the form of computer printouts, probably printouts run off especially for the litigation.

A computer printout is a document, and so when offered in evidence it can raise the same evidentiary issues that might apply to any other documentary evidence. There are four such issues: the parol evidence rule; the best evidence rule; authentication; and the rule against hearsay.[19]

The parol evidence rule applies primarily to contracts and wills, and so it seldom arises in connection with computer printouts as such. A parol evidence question might come up in connection with a contract prepared on a word processing machine, which is a computer that uses a special kind of program. But the fact that the contract document came out of a computer printing device is of no evidentiary consequence. The parol evidence issue, if there is one, will be settled exactly as though the contract had been typed out on a typewriter or written with a pen.

Authentication does become an issue with computer printouts. As with any other tangible object that is not self-authenticating, a computer printout must be authenticated before it may

---

[18]See §7.4.
[19]See §7.3.

be received in evidence. The methods for authenticating it are no different than for any other kind of document.[20] The proponent must prove that the computer printout is in fact what it purports to be. With the appropriate witness on the stand, the questioning might go like this:

Q. Your name, sir?

A. Robert Cratchit.

Q. Are you employed, Mr. Cratchit?

A. Yes.

Q. Who is your employer?

A. Scrooge & Marley Limited.

Q. What is your position there?

A. I am the chief computer operator.

Q. I hand you Defendant's Exhibit 1 for identification. Do you recognize it?

A. Yes.

Q. What is it?

A. This is a computer printout I prepared yesterday, at Mr. Scrooge's request.

Q. What is the printout a record of?

A. It shows a breakdown of the firm's current investments.

Whatever it shows, the witness will tell us. A lawyer who needs to authenticate a computer printout will proceed much as if he were seeking to put in evidence a policeman's memo book, or a lease, or any other document.

The best evidence rule, when applied to computer printouts, presents us with a more interesting question. In a common law court, the best evidence rule requires that the original of a document be offered in evidence, unless for some reason it is not available, in which case a copy will be received in evidence

---

[20]See §7.5.

instead.[21] In the minds of the judges of nineteenth-century England, who originated the rule, every document had an original, a first version of the document from which others might be copied. That original may have been lost or destroyed at some time after it was made, but the original once existed. When a copy was received in evidence, it came in as a substitute for an unavailable original.

What is the original of a computer printout? At first, we might say it is the paper that comes out of the computer. Copy that, and we have a copy; but the first paper is the original. The engineers who are privy to the inner workings of these machines would disagree. The printout itself, they say, is only a copy. But a copy of what?

Open a computer, and inside it you will find a tiny chip of silicon with wires sticking out on both sides, like a robot centipede. Engraved inside the piece of silicon are thousands of electrical circuits. Streams of electrons go coursing through those thousands of circuits. But the electrons do not stick to one path. Rather, they switch continually from one circuit to another. The total pattern is always changing, and that is what makes the computer work. It is where the electrons choose to go at any particular moment, among those thousands of circuits, that determines what the computer is doing at that moment.

At the appropriate time, certain patterns of electrons cause a printing device wired into the computer to print out certain numbers on paper. Thus, from one point of view, the computer printout itself — the very paper that comes out of the computer — is not the original at all; it is merely a copy of the electron patterns inside the chip of silicon. The true original is the inconstant pattern of electrons. There is no original to offer in evidence, save the electrons. And there never was an original; nothing, at least, that we can put before the judge.

When the Federal Rules were drafted, this problem of the nonexistent original had already been around for some years. The draftsmen recognized the problem, and they offered not one, but two solutions to it. We have already encountered one solution,

---

[21]See §7.4.

the provision in the Federal Rules saying in effect that a copy is admissible unless there is some good reason to insist on the original.[22] In the case of a computer printout, there is every good reason *not* to insist on the original, because the original never had a palpable existence.

The drafters of the Federal Rules went further, however. They put it down in so many words: "If data are stored in a computer or similar device, any printout or other output readable by sight, shown to reflect the data accurately, is an 'original.' "[23] In federal jurisdictions, at least, that takes care of the matter.

---

[22]Fed. R. Evid. 1003.
[23]Fed. R. Evid. 1001(3).

# CHAPTER 8

# Competence, Relevance, Materiality

## §8.1 Three Basic Concepts

All evidence falls into four categories. The preceding chapter examined three of those: real evidence, demonstrative evidence, and documentary evidence. Here we begin with the fourth and largest category: testimony, the kind of evidence that results when a human being takes the stand and talks. Its technical name is *viva voce* evidence, which means, literally, evidence from the living voice.

Not only is testimony the most common kind of evidence, but in the early days, it was the only kind of evidence. For historical reasons, and because it involves a human being on the witness stand under conditions of stress, testimonial proof presents many problems. This chapter discusses what the law of evidence has to say about those problems.

Three concepts are basic to any trial lawyer's ability to analyze and resolve evidentiary problems. It is most important to understand these concepts, and to be able to use them. Their names are known to every law student, and probably to most lay people in the country. We have all heard them often, if not from some more authoritative source, then because we have all spent an undue amount of time watching Perry Mason on television.

Part of the charm of that program is that every episode was constructed in accordance with a formula. Roughly two-thirds of the way through the story, we were in court, and Perry was pulling the rabbit out of the hat. He did something extraordinary, and it startled the prosecutor — Hamilton Burger, you remember, who despite being rather a nincompoop was very likable. The kindly old judge looked over at the nonplussed Mr. Burger: "Well, Mr. Burger, what do you say?"

Burger always responded the same way. "I — I — I object, Your Honor."

And the judge: "On what ground do you object?"

Burger's answer was always the same, and that answer gives us the names of the three concepts basic to analyzing any problem in evidence. His answer was, "Your Honor, I object on the ground that it is incompetent, irrelevant, and immaterial." And he would sit down. Of course, the judge always overruled the objection.

No lawyer worth his salt has ever responded to that question from a judge with a mindless invocation of those three words: incompetent, irrelevant, immaterial. To use those three words in answer to the judge's question is an open confession of ignorance as to the proper ground of the objection. One might as well stand up and say, "Your Honor, I object!"

"On what ground, Counselor?"

"On all grounds, Your Honor!"

That is, in effect, what Hamilton Burger told the judge every week. It covers the waterfront. It includes everything and specifies nothing.

**Competence.** Recall that the word "evidence" has three distinct meanings: the law of evidence; the stuff that constitutes evidence; and the status of having been received in evidence.[1]

A piece of evidence is competent if, under the law of evidence, it is eligible to be received in evidence. Competence merely means eligibility. The piece of evidence might be any item of proof: a bit of *viva voce* testimony, a document, a photograph, or a piece

---

[1]See §1.2 n.1.

of real evidence. It is competent if the finder of fact may properly take it into account in coming to a decision in the case.

Here is a purposely absurd example. Suppose the U.S. Constitution provided: "In no court of the United States, or of any state thereof, shall any document be admissible in evidence which is printed on green paper." Your opponent offers in evidence a document that is printed on green paper. The proper objection? Incompetent. The document is ineligible to be received in evidence. The document is incompetent.

In the context of *viva voce* evidence, with a human being testifying, the term applies a little differently. Normally we do not speak of putting the person himself into evidence. Instead, a competent witness is one who is eligible to take the stand and to testify, either generally or on the specific matter at issue.

**Relevance.** When a lawyer offers evidence, the lawyer is trying to prove something. Ninety-nine times out of 100, what the lawyer is trying to prove will be perfectly clear. If it is not clear, the judge will simply ask, "Counselor, what are you trying to prove?" The lawyer tells the judge what he is trying to prove, and then he proceeds to try to prove it.

A piece of evidence is relevant if it has some tendency in logic to prove what the lawyer is trying to prove. That is all relevance means. If there is no logical tendency for the evidence to prove what it is supposed to prove, then the evidence is not relevant.

Suppose, for example, that a lawyer is offering in evidence a biography of Christopher Columbus.

First objection: "Not competent, Your Honor."

Is the biography eligible to be received in evidence? Consulting our four-item checklist for documentary evidence,[2] we suspect that only the rule against hearsay will generate an issue. But let us suppose for now that the judge receives the biography under some exception to the rule.

The next objection? "Not relevant, Your Honor." Whether the biography is relevant or not depends on what the lawyer is trying to prove. Perhaps the judge does not know. The judge turns

---

[2]See §7.3.

to the lawyer and says, "Counselor, what are you trying to prove, when you offer this biography in evidence?"

Suppose that the lawyer says, "Your Honor, I am trying to prove that Columbus first saw the New World in 1492." The biography is relevant. It has a tendency in logic to prove what the lawyer is trying to prove.

Suppose instead that the lawyer says, "Your Honor, I am trying to prove by offering this biography that the defendant in *Varcoe v. Lee*[3] was driving too fast." In this instance, there is no tendency in logic for the evidence to prove what it is supposed to prove. Therefore, it is irrelevant.

**Materiality.** Relevance is rarely an issue. Lawyers do not offer biographies of Christopher Columbus on the theory that a defendant was driving too fast. The issue is more often something different, what the common law called materiality.

Evidence is relevant if it has a logical tendency to prove what it is supposed to prove. And if what the evidence is supposed to prove has some bearing on an issue in the case, then the evidence is also material.

Any good philosopher will tell us that everything is ultimately connected with everything else. Ultimately, then, everything that a lawyer might try to prove will have some bearing on an issue in the case. It comes down to a matter of degree, which is what lawyers usually find themselves arguing about.

Because materiality is more often an issue than relevance, the Federal Rules of Evidence do not treat relevance separately at all. They deal with materiality, but just to make life interesting, the authors of the Federal Rules, while addressing materiality, call it relevance. The rule reads this way: " 'Relevant evidence' means evidence having any tendency to make the existence of any fact that is of consequence to the determination of the action more probable or less probable than it would be without the evidence."[4]

Notice that the words "of consequence to the determination of the action" make this a rule about materiality. Yet the word

---

[3]180 Cal. 338, 181 P. 223 (1919). Reviewed in §6.1, the specifics of the case add nothing to the discussion here.
[4]Fed. R. Evid. 401.

"materiality" appears nowhere in the Federal Rules. The issue of materiality does, but always under the name of relevance. To help keep the distinction clear, we will continue in the common law tradition and call it materiality.

Notice too that the rule refers to *any* tendency to prove what the lawyer is trying to prove. A low degree of connection, then, between the proving evidence (sometimes called the *probans*) and the thing to be proved (sometimes called the *probandum*) will suffice.

Evidence may be both relevant and material — that is, it may have a logical tendency to prove what it is supposed to prove, and what it is supposed to prove may have a bearing on some issue in the case — and yet, if the evidence is unduly and unfairly prejudicial, confusing, or misleading, the trial judge may exclude it simply on that ground. This is an independent basis for the exclusion of evidence, and is unquestionably part of the powers of a common law judge. The Federal Rules of Evidence articulate the principle in these words: "Although relevant, evidence may be excluded if its probative value is substantially outweighed by the danger of unfair prejudice, confusion of the issues, or misleading the jury . . . ."[5]

## §8.2 Incompetence by Status

Competence means generally the eligibility of a piece of evidence to be received in evidence. When applied to a human being, competence refers to the eligibility of that human being to take the stand and to testify, either in general or on any particular subject.

Over the last six or seven centuries, the common law has done an almost complete about-face on the competence of prospective witnesses. It is essentially true, though not accurate in detail, that some centuries ago virtually everyone with any relationship to the litigants or to the controversy was incompetent to testify

---

[5]Fed. R. Evid. 403. The word "relevant" in the rule is synonymous with what the common law calls "material."

because of that relationship. In other words, a host of rules rendered people incompetent because of status. The plaintiff and defendant themselves were incompetent owing to their status as litigants. All of their friends and relatives were likewise incompetent by status, and so was anyone else who knew anything about the controversy. In those days, people with personal knowledge of the controversy constituted the jury, while the witnesses who took the stand were selected in part because they had no such knowledge.

It is painful to think about, but true nonetheless, that people used to be incompetent to testify because of their religious beliefs; and before the Civil War, one of the incidents of slavery was that black people in the South were incompetent to testify because of their race. It was not a question whether jurors would believe a slave, but rather one of the slave's incompetence by status.

Today, we have turned the roles completely around: The jurors are people who have no knowledge of the controversy, and those who testify are the people who do have such knowledge. And with respect to race, religion, and ethnic background, everyone is competent. To that extent, we have abolished incompetence by status.

In at least five important respects, however, we still adhere to incompetence by status in specific situations.[6] Each of the five may be applied or not in a particular jurisdiction, depending on the state of the law in that jurisdiction. A lawyer familiar with all of them is in a position to handle this aspect of evidence law in any of the fifty-one American jurisdictions.

The five vestigial remnants of incompetence by status make up the subject matter of the next five sections.

## §8.3 Spousal Incompetence

In every jurisdiction, at least to some extent, the spousal relationship will operate to produce an incompetence by status. The

---

[6]There are also issues of status beyond these, but they are matters of detail that we will not review here.

common law rule rendered a spouse absolutely incompetent to testify for or against the other spouse. The basis of this rule is the obvious one: the unseemliness of one spouse testifying either for or against the other. By and large, a jury is unlikely to believe a spouse testifying for another; and a spouse on the stand testifying against the other would create an ugly situation in which the law did not want to become involved. A more doctrinal basis for the rule was the common law fiction of husband and wife as one person.

There are three main forms of spousal incompetence in effect today. First, some jurisdictions have maintained the common law rule largely unchanged, resulting in absolute incompetence. Second, there is a modified form of the common law rule, usually called the federal rule. Until 1980 it provided that one spouse is competent to testify for the other spouse; but, for reasons of seemliness, one spouse was not competent to testify against the other. When one spouse does testify for the other, the federal rule leaves it to the jury to decide whether the testifying spouse is telling the truth. This form of the federal rule is followed in many states. In 1980, the Supreme Court amended the federal rule in *Trammel v. United States*.[7] Either spouse may still testify for the other. Now, however, one spouse may also testify against the other, if the testifying spouse is willing to do so. The nontestifying spouse need not consent.

The third form of the rule, which is followed in some of the states, involves a nearly total abolition of spousal incompetence. In New York, for example, one spouse is fully competent to testify either for or against the other spouse, save only with respect to issues of adultery. The exception has to do with policy considerations applicable to adultery actions, and may reflect the peculiar history of divorce law in New York.

Determining the nature of the spousal incompetence rule in any particular jurisdiction is not difficult. There is a tricky aspect to it, however, which sometimes causes trial lawyers to make mistakes. It is necessary to determine the issue of spousal competence separately from questions of spousal privilege.

---

[7]445 U.S. 40 (1980).

Competence denotes the person's eligibility to take the witness stand. In a jurisdiction such as New York, which has substantially abolished the common law rule of spousal incompetence, one spouse may be called to the stand to testify against the other. For example, if the husband is on trial as the defendant in a criminal case, the prosecutor may subpoena the wife. In such a jurisdiction the wife is competent, and she must take the stand. But once on the stand, the wife has a privilege to decline to answer certain questions. The privilege is equally applicable to the husband. Neither spouse may answer certain questions unless both spouses consent.

Suppose the husband is the defendant. The prosecutor says to the wife, "Madam, take the stand." In a jurisdiction that has substantially abolished common law spousal incompetence, she must take the stand. She is fully competent. Now, suppose the questioning proceeds this way:

Q. Madam, I direct your attention to the night of the day of the crime. Did your husband come home?

A. Yes.

Q. Did he get into bed with you?

A. Yes.

Q. What did he say to you in bed?

A. I decline to answer.

And, indeed, she need not answer. Her refusal will be sustained on the ground of spousal privilege. Competence, then, is an issue different from that of privilege. Do not confuse them.[8]

## §8.4 Lord Mansfield's Rule

This instance of incompetence by status is uncommon, but a busy practitioner may encounter it once in a career. It is Lord Mansfield's rule, which goes back to the greatest of all English

---

[8]Many courts do, by referring to the competence issue as "the spouse's privilege not to testify."

judges. So far as I know, it will be followed in every American jurisdiction.

The rule says that a married man or woman is incompetent to testify to circumstances that would result in the bastardization of a child born during the marriage. That is, given the awkward situation in which a mother wishes to testify that her husband is not the child's father, or vice versa, she or he may not do so. The matter may still be proved by other evidence, but not by the spouse's testimony.

In 1974 the Supreme Court of Utah explained the rule in these words: "It requires but little reflection to appreciate the undesirable effects it would have upon family solidarity to permit the spouses to scandalize each other by accusations of immoral conduct concerning the conception of children born in the family. Of graver moment than the disgrace to themselves, it seems repugnant to one's sense of justice to allow them to stigmatize the innocent child, whose welfare and adjustment will be so crucially affected thereby during his whole lifetime."[9]

## §8.5 Conviction for Perjury

In a handful of states, there are statutes saying, in essence, that anyone who has been convicted of perjury is forever after incompetent to be a witness: incompetent by the status of being a convicted perjuror. This is not a matter of impeaching a witness by showing that he has been convicted of perjury. We shall come to that in a later chapter.[10] Rather, these statutes say that once someone has been convicted of perjury, he may never again take the witness stand under any circumstances.

These statutes present a constitutional question under the sixth amendment, which provides for the right to compel attendance of witnesses. Whether or not the statutes are constitutional is a question separate from the evidentiary issues. The Supreme Court has not yet authoritatively spoken on the matter.

---

[9]Lopes v. Lopes, 30 Utah 2d 393, 395, 518 P.2d 687, 689 (1974).
[10]See §15.4.

## §8.6 Dead Man's Statutes

Roughly half the states have a kind of statute that presents a difficult and slippery issue, our fourth type of incompetence by status. There is no common form for this type of statute. Every state has its own way of writing it down; but however the statute is drafted, it will be called the dead man's statute. A trial lawyer must know whether the jurisdiction in which he is trying a case has a dead man's statute, whether the statute operates in his case, and if it does, how it operates.

Dead man's statutes are typically complex and difficult to work out in the circumstances of particular cases. Once a lawyer anticipates that such an issue will arise in the course of trying his lawsuit, he or she must go to the books, examine the statute in that jurisdiction, look at the cases construing the statute, and thread the needle to determine the answers to particular questions that may arise in his case. The following scenario shows the kind of issue to which the dead man's statute is addressed, and how the statute typically operates.

Imagine, if you will, that Professor Smith is delivering a lecture on the dead man's statutes in some city other than his own. Having reached the end of the day, he is putting on his jacket when he realizes that he left his wallet back at the hotel. He is penniless. He needs only a dollar to get back to the hotel where his wallet and funds are, but he doesn't have the dollar.

He approaches a member of the audience. "Ma'am," he says, "will you lend me a dollar? Tomorrow I will repay the dollar." Because he has an honest face, she lends him the dollar, and he goes back to his hotel. But between now and tomorrow, he is called to his ancestors. Come tomorrow, he is gone.

What does his benefactor do? The next day, or soon thereafter, she goes to the administrator or the executor of Smith's puny estate, and she says, "Smith borrowed a dollar from me. He promised to repay it the next day. He did not repay it before he was called to his ancestors. Repay the dollar, please."

The administrator or the executor must make a decision. He will reason something as follows: "Shall I repay the dollar? This lady says that she lent Smith a dollar. But I have no way to test the bona fides of her claim. And after all, it is my obligation to preserve the assets of the estate. It may be that hers is a fraudulent claim. She may be lying. If she is lying and I pay the dollar, why, I will thereby have diminished the estate in response to a fraudulent claim. But on the other hand, if she is telling the truth and she did lend Smith a dollar, and I don't repay it, then this lady is out the money."

That is the very decision that must be made by the legislature. On the one hand, it is concerned with protecting the assets of estates against claims the bona fides of which cannot be checked. On the other hand, claims that are justly payable should be paid.

One way of resolving this policy conflict is for the legislature to say, "In order to secure the greater purpose of protecting estates against unjust or fraudulent claims, we will pay the price that some just claims will not be satisfied. We will effect this policy decision by enacting a statute which is a rule of incompetence. The statute will be called the dead man's statute."

The nature of the resulting incompetence is just this: The lady who lent Smith the dollar is incompetent to testify that she lent him the dollar. She is incompetent because she is the one who is subject to the pressure to lie, to speak falsely about the nature of the transaction.

While it will not be true of the dead man's statute in every jurisdiction, most are written in accordance with the following points from my hypothetical scenario.

First, there was a transaction between the lady and Smith. It need not be the borrowing of money. Indeed, a transaction is anything that two human beings can do together. Borrowing money, having an automobile accident, getting into a fight — all are examples of transactions for purposes of the dead man's statute.

Second, as in my scenario, one of the participants in the transaction has died. There is another possibility that the law regards as equivalent: that one of the parties to the transaction has become insane, and hence unable to communicate with the people in charge of his estate.

Third, the other person who participated in the transaction has survived. We call that person the survivor.

Fourth, the survivor asserts a claim against the estate of the person who has become dead or insane. The claim is not against some third person; remember that the purpose of the dead man's statute is to preserve estates.

Finally, again as in my scenario, the survivor is interested in the event. It is the survivor who will be subject to the temptation to lie. The dead man's statute therefore seals the survivor's lips by making her incompetent to testify to the transaction.

None of this is to say that the transaction cannot be proved; it simply cannot be proved through the survivor. If the man in the next seat saw Smith borrow the money, he would be free to testify. He is not interested in the event, and so he is not subject to the same temptation to lie.

Or suppose that when Smith goes to borrow the money, the lady says, "Ah, now I am better informed. Now I know about the dead man's statute. I will not rely simply upon your promise to repay. I want an IOU." Smith writes, "I owe you one dollar," and signs it. He is called to his ancestors. But still, the survivor may not take the stand and say, "Smith gave me this IOU." That too is a transaction. The survivor must call some third person to the stand to say, "I recognize Smith's signature," or "I saw Smith sign the IOU." That will prove the case.

The alternative view is to say that, yes, the survivor may be tempted to lie, but juries are very good at deciding who is a liar and who is not. If there is one great theme in the development of the law of evidence and procedure and trial practice over these last several years, it is an increasing reliance upon the good sense and the intelligence of juries. It is not surprising to discover that, although several decades ago just about every state had a dead man's statute, today half the states have abolished it.

### §8.7  Incompetence of Jurors

This is the last of our five leftovers of incompetence by status, and in some ways, the most interesting. Every American jurisdiction follows or applies this rule.

One of the great themes of the common law is the idea of finality. We will do what we can to see that disputes are correctly decided; but once they are decided, it is important not to reopen them. When the thing is finally over and done with, the litigants should be able to go home and live out their lives without further regard to this particular dispute. The law, in short, frowns upon obsessions.

The value attached to finality appears in various parts of the law and in different ways. It underlies, for example, the concept of double jeopardy in criminal and constitutional law, and the concepts of res judicata and collateral estoppel in procedure. It also underlies this fifth instance of incompetence by status.

Suppose that a perfectly simple negligence case is tried to a jury. The verdict, when it comes in, surprises the lawyers. They go and talk to the jurors, for in most states there is no bar to talking with jurors once the verdict is in. The jurors need not respond to the lawyers, but they are free to do so if they wish. In the course of discussing the verdict with the jurors, it becomes apparent to the losing lawyer that the jurors arrived at their surprising verdict on the basis of a misunderstanding of the judge's explanation of the law. There is no doubt about it: The jurors made a mistake. They simply did not understand what the judge was saying to them.

The losing lawyer makes a motion to set the verdict aside. The basis of the motion is the argument that the jury made a mistake; that the verdict is not in accordance with the law; that it is an erroneous verdict. The motion is supported by one or more affidavits from jurors saying, "Well, everybody makes mistakes. We made a mistake. We did not understand the judge's explanation of the law."

Now the law must choose. The dispute has come to a conclusion. There is a verdict. The verdict is mistaken. Will we undo it and permit the dispute to be tried again? That would subvert the value we attach to finality. The dispute has been incorrectly decided, yes, but isn't it more important that it be decided once and for all?

Let us start with the original position, and then bring it up to date. The original position emphasized the value of finality. It foreclosed the losing lawyer from making his argument by refusing to receive affidavits from jurors for the purpose of attacking the verdict. There is a customary way of formulating this. To attack the verdict on the ground that the jurors made a mistake is called impeaching the verdict. The original position, then, was that no verdict may be impeached on the basis of the affidavit or the testimony of a juror. And when we say that the juror's affidavit or testimony may not be received for this purpose, we are raising a rule of incompetence — incompetence by reason of the status of being a juror. The rule is usually phrased this way: The juror is incompetent to impeach the verdict.

This is still the general rule. It is the rule found in the Federal Rules of Evidence as well. Rule 606(b) begins by stating the original position: "Upon an inquiry into the validity of a verdict or indictment, a juror may not testify as to any matter or statement occurring during the course of the jury's deliberations or to the effect of anything upon his or any other juror's mind or emotions . . . . Nor may his affidavit . . . be received for these purposes."[11]

The original position of blanket incompetence has since been qualified by exceptions. The cases that make the exceptions, however, are difficult to weave together. Probably the best attempt to find a pattern appears in the second part of Rule 606(b): ". . . except that a juror may testify on the question whether extraneous prejudicial information was improperly brought to the jury's attention or whether any outside influence was improperly brought to bear upon any juror."[12]

There are two aspects to the exception. One is misconduct outside the jury room. The misconduct need not be malicious, but it must be something that violates the law. For example, jurors are supposed to respond only to the evidence presented in court. They must not go out on their own to conduct independent investigations. A juror who does so is in violation of the law.

The film *Twelve Angry Men* illustrates the point. An important piece of the prosecution's circumstantial evidence had to do with the uniqueness of the knife used in the murder. Such a

---

[11]Fed. R. Evid. 606(b). The last sentence quoted appears at the end of the rule.

[12]*Id.*

knife belonged to the defendant; therefore he was the murderer. But Henry Fonda was on that jury. While the jury was recessed from its deliberation, he went out among the stores of the city and managed to find a knife of the very same design as the murder weapon. With it, he showed his fellow jurors that the knife used in the murder was not unique, and persuaded them that there was a reasonable doubt. They acquitted the defendant.

It made a wonderful movie. Who can oppose Henry Fonda? But if an actual juror did the same thing, there would be a problem. In one case, some of the jurors, sent home overnight in the course of deliberation, went to the scene of the crime to determine whether the sight lines were such that a witness could have seen what she purported to describe from the witness stand.[13] That sort of independent investigation is not proper. It is jurors' misconduct, and it is outside the jury room; therefore jurors will be competent to testify or to submit affidavits about it.

The other aspect of the exception concerns extraneous prejudicial information introduced into the jury's deliberation. A juror may testify to that too, and the verdict may well be impeached as a result. Suppose, for example, that in the course of the jury's deliberation in a criminal trial, the bailiff mentioned to the jurors that the defendant had been convicted several times before — information that had not come out during the trial. That would be regarded as extremely prejudicial information, and a juror would be competent to testify to the fact that such information had been revealed to the jury. In consequence the verdict would be set aside.

Likewise, in an actual New York Case,[14] the court stenographer made a mistake while reading the defendant's earlier testimony to the jury, accidentally omitting a key phrase. Under these conditions, too, the verdict can be set aside on the ground of outside influence, and the jurors are competent to testify as to what the stenographer read to them.

------

[13]People v. Crimmins, 26 N.Y.2d 319, 310 N.Y.S.2d 300, 258 N.E.2d 708 (1970).
[14]People v. Johnson, 79 Misc. 2d 880, 361 N.Y.S.2d 512 (Dutchess Co. Ct. 1974).

Occasionally there arises the situation in which a juror wishes to testify that the jury, in the course of reaching its verdict, improperly discussed the defendant's race. To set aside a verdict on this ground, using the words of Rule 606(b), the information about race must have been extraneous, prejudicial, and improperly brought to the jury's attention. Where it appears that the defendant's race was indeed a significant factor in the deliberation, though not mentioned in the evidence, it is difficult to imagine a modern court letting the verdict stand.

## §8.8 Prerequisites to Competence

We have looked at the five important incompetences by status.[15] Those aside, we have the rule with which we began: Everyone is competent regardless of status. Matters such as race, religion, ethnic background, and the like make no difference. More precisely, everyone is competent to be a witness so long as four simple prerequisites are met. They are so simple that many lawyers never take the trouble to fix them clearly in their own minds.

**Oath.** The first of the four prerequisites to competence is familiar to everyone who has seen a trial. A person is called to the witness stand. He stands up in the audience, or is called out of the witness room, and he takes a position in the well of the court in front of the witness chair. The court officer or the bailiff, or sometimes the judge, says to him, "Raise your right hand. Do you swear . . . ?" etc.

Why is that done? Today, it is a sufficient reason to say that the witness thereby satisfies the first requirement of competence, that he take an oath. The word "oath" is broader than "I swear to tell the truth." For reasons of religion or lack of religion many people prefer not to swear, and that is acceptable. Any substitute for swearing will do. A promise or affirmation to tell the truth will satisfy the first requirement of competence. But some ceremony akin to the taking of an oath is required.

---

[15]See §§8.3-8.7.

There are two reasons for the oath requirement. First, to the extent that people believe in a personal God who will judge them in the hereafter, the oath signifies that the witness has sworn to God that he will tell the truth, and that if he does not, then God will call him to account. There was a time, of course, when that was the principal reason for taking the oath.

The second reason for the oath requirement is the secular equivalent of the original religious reason. A person testifying in a trial is doing something very serious, and important consequences attend the testimony. We bring that home to the witness by insisting that he raise his right hand, put his left hand on the Bible or some equivalent, and say that he swears or promises to tell the truth. It brings the seriousness of the event to the witness's mind and conscience. The Federal Rules of Evidence say it this way: "Before testifying, every witness shall be required to declare that he will testify truthfully, by oath or affirmation administered in a form calculated to awaken his conscience and impress his mind with his duty to do so."[16]

Another way of approaching this second aspect of the oath is to note that the witness cannot be prosecuted for perjury unless he has taken the oath, because otherwise his mind and conscience were not awakened to the legal obligation to tell the truth.

Suppose that someone is called to be a witness. The judge says, "Sir, raise your right hand."

"No, I will not."

"Why not? Do you want to take an affirmation instead of the oath?"

"No. I don't want to do anything. I don't want to testify."

That person may not testify. He may be held in contempt for refusing to take the oath, and he may go to jail and stay there until he raises his right hand and takes the oath, but until then he may not testify. He is incompetent because he has not satisfied the first prerequisite of competence.[17]

---

[16]Fed. R. Evid. 603.

[17]See Gould, The Witness Who Spoke with God and Other Tales from the Courthouse (1979).

Suppose that the prospective witness is a child, nine or ten years old. Some jurisdictions have absolute dividing lines as to age, but generally speaking there are none. Very young people and very old people can be witnesses, so long as they take the oath. But it is not enough merely that they go through the cere-mony of raising the right hand; they must also possess the mental and emotional maturity to understand the significance of taking the oath. They must understand that something serious is going on, and that they have a moral and legal obligation to tell the truth.

The test is the same for prospective witnesses who are men-tally retarded. In one New York case, for example, the prosecu-tion called a sixteen-year-old mentally disabled girl, the victim of rape. After permitting the girl's teacher to testify to her men-tal condition, the court found her to be competent to take the oath. A conviction would have been very difficult to obtain without her testimony. [18]

The oath is a question of competence, and competence is a matter of law, so it is the judge who determines whether a witness is competent. It is the judge who decides whether a proposed witness understands the nature and significance of the oath. The judge may ask the proposed witness some questions, or alter-natively permit the lawyers to ask. But the purpose is not at all to decide whether the proposed witness is telling the truth. At this stage, the purpose is simply to determine whether the pro-posed witness possesses enough maturity to understand the nature and significance of the oath. A proposed witness who does not has not satisfied the first prerequisite and may not testify.

**Perception.** Assume that a person of full age and in full possession of his faculties is called to the witness stand.

The Bailiff: Sir, raise your right hand. Do you solemnly swear to tell the truth, the whole truth, and nothing but the truth?

The Witness: I certainly do.

The Bailiff: Take the witness stand..

---

[18]People v. Parks, 41 N.Y.2d 36, 359 N.E.2d 358, 390 N.Y.S.2d 848 (1976).

He does, and direct examination begins.

> Q. Sir, this case is about an accident that occurred on such-and-such a date at such-and-such a location. Did you see it?
> A. No.
> Q. Where were you on that date?
> A. In Vietnam.

Send the witness home. He has taken the oath, but that satisfies only the first prerequisite of competence. The second prerequisite is that the witness must possess first-hand knowledge of the transaction that constitutes the subject matter of the lawsuit. He perceived something of the transaction — he obtained data about the transaction through one or more of his five senses. He saw something, heard something, smelled something, touched something, or tasted something. If the witness says, after taking the oath, that in fact he perceived nothing of the transaction, he is incompetent.

**Memory.** All trial lawyers have run into problems of witness's memory. A mature person in full possession of her faculties is called as a witness.

> The Bailiff: Raise your right hand.
> The Witness: Certainly.
> The Bailiff: Do you swear to tell the truth . . .?
> The Witness: Of course.
> The Bailiff: Take the witness stand.
> Q. Madam, this case is about an accident that occurred at such-and-such a place on such-and-such a date. Did you see it?
> A. Yes, I did.
> Q. What did you see?
> A. I don't remember.

Trials always take place in time present. The transaction constituting the subject matter of the trial took place in time past.

In the courtroom we build a model, more or less accurate, of that past transaction. We must bridge the temporal gap, getting from then to now. We do that by asking the witness to remember. If he cannot remember, then the witness is not competent.

**Communication.** Assume that we have a witness of full age and in full possession of his faculties. He takes the oath, he did perceive, and he does remember. But the witness is not the decider of the case; the judge or the jurors are. We must transfer what is in the witness's head to the judge's or the juror's head. We do that by having the witness communicate. This is the fourth requirement of competence. The witness, having taken the oath, must in some rational fashion communicate what he remembers having perceived.

Usually, the communication will be by the spoken word, and in the United States, in the English language. But those are not the only possibilities. Most lawyers who try cases have had witnesses who do not speak English. Very well; the witness may speak through an interpreter. In some instances, there is a witness who, because of a physical disability, uses the international sign language. He too may communicate through an interpreter. There must, of course, be reason to believe that it is the witness, not the interpreter, who is providing the answers.[19] On very rare occasions there may be a witness who does not speak in any language, but instead will write the answers down. It is clumsy, but it satisfies the fourth prerequisite. If the witness cannot use any rational mode of communication, however, the witness is incompetent.

### §8.9 Competence and Credibility

The question of competence is a matter of law. We have already seen that the judge, not the jury, determines whether a child, a senile person, or a mentally disabled person understands the oath, and so is competent with regard to the first prerequisite.[20] Here we look further at the question of deter-

---

[19]*See* People v. Walker, 231 P. 572 (Dist. Ct. App. Cal. 1924).
[20]See §8.8.

mining competence with regard to the second, third, and fourth prerequisites: perception, memory, and communication.[21] We must deal with a certain amount of garden-variety psychology in the process.

No one perceives everything. People who did would go out of their minds very quickly. As we mature, we develop barriers to the flood of sensory impressions constantly coming in on us. We block out most of the flood; we all know that.

Likewise, no one remembers everything. If I asked fifty people what each had for breakfast yesterday morning, most would not be able to give me a fully accurate answer. And no one is supremely eloquent. Most of us have no special gifts with respect to the use of language. We cannot communicate all that we want to communicate.

As an aid to discussion, let us postulate three ideal scales from zero to 100. Someone who perceived everything would score 100; someone who remembered everything would score 100; and someone who was perfectly eloquent would score 100. If we used these scales to measure any particular prospective witness, nobody would score 100. Most of us would score surprisingly low, probably well under 30 on all three scales.

Everyone who has tried a case has run into the following situation. We have a witness, an adult person in full possession of his faculties. Let us say that he was the victim of a mugging. There is no question about his satisfying the first prerequisite of competence, the oath. He takes the stand. His testimony goes something like this:

Q. Sir, at what time did it happen?
A. Eleven-thirty at night.
Q. What were the lighting conditions?
A. Very bad. It was a badly lit street. There were street lights about a block and a half away.
Q. How long did the whole thing take?
A. About ten seconds.

---

[21]See *Id.*

Q. From what direction did he come at you?

A. From behind.

Q. What was your mental state?

A. I was terrified out of my mind.

It adds up to a witness who perceived something, but not much. He certainly does not score 100 on our scale, not even 20 or 30. At best, he might score 4 or 5. Is he competent?

The same can happen with memory.

Q. Sir, did you see the accident?

A. I did.

Q. How long ago was this?

A. Five and a half years.

Q. What did you see?

A. Well, I really don't remember very much, but what I remember is . . .

Again the witness is not scoring 100, or even 30, but 4 or 5 at best. The same can be true with respect to the ability to communicate. Everyone who tries cases has occasionally run into a witness of thin faculties who has difficulty articulating. He, too, is scoring 4 or 5 on the scale of 100. Is he competent?

It is rare to hear a challenge to competence on this ground. A lawyer will not often stand up and say, "I object, Your Honor. I don't think this witness perceived enough to be competent. I don't think he remembers enough. I don't think he can communicate enough." But if a lawyer does raise that objection, what will the judge do?

In a manner of speaking, the judge measures perception, memory, and communication. If each is anything more than zero, even though it is only 1 or 2 out of 100, he will hold the witness to be competent. And he will go on to say, "Counselor, I agree with you. This witness didn't perceive much, doesn't remember much, can't communicate much. But he has enough of each to be competent. You may bring out his deficiencies on cross-examination, and you may argue them to the jury in summation.

The jury will decide whether the witness's deficiencies render him less than fully credible."

This point is important. Once the witness meets the above-zero minimum, the issue of competence changes its form. It becomes an issue of credibility or weight. The jury, in determining credibility, by no means second-guesses or overrules the judge. Each is answering a different question. The judge answers the question, "Does the witness possess enough?" — with respect to each of the four elements of competence, yes or no. The jury, for its part, asks itself whether this witness possesses enough of each element to be credible, to be worth believing. The jury's answer has no necessary connection with the answer to the judge's question.

Competence and credibility must be sharply contrasted. They are entirely different issues.[22]

---

[22]The matter of credibility, in the context of cross-examination, is taken up in Chapter 15.

# CHAPTER 9

# Preparing Witnesses

## §9.1 The Importance of Preparation

The opening statements are over, and now the jury expects us to call the first witness. The jury does not know it, but a good deal of work must have been accomplished before anyone can take the stand. The witness — all of the witnesses — must be prepared.

This is one of the very few outright admonitions that must be offered: *Never* call a witness whom you have not prepared. There is, of course, an unavoidable exception to the rule, when a witness whom we have no choice but to call — because he is the only witness to some fact essential to our case — declines to meet with us. A lawyer in private practice has no way of forcing the witness to come and talk, and so must put that witness on the stand without preparing him. It is a terrible spot to be in. The prosecutor can force a reluctant witness to speak before trial by serving a grand jury subpoena, but that is a special situation.

Sometimes, a witness agrees to meet with us but does not show up in time. Let us say that the judge breaks for lunch and indicates that we shall resume at 2:15. We plan to call the witness right after lunch; we have been pressed for time, and his testimony is not very elaborate. We told him to meet us at one o'clock, so that we can work over lunch. But he gets lost, or his car breaks down, or something else happens to him. He does not show up. It's 2:15, the judge takes the bench, and he says, "Call your next witness." At the very moment the witness walks in.

Most of us are afraid of judges. We are reluctant to say, "Your Honor, can I have a couple of minutes to talk to the witness?" But we must say it. The judge might complain but will give us the couple of minutes.[1]

Depending upon where they practice, lawyers have several slang expressions for preparing witnesses. In some states it is called horse-shedding the witness, reminiscent of taking the witness out in back to the stable and having a little talk. Elsewhere it is called sanding or planing the witness — smoothing the witness down and taking the splinters off. Regardless of what it is called, it is extremely important.

## §9.2 Preliminaries

We can arbitrarily divide the many kinds of witnesses into two categories. The first consists of witnesses who spend a good

---

[1]In my days as a criminal prosecutor, I once tried a case before a judge who looked formidable but in fact was a very gentle man. The judge took the bench at 2:15 and growled to defense counsel, "Call your next witness!" — at which moment the witness walked in. It was clear to all of us that he was supposed to be a character witness for the defense, but there had been no opportunity for defense counsel to prepare him. Unaware of the kindliness behind the judge's fierce demeanor, defense counsel was afraid to ask for a little time. Instead he stood up and went ahead with his direct examination:

Q. Sir, do you know the defendant?
A. No.
Q. Well, then, do you know anybody who knows him?
A. No.
Q. Have you ever *heard* of the defendant?
A. No.

At that point the judge, who had a fine sense of humor, made a friendly gesture and said, "Mr. Witness, thank you for coming to court and helping us. You are free to go home now." That was comedy. More often, when a lawyer puts a witness on the stand without preparing him, it blows up in the lawyer's face.

deal of time in court — FBI agents, doctors, other experts, and so on. The second category consists of everybody else. Preparing the expert witness is a special kind of task, and we shall mention it later on.[2] For now, we consider only John Q. Bystander, the fellow who happened to be standing on the corner when two cars collided. He has never been a witness before. He has never been a juror or a litigant. In fact, this is the first time in his life that he has been in court.

It is safe to assume that John Q. Bystander is terrified beyond his capacity to describe. That is very important to remember. Lawyers are frightened too, of course. I have known a lawyer to throw up in front of the jury. Every one of us visits the restroom five times every morning of a trial. If that feeling ever goes away, it will mean that we are no longer putting everything we have into the job, and it will be time to quit. But for most witnesses it is far worse, because the whole process is alien to them.

Consider the situation from the witness's point of view. He must come to the courthouse, a building that houses government. If the witness's people are from almost anywhere in Europe, then he knows from his grandparents that people who walk into a government building never come out. He knows too that in this country things are different, but the very building terrifies him all the same.

Never having been through it before, John Bystander does not know what to ask us. We shall have to ask the questions for him, and answer them. We must think of everything that we can to discuss with him. Doing so will not make his fright go away; nothing can do that. But the more we talk with him, the more we can help him to deal with the fright, to control it, and to render it less inundating.

We begin with the location of the courthouse. No one, including cabdrivers, can ever find the right courthouse on the first try. We give him detailed directions for the cab, or we talk him through the streets from the bus stop. And once we have led him to the building, we tell him how to find the room where he is

---

[2]See §9.6.

to go. In New York, for example, they call the rooms "parts." They assign the numbers at random, they put up the numbers in Roman numerals to make sure that no one can read them — and to be absolutely certain, they change all the numbers every Monday. In New York, the only place that witnesses can find is the cigar stand, and so we arrange to meet him there.

We tell the witness what will happen to him then. "When I meet you at the cigar stand, we'll go to the courtroom." Or there may be a witness room where he will wait. We explain that to him. We say who will come to fetch him, and what they will say.

In the usual case, we assure the witness that the courtroom is not like those in the movies, with crowds, reporters, and television cameras. It is nearly always empty of spectators. There will be just the other lawyer, the jury, and the judge. We talk about that sort of thing, generally as much of it as we can think of. The more that the witness knows about what to expect, the better controlled his fears will be. And because witnesses seem to worry most of all about how they are to take the oath, we make it a point to rehearse the oath with him.

## §9.3 Direct Examination

In preparing the witness for direct examination, I find it most productive to say to him, "Tell me what happened," and then to let him tell it in his own words. I do not take notes, because then he will think about what I am writing down instead of about the story. A tape recorder is even worse; the black box is formidable, and it will tongue-tie him. I have the witness simply tell the story while I listen and concentrate. Most lawyers who do it this way find it easy to remember everything.

It is best to let the witness do it in one take, without interrupting. If we are preparing the chairman of IBM in an antitrust case, of course, we cannot do it quite that way. Instead we have to break the story down into segments, but we still let him go through each segment without interruption. Then, having noted those parts that need work, we can go back.

Perhaps I should make it clear that working with the witness is not the same as suborning perjury. There are many ways to say anything. Some ways are more effective than others, and so we help the witness to find the best language. When his recollection is hazy, we try to help him remember. It may be necessary to go back and forth several times over the parts that need sharpening, and it may take half a day or more.

The next decision is whether to rehearse the witness in question-and-answer form. The consensus among some very able and experienced trial lawyers is usually to forgo the Q and A. We want a witness who will come across to the jury as sincere, credible, telling the truth. But the witness is terrified. In his terror he will grasp at any straw that he thinks might keep him out of trouble. His terror gives him a power to concentrate beyond his knowledge. If we Q and A it, he will unwittingly memorize the answers. Then, he thinks, nothing can go wrong; all that he has to do is recite the answers on the witness stand.

The problem with memorized answers is highlighted in one of the great true stories of the American trial bar. People who saw Max Steuer work say that he was the greatest trial lawyer who ever lived. He could violate all the principles of effective cross-examination[3] with impunity; he was a virtuoso.

In the early part of this century, great waves of immigration from Eastern Europe hit New York City. The Lower East Side was full of poor Jewish people from Poland and Russia. Many of them earned a meager living in the garment industry. That was the heyday of the sweatshop, when children worked seventeen hours a day, seven days a week, for five dollars a week.

One of the sweatshops of those days was the Triangle Shirtwaist Company. It occupied a large building on the east side of Washington Square, what is now the site of New York University's College of Arts and Sciences. There they manufactured ladies' blouses. In a factory building ten stories high, several hundred girls stitched blouses seven days a week. The owners learned that sometimes the girls went out on the fire escapes and smoked a cigarette. That meant the girls were working only fifty minutes

---

[3]See §15.8.

an hour instead of sixty. The owners put a stop to it by nailing the fire doors shut.

In 1911 the notorious Triangle Shirtwaist fire occurred. One hundred forty-five employees, most of them young girls, were burned to death. It was a disaster beyond our capacity to understand. To this day the International Ladies Garment Workers Union commemorates the anniversary of that fire, because it aroused the public concern needed to get the union movement off the ground.

Nailing the fire doors shut was a misdemeanor, and the owners of Triangle Shirtwaist, Isaac Harris and Max Blanck, were indicted on 145 counts of misdemeanor manslaughter. The public was out for blood. When Harris and Blanck appeared for their trial, 300 women tried to attack them on the street.[4] Because the owners had plenty of money and were in desperate trouble, Max Steuer was at their side. The courtroom filled up with journalists from all over the world.

The prosecution called their first witness, a young girl. She spoke in heavily accented English.

Q. What is your name?
A. Sophie Shapiro.
Q. How old are you?
A. Seventeen.
Q. How long have you been in this country?
A. One year.
Q. Where did you come from?
A. Poland.
Q. Do you live with your parents?
A. Yes.
Q. Where?
A. Lansing Street.
Q. Did you work?
A. Yes.

---

[4]See S. Speiser, Lawsuit 136 (1980).

Q. Where?

A. Triangle Shirtwaist Company.

Q. Were you working on the day of the fire?

A. Yes.

Q. Tell us what happened.

A. Well, we were working. It was a Saturday, just before closing time. I was on an upper floor with about fifty girls in my room. One of the girls said that she was going to have a cigarette. We used to go out on the fire escape, but we couldn't because the doors were nailed shut. So this girl went out in the stairway, and she smoked a cigarette. She came back, and she said, "You know, it is funny, I smell smoke." And we all said, "You are smelling your own cigarette, there's no smoke." We went back to work. In about five minutes we all smelled the smoke, and then the girl who was nearest the door to the stairway went out, and she came back in and she said, "There's fire coming up the stairs." Now the girls who were nearest the fire exit went to open the door, but of course they couldn't. It was nailed shut. And they began to try to pull the door open, but they couldn't; the nails were so strong, and now the fire had reached the top of the stairs and was coming into the room.

Well, the girls at the far end of the room came piling up on top of the girls who were near the fire door, screaming, "Let us out, let us out," but they couldn't get out. And the girls who were near the door were screaming, "You're crushing me, you're crushing me," and they were underneath the pile of fifty girls, and the girls were crying and trying with their fingernails to pull the fire door open, and they couldn't and the flames came in the room, their hair started to burn, and the screaming was awful, and I didn't know what to do.

There was a broom closet. I stepped into the broom closet and I closed the door. After that I couldn't see what happened, but I could hear it, and I could smell

it, and the girls screamed, "I'm burnt," and I could
smell it, the burning flesh.

And then I fainted, and when I woke up, a fireman
was carrying me out.

"You may inquire," said the district attorney.

How can a lawyer possibly cross-examine that witness, a girl
who in real life had experienced that horrible tragedy? Max Steuer
had a photographic and phonographic memory; he remembered
everything that he had ever read or heard. Steuer stood up and
proceeded to violate the principle of cross-examination that tells
us never to give the witness the chance to repeat her direct
testimony.[5]

Steuer's first question was, "Sophie, tell it again." She told
it again, in exactly the same words. When she finished, he said,
"Tell it again, Sophie." Again she told it, in the same words. And
a third time: "Tell it again." She told it again. But this time she
made a mistake. Halfway through the narrative, she transposed
a "that" for a "which." Steuer heard it and remembered. When
she finished, he said, "Sophie, didn't you make a mistake? Didn't
you say 'that' instead of 'which'?" And she said, "Oh, yes. I'm
sorry. I did make a mistake." Steuer sat down. That was the end
of the cross-examination.

The defendants were acquitted. The jury acquitted them in
part on Steuer's argument that the district attorney was patroniz-
ing the jury. He did not trust them to decide the case on the actual
evidence. Instead, to use a metaphor from a later age, he turned
the witnesses into tape recorders, and had them parrot back to
the jury what the district attorney wanted them to hear.

An analogy from popular culture might help explain what
it is that jurors sense in memorized answers. In the *Star Trek*
films and in the television series, protagonists are Captain Kirk,
an earthling, and Mr. Spock, who is an alien being. We have three
ways of knowing that Mr. Spock is an alien. First, he has pointed
ears. Second, he has a green complexion, because his blood is
based on copper rather than iron. But the third distinction is just
as obvious. Mr. Spock speaks perfect English. In science fiction

---

[5]See §15.8.

movies, all aliens speak perfect English. Captain Kirk is well spoken, but his speech is not perfect.

In other films, too, the actors who play the good guys — Spencer Tracy, Jimmy Stewart — are well spoken but not perfectly so. For contrast there is Vincent Price, a fine actor and a veteran of countless suspense and horror films. His voice is a drop of salad oil running down a stalk of celery. Every syllable is perfectly spoken. The moment he opens his mouth, we know that he is a homicidal maniac.

If we put John Q. Bystander on the witness stand with his Q and A testimony memorized, it will come out letter perfect. It will sound as though Mr. Spock or Vincent Price were testifying. To the ears of the jury, that bespeaks something other than credibility. "He is an alien being," they will think. And they will not believe what he tells them.

A compromise is possible, and some lawyers recommend it. We can Q and A the three or four most crucial questions, and leave the rest for an extemporaneous Q and A in the courtroom.

The problem of overrehearsal applies just as much to the lawyer as to the witness. When extemporizing, the lawyer will sometimes get tangled in one of those sentences that seems forever unable to reach a question mark. We break off and we say, "Your Honor, may I withdraw the question and try it again?" He says, "Sure." The jury loves that, so long as we do not do it too often. It tells them that we are not a cold and perfect lawyer after all, but just a human being who makes mistakes like everybody else.

## §9.4 Cross-Examination

If we somehow forget to prepare the witness for cross-examination, he will be tugging at our coattails to remind us. John Q. Bystander dreads cross-examination. He has watched Perry Mason. He understands that he will take the witness stand and, on direct examination, tell what he saw when the two cars came together at the intersection; and then, on cross-examination, he will be made to admit having committed the murder.

Perhaps the simplest and therefore the most effective way to prepare the witness for cross-examination is to speak with him along these lines:

> Listen, John, every lawyer conducts cross-examination differently, so I really can't prepare you for what the other lawyer will ask. But I know that you want to do well, and not be humiliated in public. I know you want to do everything you can, everything that is proper to help us win. I can only give you one piece of advice. If you follow it, there's nothing to be concerned about. You'll be pleased with your performance, and the case will come out as it should. This is the advice. On cross-examination, listen to the question, and be sure you understand it. Then answer it with the truth. That is all you are to say — the truth.

Then we have to go on:

> But in a courtroom, John, the truth means what you know through your five senses. It does not mean what you have figured out to be true, or what you surmise to be true, or what you sincerely believe to be true. It means only what you *know* to be true.[6]

When the witness has digested that, we say to him, "Now, John, I can't predict what the other lawyer will ask. But if you want, I'll cross-examine you myself right now." He nods enthusiastically. "Fine. Before we start, tell me — what is the one thing you have to do?"

"Tell the truth."

"Good. Remember, now, I'm not Younger any more. I'm the other lawyer. Just tell the truth."

---

[6]See §12.1.

Q. All right, you. Before coming to court, did you discuss your testimony with Younger?

A. No, sir.

Every time.

"Just a minute, John. What have we been doing for the past two and a half days?"

"Discussing my testimony."

"That's right. Then why did you answer that question 'no'?"

I quote here from a particular John Q. Bystander who said it to me: "I'm not supposed to admit it, am I?"

"Of course, you're supposed to admit it! No lawyer puts a witness on the stand without preparing him. No one will believe you if you deny it. Besides, it's the truth. You're supposed to tell the truth, right?"

"Oh, you really mean it?" — which gives a fascinating insight into what the public thinks about lawyers.

"*Yes*, I really mean it! Just tell the truth. All right; let's try it again."

Q. Did you discuss your testimony with Younger?

A. Yes, sir.

Q. And did Younger tell you what to say on the witness stand?

A. Yes, sir.

Every time.

"Just a minute, John. What did I tell you to say on the witness stand?"

"The truth."

"If the lawyer asks, then, shouldn't you tell him that?"

We go through it a few more times, and finally, in the courtroom, it comes out like this:

Q. Did you discuss your testimony with Younger?

A. Yes, sir.

Q. Younger told you what to say, didn't he?

A. Sure. He told me to tell the truth.

The other lawyer will instantly back away. Not only does he realize that he is dealing with a witness who has been prepared, but he also knows that he is dealing with a lawyer who understands how to prepare a witness.

## §9.5 Clothing

Recall the analogy between the courtroom and the theater.[7] Any actor or director will agree that costume is a crucial part of communication from the stage. We lawyers, however, tend to forget the importance of costume, perhaps because we feel uncomfortable telling someone else what to wear. And so, on the morning of his testimony, John Q. Bystander stands unadvised before his closet. He is likely to decide that because court is formal, he should wear something formal. But there are many kinds of formality, and the witness may need a few words of help.

Years ago, when I was in practice before going on the bench, a national firm of supermarkets was among my clients. My job for them was to fly around the country in their company jet, losing slip-and-fall cases. The cases were all pretty much the same. A customer with a fractured ankle sues the company alleging that she slipped on a piece of lettuce in the store. There is no way to prove otherwise. The defense on the issue of liability usually consisted of my saying, "Well, I guess she slipped. We sweep up the store every thirty minutes. If that's not often enough, then I suppose we're liable, and the public can pay for the extra sweeping in the form of higher prices."

On this one occasion, however, we were really going to contest liability. Our only witness was a kid who sweeps up in the store. That is a term of art in the supermarket business; regardless of age and gender, it is always "the kid who sweeps up." His

---

[7]See §3.6.

testimony was going to be, "I swept up at 10 a.m. I was going to sweep up again at 10:30, but she fell at 10:15. That's all I know."

The day before trial, I went to the supermarket and met the kid. He was wearing the regulation white smock smeared with regulation cabbage juice. Across the street over a cup of coffee, we talked. He was bright and he expressed himself very well. It took all of fifteen minutes to prepare him.

The next morning he showed up in court. And in place of the smock, he had on a Brooks Brothers three-piece suit. There was a gold watch-chain across the front of the vest, and dangling from it was a Phi Beta Kappa key. "Where did you get that?" I asked.

"Princeton."

"What are you doing sweeping up in a supermarket."

This was back in the 1960s, and so he answered, "Well, I'm getting my head together." I have no quarrel with that; he was doing honest work, and for all I know he went on to law school. But when I put him on the witness stand, his appearance and his testimony did not add up. His testimony said, "I'm the kid who sweeps up." His costume said, "I'm an assistant professor of history at Yale." The disparity between the two struck the jury as phony, and in the verdict they told me so in no uncertain terms.

## §9.6 Expert Witnesses

The purposes of preparing an expert witness are the same as those for a lay witness: to make sure that the testimony comes out as we want it to. A novice expert witness will need the same kinds of reassurances that John Q. Bystander does. If he is experienced, the expert will probably have learned to control his fear; he will know what to expect in the courtroom, how to take the oath, and the like. Especially if he is from another city, however, the expert may not be familiar with the particular courthouse. Even experts get lost. It is still important to arrange a meeting place that he will be able to find easily.

The preparation of an expert witness has another purpose as well. The expert will be helping and advising us. But experts in every field have a tendency to slip into jargon. Lawyers are probably the worst of all; we have already noted the importance of the lawyer's speaking plain English.[8] John Q. Bystander cannot help speaking plain English; it is the only language he knows. But the expert, given a chance, will express himself in a string of polysyllables that no one but another expert can understand. We must help him to say his piece in short, easy words. Just as important, he must help us to frame our questions in short, easy words. The jury must understand both the questions and the answers, for they cannot be convinced by what they do not understand. If the first pass through the testimony has too much unexplained technical language — and almost any amount is too much — we shall usually need the expert's help in simplifying it. The simplifications are better planned out in advance, because we do not want the expert splitting hairs with us while he is on the stand before the jury.

Remember that an expert can be helpful in planning the cross-examination of the other side's experts. Our expert is in a good position to know of likely weaknesses in their testimony, and often he may be able to guide us to written authorities that we can use to impeach.[9]

In preparing the expert for cross-examination, we should advise him about the possible use of hypothetical questions from the other side. As far as possible, we should try to anticipate those questions and put them to him in advance of trial. If there are any authorities that contradict his position, it is wise to find out about them ahead of time, so that they can be raised and dealt with in the direct examination.

### §9.7 Other Matters

Most lawyers find it helpful to have an outline for each witness's testimony. Use of the outline eliminates the need to go back and forth through the sequence of events, and so the presentation becomes more orderly, more logical, and less confusing

---

[8]See id.
[9]See §15.6.

to the jury. With an outline, the testimony will take less time, and that aids the jury's comprehension and memory. The outline also helps to save the lawyer from overlooking an important piece of evidence. An experienced lawyer may not always put the outline in writing, but will nonetheless have thought in detail what the sequence of the testimony should be.

When several witnesses will be testifying, it is generally better to interview and prepare them separately. When they are together, what the first few say will tend to influence not only what the others say, but also what they believe. Worse, the witnesses who hear one another rehearse may all come to testify in more or less the same words. If the jury notices that, it will greatly diminish credibility all around. Most courts, moreover, now exclude witnesses from the courtroom while others are testifying.

# CHAPTER 10

# Planning for the Trial

## §10.1 The Theme

Every lawsuit involves a story of human beings in conflict.[1] Sometimes the story is obvious; sometimes it is hidden and needs to be brought out. All stories, however, have certain properties in common. The study of literature and drama can give us useful insights into how some of those properties can be used to advantage in the courtroom.

Every good story, be it a novel, short story, epic, or play, has a unifying theme. When we pull the theme out and state it separately, it is always absurdly simple in comparison with the complexity of the finished work. That is why artists themselves will never discuss their themes. All the same, unity in the story enhances the story's effect upon the audience; and for the artist, the theme is a device that serves to provide that unity. Once the artist has a theme, he must let it do the job of unification for him. No matter how wonderful a character or a scene or a turn of the plot may be otherwise — if it is not related to the theme, it stays out, or it goes into the notebook for the next novel. The artist knows that each piece of material unconnected with the theme detracts from the total aesthetic effect.

---

[1]See §5.3.

Exactly the same is true of a trial. The trial must have a theme — a central idea that gives unity to the drama we shall unfold before the jury. Like the literary artist, the trial lawyer must let the theme do its job. Every witness, every exhibit, every bit of testimony must share a relationship to the theme. If a witness's testimony seems helpful in some abstract sense, but is not related to the theme, we do not put that witness on. Otherwise we shall be committing the mistake that trial lawyers call "overtrying the case." It might also be called the kitchen-sink approach. Putting in everything that comes to mind — failing to discriminate between what is relevant to the theme and what is not — shows a lack of self-confidence on the lawyer's part. To the extent that everything we do for the jury has an articulable relationship to the theme, we enhance the likelihood of achieving the aesthetic effect that we want, namely, persuasion of the jury.

The theme is easy to ascertain. In fact, we have already written it down. The theme of the trial appears in the second sentence of the trial memorandum.[2] Our first sentence read, "This is an action for damages for personal injury and property damage arising from a collision that took place at the intersection of Main and Market Streets . . . . " And then came the second sentence: "It is the plaintiff's position that the collision occurred because the defendant did not stop for the red light." That is the theme. The only evidence we will put in is evidence that bears upon that theme. If we have a witness who can testify that the defendant had a couple of beers before he got behind the wheel that day, we do not call that witness. The testimony is not related to the theme; we cannot call that witness without diffusing the theme. If we do want to call the witness, we can always change the theme: "It is the plaintiff's position that the collision occurred because the defendant was driving while intoxicated." That gives the case a different posture, of course; and once adopted, it sets new boundaries on the evidence we should introduce.

There is no one way to present the theme. There are only foul lines, and within those, room for a great deal of creativity.

---

[2]See §4.2.

We must think about what is possible, what will make the best impression, how we can make best use of the witnesses, and so on. Once we have the theme, it operates as a principle of exclusion. It tells us what not to put in, namely, anything not related to that theme.

## §10.2 The Props

Many lawyers who are meticulous in preparing their own opening, direct examination, cross-examination, and summation pay no attention to what the jurors see in between, when the opponent is on his feet. Suppose that our opponent is summing up. She is doing a good job; there is nothing to object to. She will go on for at least fifteen minutes. But jurors have about the same attention span as the average human being, or about two minutes. When the opponent has been talking for a minute and half, Juror No. 3 runs out of attention. What he really needs is a walk around the block, but he cannot do that, and so his eyes take a walk around the courtroom instead. Finding nothing much else to look at, he looks at us, and then, restored, he goes back to listening to the summation. That is when the next juror tires out, and he too looks at us.

We must always assume that at least one juror is looking at us. To be sure, a lawyer invariably sits in an attitude of respectful attention. But the table in front of us is equally of interest to a bored juror. To take one example: Most of us use yellow legal pads. One by one, the pages we have written on fall out. By the time we get to summations, the table is a rat's nest of yellow papers, pads, exhibits, file folders, pencils, pens, and everything else. We are not confused, of course; we can find instantly whatever we need. But that is not the point. The table looks as though we are confused. The jury thinks, "A tough case, too much for the kid. Look at him. He's drowning in paper." We are not communicating the Joe DiMaggio effect; we are not giving the jury absolute confidence that the ball will be caught.[3] The table

---

[3]See §1.3.

should suggest that we have mastered the case, not vice versa.

It is best not to take notes at all in court. If we are thoroughly prepared, and then use all of our attention to concentrate, notes are unnecessary. Even when there is a witness testifying on direct whom we shall have to cross-examine, we will accomplish much more by watching the witness's face than by taking notes. What he is going to say is no secret. We know what it will be, and we have already prepared for the cross. And so we simply watch him, for two reasons. One is to observe his face — to see the clouds passing over it and gain a sense of where he is vulnerable. But even more important, he must know that we are looking at him. We fix him with a steely gaze and do not let go. We are the snake; he is the bird.

There are always materials, and to hold them, a large three-holed looseleaf binder is best.[4] The binder is primarily a prop. So long as the jury is in the box, we hardly ever open it. The binder communicates to the jury our total mastery of the case, so total that everything we ever need is somehow in that magic notebook. For example, we have a policeman on the stand:

Q. Officer, did you investigate the accident?

A. Yes.

Q. And did you look for skid marks?

A. Certainly.

Q. Did you find them?

A. Yes.

Q. Did you measure them?

A. Of course.

Q. How long were they?

A. That was a long time ago. I really can't remember.

Q. Officer, is there anything that might help you to remember.

A. Yes, sir.

Q. What is that?

---

[4]We see the contents of the binder in §10.3.

A. The accident report I filed in the station house that night.

We hand him the binder, opened.

Q. What is that?
A. My accident report.
Q. Read it to yourself.

After a few such episodes, the binder becomes a totem object in the courtroom. Everything is in that one notebook, and it is ours.

In addition to the notebook, I keep only one thing on the table: a brand new No. 2 yellow pencil, sharpened to a brilliant point, placed parallel to the upper edge of the notebook with its point toward the jury box. (I once climbed into the jury box to see which way it looks best.) No one ever wins a case because of the placement of a pencil, but lawyers who pay attention to detail do win more cases — even details as small as this one.

A few items will not fit into the notebook: three-dimensional exhibits, large stacks of documents, and things of that kind. It does not matter where we put them, so long as they are not piled loose on the table. A portable cardboard filing cabinet to hold such things costs less than ten dollars. It can fit under the table or it can go at the far end of the table, where it creates a storeroom area while our end becomes the study. The point is to make the materials seem to be under control. That is part of conveying to the jury our mastery of the case.

## §10.3 Trial Notebook

In one looseleaf binder, the trial notebook contains every piece of paper that we shall need in trying the case. It is helpful to tab the various sections of the binder, so as to find them very quickly. Among other things, there may be a sheet for each witness who will be called, containing the outline of that witness's testimony.[5]

---

[5]See §9.7.

For witnesses whom we shall call, the outline should show only the answers, so that we may extemporize the questions.[6] Questions for cross-examination are probably better written out, because there we need a higher degree of control and planning. If it will be necessary to refer to a document during a witness's testimony, that document too should be in the binder.

One very successful lawyer I know organizes his trial notebooks this way:

1. pretrial motions
2. voir dire
3. opening statement
4. leads to be covered
5. research — evidence
6. research — substantive
7. argument — motions during trial
8. theories — ours/theirs
9. cross — opposition witnesses
10. cross — opposing party
11. rebuttal
12. instructions — ours
13. instructions — theirs
14. final argument
15. jury (post-retirement) matters
16. notes during trial

For a long trial, it is still best to use only one notebook, and to refill it each day as needed.

## §10.4 Supporting Characters

Just as important as the props are the supporting characters in the courtroom. On the defense side, I try to have a client

---

[6]See §9.3.

sitting with me who looks presentable. Some lawyers like the client to talk to them, on the theory that it helps the jury to see the client as more human. That is why I introduce the client.[7] But my instructions to the client are almost always these:

> Charlie, don't talk to me. And don't pass me notes. So long as the jury is in the box, I want them to focus on me, not you. If they focus on me, they may acquit. They're not going to convict me. But let them focus on you, Charlie, and you're going away. Just sit there in a catatonic trance. We'll talk together when the jury is somewhere else.

Being one of several plaintiffs or defendants in a multiparty case can create a different kind of difficulty: What if the other lawyers on our side are all certifiable idiots? What if they seem to be methodically losing the case, becoming more of a problem to us than the opponent is? One solution is quite literally to distance ourselves from the other lawyers. Every morning we arrive early and move our chair a couple of inches away. In the theater it is called "cheating"; no one will notice. By the time of summations, we are sitting on the other side of the room. The masters do it, and it works.

Typically the judge in such cases calls a sidebar conference every ten minutes, and everybody goes running up to the bench. But a master will stay in his chair. He knows that he will not miss anything important. He looks over at the jurors, who of course do not know what goes on at a sidebar. When the lawyer has the attention of all twelve jurors, he gives an eloquent shrug. It says to the jury, "I don't know what's going on up there, either. Why are we here? Come on, let's all go home." Little things like that add up.

Many of us begin to learn the business by prosecuting. In the U.S. attorney's office where I served, it is the custom for the case agent — the FBI agent, Secret Service agent, or whoever it may be — to sit with the prosecutor. When I had gained a little

---

[7]See §5.3.

experience, I refused to go along with the custom. I wanted the jury to look at the table and see me sitting there alone. There then goes through the jurors' minds something like this: "Look at that! The kid can't be more than a couple of years out of law school, but he can handle this case all by himself. He's obviously not very good, but the case is so clear that he doesn't need any help." If I am the prosecutor, that is precisely the message I want to get across: The case is very clear.

## §10.5 Sequence of Witnesses

There is never one best sequence in which to call witnesses. The only poor sequence is one arrived at accidentally, with no planning at all. One common method is a chronological presentation, which is easy for the jury to follow. Another is to start with a powerful, substantial witness, so as to form a strong early impression in the jurors' minds. A weak but essential witness is best sandwiched in between two good ones. It is important, however, not to end the day with a poor witness.

The degree of repetition in witness's testimony needs some thought. Repetition may be helpful to the case, especially if the issues are complex enough that the jury may not fully understand them the first time around. Repetition also emphasizes the points being made. It does, however, risk boring the jury. In a criminal case, character witnesses for the defendant are best scattered, so that their testimony does not sound repetitious and mechanical.

## §10.6 The Final Note

It is most important to end the entire case on an affirmative note. It is also best to end each day, and certainly each week, on an uptick. The jury will think about the testimony at home, and they will almost certainly form tentative opinions. We want them to be thinking about the case from our point of view, and in a positive frame of mind.

# CHAPTER 11

# Direct Examination

## §11.1 Sequence of Examination

In England, the United States, and other countries that trace their legal tradition back to England, the custom is that witnesses do not make speeches but rather respond to questions from the lawyers. Whether we are considering a state case or a federal case, whether the matter is criminal or civil, there are certain mechanical terms, common currency among lawyers, to describe the basic process.

Almost always, a witness is called to the witness stand by one lawyer or the other. The lawyer who calls him is the proponent of that witness, a word denoting merely the mechanical function of saying to the witness, "You take the stand." The other lawyer in the case is the opponent or adversary, of whom there may be more than one. With respect to a witness, then, we speak not of plaintiff and defendant, or of prosecutor and defendant, but of proponent and opponent.

It is the custom that the proponent question the witness first. The questions that the proponent asks, together with the witness's answers, are collectively called direct examination. A point worth emphasizing, because even experienced lawyers and judges frequently lose sight of it, is that "direct examination," as a term and as a concept, says nothing about the emotional temperature of the examination. It can be friendly or unfriendly. Direct examination is simply examination conducted by the proponent, the lawyer who called the witness. It means nothing more.

When the proponent finishes, the other lawyer in the case stands up and asks questions. If more than two parties are represented, more than one lawyer may do so. The questions asked by the opponent, together with the witness's answers, are collectively called cross-examination. Once again, "cross-examination," as a term and as a concept, says nothing about the emotional temperature of the examination. The word has simply a mechanical significance. Cross-examination is nothing more than the examination conducted by the opponent, whether it be friendly or unfriendly, hostile or otherwise, destructive or the reverse.

After the opponent completes cross-examination, or after each opponent does, if there are more than one, the proponent has another turn. We call those questions, and the answers given, re-direct examination. After re-direct, the opponent may want another turn, and we call that re-cross. After re-cross, conceivably the proponent may want to go again, and that, once more, is re-direct. It can go back and forth between re-cross and re-direct until finally the judge says, "Enough!" — because, now, all the lawyers are fighting over is who will have the last word.

As a matter of elegance and terminology, one does not multiply prefixes. The sequence is direct; cross; re-direct; re-cross; re-direct; re-cross; and so on for as many turns as there are. There is no re-re-re-direct examination.

## §11.2 The No-Leading-Question Rule

The law of evidence has a major and celebrated rule that regulates how the proponent may ask questions on direct examination. In each of the fifty-one American jurisdictions, the law says that on direct examination, you may not ask leading questions. The Federal Rules of Evidence say, "Leading questions should not be used on the direct examination of a witness . . . . "[1]

---

[1]Fed. R. Evid. 611(c). The same rule goes on to sketch out exceptions, discussed in §11.3.

A leading question is a question that suggests the desired answer. While it is true that a leading question can always be answered with yes or no, so can some nonleading questions. The possible answers to a question, therefore, do not identify it as a leading question. Rather, a leading question is one that puts the answer in the witness's mouth.

Bear in mind that at least nine times out of ten, the proponent has interviewed the witness before the trial. He has prepared the witness. If the witness is also a friendly witness, then with leading questions allowed on direct examination, all the witness need do is switch the automatic pilot to "Yes." The lawyer would testify, and the witness would interrupt occasionally with "Yes . . . Yup . . . That's how it was . . . Just like that." It would be the lawyer, not the witness, who tells the story.

The law says that the lawyer may not tell the story, simply because the lawyer is not competent to be a witness. He did not take the oath. And even if he were to take the oath, he was not present to perceive the transaction at issue. Thus he is incompetent. That is why the no-leading-question rule makes sense.

Here are a few examples:

Q. Your name is John Smith, isn't it?
A. Yes.

That is a leading question. I told the witness what I wanted him to say. But we can put it in nonleading form.

Q. What is your name, sir?
A. John Smith.

Now it is not a leading question. But this one is:

Q. You live here in the city, don't you?
A. Yes.

In this version, though, it is not a leading question:

Q. Tell us where you live.

A. Here in the city.

These are easy examples. In the real world of the courtroom, though, it is sometimes very difficult to determine whether a question is leading or nonleading. Out of the universe of all possible questions, I would say that perhaps thirty percent are mainly leading. At the other end, about thirty percent are plainly nonleading. Both kinds are in the examples above. But in the middle, perhaps forty percent of all possible questions may be either leading or nonleading in the sense that reasonable people might differ. Much might depend upon the temperament of the judge, on the sense of the occasion, and on how much the judge wants to move things along. It may depend upon the tone of voice in which the question is asked. Thus, while the rule is easy to state, putting it to work in the courtroom is more difficult than a novice might think.

## §11.3 Exceptions to the No-Leading-Question Rule

Read in its entirety, Rule 611(c) says, "Leading questions should not be used on the direct examination of a witness except as may be necessary to develop his testimony. Ordinarily leading questions should be permitted on cross-examination. When a party calls a hostile witness, an adverse party, or a witness identified with an adverse party, interrogation may be by leading questions.[2]

The situations in which leading questions become permissible are common and important. When they are necessary or appropriate, the judge has considerable discretion to allow leading questions on direct examination. Here are scenarios illustrating the ten situations in which judges will usually allow leading questions on direct examination.

**Preliminary Matters.** The proponent may lead with respect to preliminary matters, whether they are preliminary to the

---

[2]Fed. R. Evid. 611(c).

entire direct examination or to a particular part of it. Such leading questions affect the adversary hardly at all, and they can save a great deal of time.

Q. Your name is John Smith?

A. Yes.

Q. You live here in the city?

A. Yes.

Q. You work at the supermarket on Main Street?

A. Yes.

Q. Were you working at the supermarket on the morning of January 5 of this year?

A. Yes.

Q. At about 10:30 in the morning?

A. Yes.

Q. You were working right in front of the fresh fruit counter; is that right?

A. Yes.

Q. What happened?

A. Well, I saw . . .

As soon as we leave the preliminary matters, it is necessary to switch to nonleading questions.

**Uncontroverted Matters.** With respect to matters not in controversy, the proponent may lead. Which facts are uncontroverted can be determined by examining the pleadings, by listening to the opening statements and the testimony of witnesses, by asking the opponent, and by getting a sense of the courtroom generally. Another method, one too often ignored, is a notice to admit or a request for admissions. Though not part of our agenda here, these procedural devices will have the consequence of removing facts from the areas of controversy, thereby making it permissible to elicit those facts by way of leading questions. Again, the adversary cannot complain, and a great deal of time will be saved.

The following example assumes that all of the facts brought out are not in dispute, having already been admitted by the adversary.

Q. On February 15 at about 2 p.m., you were driving your car on Main Street?

A. Yes.

Q. Heading downtown?

A. Yes.

Q. Your car was a blue Buick?

A. Yes.

Q. At the intersection of Main and Broadway, you collided with another car?

A. Yes.

Q. The other car was a yellow Plymouth?

A. Yes.

Q. How did the collision happen?

A. Well, I saw . . .

There we have gone beyond the ambit of facts not in dispute, and therefore must revert to nonleading form. Note that by varying leading questions with nonleading questions, the use of these rules can bring pace and shape and rhythm to a direct examination, focusing the jury's attention on what the lawyer wishes them to have in mind.[3]

**Inconsequential Matters.** Inconsequential matters by definition will be immaterial. They have nothing to do with the lawsuit. Nonetheless, and not infrequently, we may wish to bring out inconsequential matters. Suppose, for example, that the witness has knowledge of events of Monday and Wednesday, both of which are material. If the witness goes directly from Monday to Wednesday, the testimony will be choppy and discontinuous. Because to the jury, a trial is a kind of theater, the jury will wonder about Tuesday. As a matter of tactics, then, we may want the jury to hear a smooth, narrative flow, even though the events of Tuesday are immaterial.

---

[3]We consider the rhythm of the direct examination in §11.4.

Q. Have you told us everything you remember about the accident on Monday?

A. Yes.

Q. On Tuesday, you went to work as usual?

A. Yes.

Q. Ate as usual?

A. Yes.

Q. Went to bed as usual?

A. Yes.

Q. Slept well?

A. Very well.

Q. What happened on Wednesday?

A. Well, I woke up feeling . . .

Those few seconds of leading questions give the testimony a continuous and legally permissible flow.

**New Topic.** For tactical reasons, it is sometimes prudent deliberately to make the testimony discontinuous — in our same example, to skip altogether the immaterial evidence of events on Tuesday. This fourth exception allows the proponent to lead the witness over the gap.

Q. Sir, have you told us everything you remember about Monday?

A. Yes.

Q. I direct your attention to the following Wednesday, at about 10 a.m., in front of the supermarket at Main and Broadway. Were you there?

A. Yes.

Q. What happened?

A. Well, I saw . . .

We have led the witness to the new topic by putting the words in his mouth, and that is permissible.

**Refreshing Recollection.** A witness who cannot remember may be prompted with one or two leading questions. We shall defer a more complete discussion of this exception until we take up generally the problem of the witness who forgets.[4]

**The Boorish Witness.** The cases supporting this sixth exception ordinarily refer to a "hostile witness." As that term covers no fewer than three distinct situations, however, it is better to use separate words for each. Here, I refer to the witness who is simply a boor — who misbehaves on the witness stand. Such a witness is very rare. Most people are either accustomed to testifying, and so are well behaved; or else they are unaccustomed to testifying, and therefore too frightened to misbehave. But with a boorish witness on the stand, leading questions are permitted even on direct examination. There is little danger of leading him to say something he does not wish to say, or is incompetent to say, and the need to proceed expeditiously is great. This example is adapted from a real case:

Q. What happened next?
A. One step closer, you son of a bitch, and I'll punch you in the nose.
Q. All right, now, what happened next is that you wrote out a check for $25,000?
A. Yes.[5]

**The Reluctant Witness.** Once in a while every lawyer encounters a witness who is not boorish, whose manners are perfectly acceptable, but who, for one reason or another, is simply reluctant to testify. The examination becomes awkward, drawn out, and tedious. Since the dangers of leading the witness yield to the need for dispatch, leading questions are allowed.

**The Predisposed Witness.** Again the cases will speak of a "hostile witness," but the witness here is not boorish. He is merely predisposed. His circumstances make it reasonable to assume that he is inclined against the proponent. Under this eighth

---

[4]See §§11.5-11.6.
[5]Reynolds v. Pegler, 223 F.2d 429 (2d Cir.), *cert. denied,* 350 U.S. 846 (1955), *discussed in* L. Nizer, My Life in Court 84-85, 90-91 (1st ed. 1961).

exception, the proponent may interrogate him by way of leading questions.

> Q. Sir, you saw the collision between the yellow Plymouth and the blue Buick, did you not?
> A. Yes.
> Q. You understand that I represent the driver of the yellow Plymouth?
> A. Yes.
> Q. And the other litigant is the driver of the blue Buick; is that right?
> A. Yes.
> Q. Now, you know the driver of the blue Buick, don't you?
> A. Yes.
> Q. As a matter of fact, he's your brother, isn't that right?
> A. Right.

Although he is perfectly well behaved, this is a predisposed witness. The proponent may interrogate by leading questions.

**The Adverse Party.** This is a special case of the preceding exception, the predisposed witness. In a civil case, there is no constitutional problem with one party calling the other as a witness. The calling party is then the proponent of the adverse party, and may interrogate by leading questions.

**The Witness of Limited Capacity.** Occasionally it is necessary to call a witness whose capacity to speak is limited because of mental deficiency, immaturity, senility, or some physical disability. If he had no capacity to communicate at all, the witness would be incompetent,[6] but he may still be competent with capacities so limited that the direct examination will be a clumsy and awkward process. In that event, in this tenth and last exception, leading questions are allowed.

---

[6]See §8.8.

## §11.4 The Rhythm of Direct Examination

Direct examination is a most difficult thing to do well. There is no particular problem if it will run for only five minutes; we simply do it. But if the direct examination will be reasonably protracted — anything on the order of fifteen minutes or longer — it becomes a different matter. Then, if we are to hold the jury, we need forward motion, impetus, and rhythm — a sense of irresistible progress. That is difficult to bring off, sometimes so difficult that we are tempted to throw in the towel and find some other way to make a living.

The direct examination can sometimes go on for days, as when the witness is a personal injury plaintiff, or the chief executive officer of a corporation being sued for antitrust violations. It is hard enough to keep the jury awake, let alone to sweep them on ahead of us. Every trial lawyer knows how it sounds. We ask, "What did you do?" The witness answers. "Then, what did you do?" The witness answers. "And what did you do after that?" The witness answers. There is no feeling of propulsion to it, no sense of inevitable forward motion.

Having drawn analogies from theater and literature, I turn now to yet another art form: What is the difference between noise and music? The difference is rhythm — the essence of all music and dance, because rhythm engages itself right into the bloodstream and the central nervous system.

Hum to yourself, if you will, the opening two bars of Beethoven's Fifth Symphony in C Minor: Di-Di-Di-Dummmm. Beethoven plucked out of the air that most famous rhythmic segment in all of Western music, the three eighth notes and a protracted half note. Probably he would not have been able to put it into words, but with those four notes, Beethoven showed that he knows something important about how the human nervous system operates. Listen to the first movement of the Fifth all the way through, and try to hear it as though for the first time. Depending upon the conductor's tempo and on whether he takes the repeat back to the beginning, the performance can run as long as nine or ten minutes. And yet it seems to go by in about thirty seconds.

Like the first movement of the Fifth, we want the hours and days of the direct examination to seem to go by in seconds. And indeed, the technique that Beethoven used in that movement is precisely the secret of conducting a lengthy direct examination. Just as Beethoven manipulates his audience's nervous systems to keep them alert, engaged, and receptive, we can do it with the jury. As the first movement seems to pass in a flash, so will the direct examination. The secret lies in the same bit of human psychology that Beethoven exploited so well.

Every one of us has a limited attention span. Attention drifts. But we can restore the attention span, rather like winding up the key of a spring motor. With the drawn-out fermata on the fourth note of the sequence, the half note, Beethoven uses up the audience's attention span. Then, with the short notes, he winds the audience back up again. The pattern goes back and forth all through the movement, alternately preparing the attention span and wearing it out. It repeats several hundred times in a few minutes, yet we never tire of it.

We can rarely achieve that same degree of mathematical precision in the courtroom, but we can do enough of it to impart some pace and forward motion. We construct the direct examination as nearly as possible in a series of rhythmic segments. Each consists of several short notes, followed by a long note — our "notes" being the witness's answers. We repeat that pattern, several shorts and a long, over and over again. The precision sometimes fails, because we cannot always get to the shorts just when we need them; but we try.

We elicit the courtroom equivalent of Beethoven's short eighth notes with questions like these:

Q. Were you there?
A. Yes.
Q. Was it ten in the morning?
A. Yes.
Q. Was the sun out?
A. Yes.

And then a long:

> Q. What did you see? What happened then?

In brief, then, the secret of an effective direct examination is the adept use of leading questions. Those give us the short notes. Interspersed among them, nonleading questions provide the long notes. Deliberately, then, we lay the thread of the direct examination so that as often as possible, we are within the ambit of one exception or another to the no-leading-question rule.[7]

The ten exceptions, once again, are:

1. to elicit preliminary matters
2. to elicit noncontroversial or undisputed facts
3. to elicit inconsequential matters
4. to introduce a new topic
5. to refresh recollection
6. to question a boorish witness
7. to question a reluctant witness
8. to question a predisposed witness
9. to question an adverse party
10. to question a witness of limited capacity.

The first four exceptions can be used with any witness, which makes them especially valuable. These four, moreover, can always be anticipated in advance, and so can be relied upon in planning any direct examination. Of the next two, the forgetful witness is always a surprise, and sometimes the boorish witness is also. The last four exceptions on the list, however, are completely predictable for the witnesses to whom they apply. If we have planned the thing out in advance, the exceptions taken together give us enough latitude to change the rhythmic pattern almost any time we wish to. That makes it possible to conduct a direct examination that keeps the jury moving right along with us, paying attention all the way.

---

[7]See §11.3.

## §11.5 The Witness Who Forgets

Here we take up a problem that concerned English trial lawyers before American independence, and it's one that every trial lawyer still deals with every day. The problem is that of the witness who forgets. Not that he was bribed or threatened — that happens rarely. More often, the problem arises when we call to the stand someone who is not an experienced witness. He is John Q. Bystander who, for the one and only time in his life, happened to be standing on a street corner when two cars collided. For the one and only time in his life, he is on the witness stand. All he knows about it is what he has seen on television or in the movies, and that is terrifying. He sits on the witness stand under extraordinary pressure. Not infrequently, as a consequence of that pressure, he forgets. It is astounding how often witnesses forget matters that in other circumstances would be unforgettable.

I was once present in court when the witness could not remember his own name. It was a nonjury case. The judge's name was Smith. The witness, whose name was Shapiro, was a mature man but certainly not senile. He took the stand. The questioning proceeded as follows.

Q. What is your name?

A. Smith.

Q. No, no, not the judge's name. Your name. What is your name?

A. Smith.

Q. (with some exasperation) Mr. Shapiro, what is your name?

A. Smith.

At that point the judge interrupted and said, "Walk him around the block a few times." They did, and by the time he was back on the witness stand, he had calmed down enough to remember his name.

This is a melodramatic example, but melodrama is not essential to the situation. In an earlier discussion, the witness was a policeman who had investigated an accident.[8]

> Q. Officer, in the course of your investigation, did you find any skid marks?
> A. I did.
> Q. Did you measure them?
> A. Yes.
> Q. How long were they?
> A. Counselor, that accident was five years ago. I've investigated a thousand accidents since then. I can't possibly remember.

Recall the elements of competence.[9] The witness took the oath; he perceived; and he can communicate. But he does not remember. He is therefore incompetent. He may not testify. Unless we can do something to help him remember, we shall have to send him home.

This is the situation that our English progenitors had been dealing with for centuries. In response to it, they developed four possibilities that every trial lawyer must have in his armory. If one of these four methods works, the problem is solved. If none of them do, the witness must go home as incompetent. Of course, of the four items on the checklist, a lawyer will use only whatever seems sensible in the circumstances.

Your chief witness is on the stand. You ask him his name, and he forgets. With a sublimely self-confident expression, the one you must always put on when things go wrong, you turn to the judge and smile. Your demeanor says that, of course, you had planned it this way all along. With a little laugh, you say, "Your Honor, may we have a recess?"[10]

---

[8]See §7.5.

[9]See §8.8.

[10]We discussed the exigency of seeking a timeout in the context of witness preparation, §9.1.

The request for a recess is always available, although it is not always advisable. If the judge is in the right mood, and if he understands what the problem is, he will grant a recess. You take the fellow out to the corridor for an emphatic word or two. Back on the stand, if he remembers, the problem is solved. He is competent.

Sometimes, for tactical reasons, a recess is not appropriate. The witness has the words on the tip of his tongue; he knows what he wants to say, but he can't quite get it out. It may be enough to start him off, and then he will remember the rest of it. You can start him off by putting the first few words in his mouth with a leading question.

Q. What happened next?

A. I don't remember.

The proponent: Your Honor, may I have the Court's leave to ask a leading question or two, just to help the witness remember?

The Court: Proceed.

Q. Isn't the next thing that happened that you met the defendant on the street?

A. Yes, of course. How could I forget?

Q. What did he say to you, and what did you say to him?

A. Well, he said . . .

This is the fifth exception to the rule against leading questions on direct examination.[11] It is still not permissible to conduct the entire direct examination by way of leading questions, but one or two are allowed to help the witness remember.

The possibility of a leading question in this situation is one of the countless things that a trial lawyer must be alert to. The lawyer should be fast on his feet. Things should seem to go smoothly, in accordance with plan, because that is the impression to convey to the jury. Asking the judge's permission is not always necessary.

---

[11]See §11.3.

Q. What is your name, sir?

No answer from the witness.

Q. Don't remember? Let me help you. Your name is John Smith, isn't it?

A. Yes.

The problem is solved, and the testimony goes on from there.

If neither a recess nor one or two leading questions do the trick, two other methods are available. We take them up in the following two sections.

## §11.6 Present Recollection Refreshed

Of the four methods for aiding the witness who cannot remember, the preceding section dealt with the short recess and the leading question. The next method was called "present recollection revived" by the great John Henry Wigmore,[12] and is referred to everywhere by that name or its equivalent, "present recollection refreshed."

The law understands that memory is an associative process, in that the human mind can often best retrieve particular memories when presented with particular objects and sensations. When a witness forgets, there may be something to help him to remember. In the courtroom, anything may be used to refresh recollection. There are no limits, and there is an important reason for this absence of limits: The memory-refreshing thing, whatever it may be, does not itself go into evidence. Rather, the evidence will be the witness's testimony drawn from his refreshed memory.

Q. Officer, did you investigate the accident?

A. Yes, I did.

Q. Did you look for skid marks?

A. Yes.

---

[12]3 Wigmore on Evidence §758 (Chadbourn rev. 1970).

Q. Did you find skid marks?

A. Yes.

Q. Did you measure them?

A. Yes.

Q. How long were they?

A. I don't remember. It was too long ago.

Q. Is there anything that might help you to remember?

A. Yes.

Q. What is that?

A. My memo book. When I measured the skid marks, I wrote down the lengths in my memo book.

Q. Officer, I hand you what has been marked as Plaintiff's Exhibit 1 for identification. What is this?

A. This is my memo book.

Q. Read it to yourself. . . . Have you read it?

A. Yes.

Q. Now do you remember?

A. Yes, now I remember.

Note that the policeman's memo book is not evidence. It cannot be read or shown to the jury. It is for the officer alone. Having read the memo book, and with his memory thus refreshed, the officer goes on to testify in the usual fashion.

Here is one other example of the technique, this one contrived to illustrate the point that there are no limits on the things that can be used for refreshing the witness's memory.

Q. Sir, did you talk to her?

A. Yes, I did.

Q. And where were you, when you talked?

A. We were in the middle of the dance floor, dancing.

Q. What did she say to you?

A. I don't remember.

Q. Is there anything that might help you to remember?

A. Well, as we spoke, they were playing our song.

Q. And what is that, sir?

A. "Stardust."

The proponent: Your Honor, I have here a portable phonograph and a record of Hoagy Carmichael himself playing "Stardust." May we play it for the witness?

The judge does not have the power to say no. He may or may not send the jury out. Unlike the policeman's memo book, the song has no direct connection with the contents of the witness's memory, so there is no particular harm in having the jury present. With the jury there or not, and it makes no difference, we play the song for the witness.

Q. Have you heard the song?

A. Yes.

Q. Does it bring it back?

A. It brings it back.

The witness goes on to testify on the basis of his present recollection refreshed.[13]

---

[13]The memory-refreshing thing must of course be shown to the opponent. Fed. Evid. 612. The opponent may use it as he wishes on cross-examination and may, if he chooses, put it into evidence. The prohibition against the receipt in evidence of the memory-refreshing thing applies only to the proponent. For example:

Q. [by the opponent] Officer, you say that, after looking at your memo book, you remember that the skid marks were forty-five feet long?

A. Yes, sir.

Q. Officer, you've said that Plaintiff's Exhibit 1 is your memo book?

A. Yes, sir.

Q. And is this page, numbered five, the one of which you made notes of your investigation in this matter?

A. Yes, sir.

Q. Isn't it a fact, Officer, that nowhere on page five do you say that the skid marks were forty five-feet long?

A. That is so.

Counsel: Your Honor, the defense will offer in evidence page five of the officer's memo book.

## §11.7 Past Recollection Recorded

This is the fourth and last of our methods for coping with the situation in which the witness cannot remember. As in the preceding section, a policeman is on the stand.

Q. Officer, you measured the skid marks?

A. Yes.

Q. How long were they?

A. I don't remember.

Q. Is there anything that might help you to remember?

A. Yes.

Q. What?

A. My memo book.

Q. I hand you Plaintiff's Exhibit 1 for identification. What is it?

A. It's my memo book.

Q. Read it to yourself, please. . . . Have you read it?

A. Yes.

Q. Now, tell us how long the skid marks were.

A. Counselor, this is my memo book. I recognize my handwriting. But I still can't tell you that I remember — not an accident five years ago, and a thousand accidents between that one and today. I know I wrote it down, but even having read it, I don't remember.

The witness is breathtakingly honest. He is also forever incompetent. He has told us, in essence, that he has no way of remembering. His recollection is permanently unavailable. If his memo book containing the notes he made at the time does not bring back his recollection, then a conference, a recess, or a leading question will not bring it back either.

This problem has been happening for so long that our English progenitors invented a fallback position: When something like a memo book contains the needed information, then the proponent can place the thing itself, the memo book, in evidence as a substitute for the witness's forever unavailable recollection.[14] The witness once knew, but no longer remembers, and we have no way of bringing the memory back. When he did remember, he wrote it down. We put that writing into evidence as a substitute for the memory. The device is called, appropriately enough, past recollection recorded.

Note two important distinctions between this method and that of present recollection refreshed.[15] First, with present recollection refreshed, anything whatsoever can be used to refresh the recollection — a memo book, a record of any kind, a physical object, a song. With past recollection recorded, however, the thing introduced in evidence must itself contain the needed information. Sometimes the same object, as the policeman's memo book, might serve for both purposes, but sometimes an object will serve for one and not the other.

The second difference between the two is that with present recollection refreshed, the thing that refreshes the witness's memory is for the witness only. It is not for the jury. It does not go into evidence. But with past recollection recorded, the thing does go into evidence precisely because the witness cannot be helped to remember. It is read to the jury, and in some jurisdictions will actually be given to the jury to examine.[16]

There are four prerequisites to invoking past recollection recorded.

- The witness once was competent. He once perceived and once remembered.
- The witness is now incompetent solely because he does not remember.
- At a time when the witness did remember, he wrote the information down, or someone else wrote it down and the witness read it while his memory was still fresh.[17]

---

[14]This device appears briefly in §7.5.

[15]See §11.6.

[16]*See* Fed. R. Evid. 803(5).

[17]It is sometimes said that the witness must have written it down soon after the event, which is merely a different formulation of this third prerequisite.

- The witness can give us assurances that the document is accurate.

With all four prerequisites met, the document goes into evidence. It might sound something like this:

Q. Officer, have you read your memo book?

A. Yes.

Q. Now do you remember how long the skid marks were?

A. I do not, Counselor. I recognize my handwriting, but I really don't remember that particular occasion.

Q. Officer, that memorandum book is very important to a policeman's work, isn't it?

A. Yes.

Q. You're supposed to write down everything you do, as accurately as you can?

A. That's right.

Q. And you write down nothing that you do not do?

A. Yes.

Q. So that everything that you wrote down, you did do?

A. Yes.

Q. Officer, did you write down the lengths of the skid marks at just about the time you measured them?

A. Yes.

Q. Did you write down the measurement accurately?

A. I certainly did. I always do.

The proponent: Your Honor, I offer in evidence . . .

And in it goes, as past recollection recorded.

Keep an eye on the changing nature of the evidence. What began as viva voce evidence, testimonial evidence by the officer answering questions, is no longer that. At the moment that the memo book went into evidence, it shifts to documentary evidence.

And as soon as the form of the evidence changes, the four-item checklist for documentary evidence comes into play.[18]

Let us run through the checklist. First, the parol evidence rule is inapplicable here. Second, the best evidence rule does apply; the proponent must offer the original memo book, not a copy of it, unless there is some good reason to offer a copy instead.[19] Third, the memo book must be authenticated by having the policeman testify that it is indeed his memo book.[20] And fourth, the memo book is indeed hearsay, although it comes within an exception to the rule against hearsay,[21] called, pleasingly enough, past recollection recorded.

## §11.8 Pulling the Teeth

We have seen that any problems in the case should be brought out early — if not in the course of jury selection, then at the very latest, by the opening statement.[22] If a problem is serious, that may not be enough. One class of problems in particular may need further handling on direct examination.

Suppose that we represent the defendant in a criminal case. He is going to take the stand in order to give the jury his alibi. At the time that the crime was committed, he will say, he was at the movies with his mother. Unfortunately, there are incidents in his background that may incline the jury not to believe him: The defendant was convicted seven times before. And there is little doubt that the prosecutor will bring out those convictions on cross-examination.[23]

We will have done our best to minimize the shock value by deliberately exposing the defendant's prior convictions ourselves, very early in the trial. Now he is on the stand. Rather than wait for the cross-examiner to bring out the convictions, we can fur-

---

[18]See §7.3.
[19]Fed. R. Evid. 1003. See §7.4.
[20]See §7.5.
[21]Fed. R. Evid. 803(5).
[22]See §§3.6, 5.3.
[23]See §15.4.

ther contain the damage by eliciting them ourselves, on direct. This technique has two advantages. It lets us put the facts in as sympathetic a light as possible; and the mere fact that we are bringing out the information ourselves tells the jury that it must not be so terrible after all. Trial lawyers call it "pulling the teeth," and it sounds something like this:

Q. It's been a tough life, hasn't it, Charlie?
A. Yeah.
Q. You've been in trouble with the police before, haven't you?
A. Yeah.
Q. And you've been convicted a few times, right?
A. Yeah.
Q. Let's tell the jury about that, okay?
A. Yeah.

But we must tread carefully, or it can go very wrong.

Q. Tell me, Charlie. How many times have you been convicted?
A. Well, lemme see. There was that murder, a couple of rapes, the aggravated cruelty to animals . . . seven times, I guess. So this time will make eight.

# CHAPTER 12

# Opinions

## §12.1 The Non-Opinion Rule

Recall the four categories of evidence: real evidence, demonstrative evidence, documentary evidence, and testimony from witnesses.[1] Here we seek a way to categorize witnesses in the last category. Not all categorizations will serve us. For example, it is true, but not helpful, that all witnesses are either male or female. It is true that all witnesses are either credible or not credible, but that also is not a useful categorization for our purposes.

Only one way of classifying witnesses ever suggested seems to be at all helpful. Every witness testifies in one of two capacities. To say it more precisely, any witness at any given stage of his testimony is testifying in one of two capacities. The first possibility is the capacity of the expert witness. When we describe a witness as an expert witness, we really mean that at the moment in question, the witness is testifying as an expert. The second category includes everybody else, anyone who is not testifying as an expert witness. We usually refer to everybody else as lay witnesses, ordinary witnesses, or nonexpert witnesses.

---

[1]See §§7.1-7.3.

The law of evidence tells us that anyone is competent to be a witness if he bears no incompetence by status[2] and takes the oath, did perceive, does remember, and can communicate.[3] The law of evidence goes on to limit the style of questions available to the lawyer conducting the direct examination: With ten exceptions, he may not use leading questions.[4] The law of evidence further restricts the style of the answers that the witness may give. This restriction is commonly called the opinion rule. A better name is the non-opinion rule, thus giving the content of the rule in its name. The non-opinion rule does not address questions of competence; it presupposes that the witness is competent. The rule refers only to how the witness may answer questions.

The non-opinion rule says that the witness must not testify as to his opinions, conclusions, or characterizations. Rather, the witness must respond to questions with the bare bones of perception. Without any emotional overtones whatsoever, the witness must say, in effect, "This is what I saw," or heard or smelled or tasted or touched. The non-opinion rule says that the witness must give us just the news, no editorials. The rule applies in every jurisdiction in the land.

## §12.2 The Lay Witness Exception

There is a basic problem with the non-opinion rule.[5] Suppose that I ask a colleague, "How are you this morning?" He will reply along the lines of, "I am fine, thank you." But that violates the non-opinion rule. He has given an opinion, a conclusion, a characterization, an editorial. Yet, to answer otherwise is very difficult. "How am I? Well, let me tell you. I have a dull pain between my eyes. My tongue, when I examined it in the mirror, was coated with a green, scum-like substance. I failed to move my bowels this morning . . .," etc.

---

[2]See §§8.2-8.7.
[3]See §8.8.
[4]See §§11.2 and 11.3.
[5]See §12.1.

The truth is, most of us, speak almost wholly in opinions, conclusions, and characterizations. "How are you this afternoon?" "Fine." "How did you feel this morning?" "Not so good." "How were you yesterday?" "Okay." All of those are opinions.

The same problem arises in testimony. One example appears in *State v. Garver,*[6] an Oregon case back in 1950. Garver, the defendant, was charged with murder. He was in very serious trouble. The prosecution called numerous eyewitnesses against him — the testimony amounted to everything but a motion picture of the murder being committed. When the prosecution has the goods on your client to that extent, there is only one possible defense: insanity. And who does a person call when he is in very bad trouble? His mother of course.

Picture Garver's mother — her name by then was Mitchell — a nice, gray-haired woman in 1950 trying to save her son from the gas chamber. If we fill in the gaps in the published opinion, we find defense counsel's efforts at direct examination going something like this:

Q. Now, Mrs. Mitchell, during those times, did your son live with you?

A. Yes.

Q. Did you see him for many hours each day?

A. Oh, yes.

Q. How was he?

A. He was in such a terrible shape.

The district attorney leaps to his feet: "I object! That violates the non-opinion rule!"

"Objection sustained," says the judge. He turns to the lady and he says, "Madam, tell us only what you know." When a lawyer says those words, he wants the witness to report only what she perceived, and to report it in the language of perception. A layperson cannot know that, but the mother resolves to do the best she can.

---

[6]190 Or. 291, 225 P.2d 771 (1950).

Q. All right, Mrs. Mitchell. How was your son?

A. He was crazy.

Prosecutor: Objection! Non-opinion rule.

The Court: Sustained.

Q. Mrs. Mitchell, only what you know, please. Now, how was he?

A. He was as sick as could be.

Prosecutor: Objection.

The Court: Sustained.

Mrs. Mitchell was a fairly intelligent witness, the opinion tells us. But at around that point, "she became so confused by the objections and rulings that . . . she said to counsel for the defendant, 'Mr. Johns, I don't know what you mean by— when you ask me a question and I answer it to the best of my ability; I don't know what you mean for me to answer. I just try to tell you what you ask me.' "[7] The situation did not improve. After further objections had been sustained, the poor woman turned to the judge in what must have been complete frustration, and she said, "I don't know how to express it; when I say what was in my heart then it is stricken from the records."[8]

The jury convicted Garver, but the Supreme Court of Oregon reversed. It did so under the first of our two exceptions to the non-opinion rule.[9] This exception, in the words of the Supreme Court of Oregon, "leaves the witness free to speak his ordinary language, unbewildered by admonitions from the judge to testify to facts, when all the while the witness is sure in his own mind that he *is* testifying to facts. The jury understands what the witness means, and the right of cross-examination removes the likelihood of harm to the other side."[10]

This is the exception to the non-opinion rule for the lay or ordinary witness. It has no precise formulation, but in general

---

[7]*Id.* at 316, 225 P.2d at 783.

[8]*Id.* at 317, 225 P.2d at 783.

[9]We take up the other exception, for expert witnesses, in Chapter 13.

[10]190 Or. at 316, 225 P.2d at 782.

it runs something like this: When a competent witness has first-hand knowledge, and wishes to report his perceptions in an opinion that is part of everyday language, and the jury will unquestionably understand what the witness means, and it would be a waste of time to insist upon compliance with the non-opinion rule, then a lay or ordinary witness may state the opinion. The Federal Rules of Evidence agree.[11]

Nearly all permissible instances of the lay witness exception fall into just four categories. Others occasionally slip in, but these four account for most of the cases.

First, assuming firsthand knowledge, a lay witness may give an opinion as to the physical condition either of himself or of another person. "I felt fine." "He was sick." All such verbal variations are permissible.

Second is the *Garver* situation. Again assuming firsthand knowledge, a layman may testify as to mental condition. "He struck me as crazy." "He seemed perfectly sane." Obviously, lay witnesses cannot give complicated psychiatric diagnoses, but they may report on mental condition in the terms of everyday speech.

Third, a lay witness may testify as to alcoholic intoxication. The reasoning is that this is part of everyone's experience. We all know what a witness means by saying, "The defendant was drunk." This branch of the exception applies only to alcoholic intoxication, not to intoxication from other drugs, because those others are not considered to be part of the universal experience.

Fourth and finally, lay judgments as to the speed of a car will be admissible, again on the theory that everybody nowadays knows about cars. A particular judge may not allow the witness to say that a car was going sixty-five miles per hour, but the witness may say it was going pretty fast. How exact the testimony can be will vary with the individual judge.

---

[11]"If the witness is not testifying as an expert, his testimony in the form of opinions or inferences is limited to those opinions or inferences which are (a) rationally based on the perception of the witness and (b) helpful to a clear understanding of this testimony or the determination of a fact in issue." Fed. R. Evid. 701.

For any opinion under this exception, the adversary on cross-examination can always bring out the underlying data. "What makes you think he was drunk?" "I saw him stumble when he walked. I smelled alcohol on his breath. I heard him bark" — or whatever it was that led the witness to say on direct, "He was drunk."

# CHAPTER 13

# Experts

## §13.1 Making the Lay/Expert Distinction

We saw in the previous chapter the exception to the non-opinion rule that applies to a lay witness. The second exception applies to an expert witness. The exception says simply that an expert witness may testify as to his opinion, under the proper circumstances. We examine those circumstances in this chapter.

Expert witnesses are taking on an increasingly important role in the law. With ever increasing frequency, trials in the state and federal courts, civil and criminal, tort and otherwise, turn upon expert witnesses. It is fair to say that it is impossible for a lawyer to proceed with any confidence these days unless that lawyer has a very good grasp of the considerable body of law that has been developed with respect to expert witnesses. The relevant body of law includes segments of three separate structures of doctrine: the law of evidence; the law of professional responsibility; and the law of trial advocacy.

To put into context the questions that a lawyer is likely to ask when preparing a case involving expert witnesses, we will pay attention to the federal jurisdiction and the twenty or so states

Portions of this chapter are drawn from "A Practical Approach to the Use of Expert Testimony," by Irving Younger, which appeared in the Cleveland State Law Review, vol. 31, no. 1 (1982). © Cleveland State Law Review. Used with permission.

that have enacted the Federal Rules of Evidence. Then, by way of contrast, we will refer to some New York cases. New York is the major jurisdiction on the other side of the road from the Federal Rules of Evidence.

Whatever the jurisdiction, it is incorrect to label a witness as lay or expert, and to leave the label in place for as long as the witness is on the stand. The purpose in calling the witness is to prove certain facts. The witness's status will therefore vary with the sort of fact about which the witness testifies.[1] At one moment the witness may be a lay witness, at the next an expert, and so on.

Consider the treating physician. When he testifies that he examined the plaintiff and felt a stiffness in the muscles at the back of the neck, he is testifying to his own perceptions, and so is a lay witness. When he testifies that from these observations, and from red, swollen patches on the back of the plaintiff's throat, he diagnosed a strep throat, he becomes an expert witness, for that is a fact provable only by expert opinion.

One practical consequence of the distinction turns on the common law rule that lay testimony is compellable, while expert testimony is not. For the lay elements of his testimony, it would have been proper to subpoena the physician. Only as to the diagnosis would the traditional arrangements for compensation be necessary. Nonetheless, a case discussed below suggests that certain kinds of expert testimony may now be compellable along with lay testimony.[2]

The lay/expert distinction becomes important also in determining whether any of the elements necessary to a prima facie case require expert testimony. Take, for example, *Meier v. Ross General Hospital*,[3] an action for wrongful death. Plaintiff's deceased had a long history of mental trouble, evidenced chiefly by an attempt at suicide. He was placed in the care of the defendant hospital, which, despite its knowledge of the deceased's history, assigned him to an unsecured upper-story room. Result: defenestration. On which note the plaintiff rested.

---

[1]See §2.2.
[2]Kaufman v. Edelstein, 539 F.2d 811 (2d Cir. 1976); See §13.2.
[3]69 Cal. 2d 420, 445 P.2d 519, 71 Cal. Rptr. 903 (1968).

The plaintiff had produced no expert opinion to the effect that the hospital had been unreasonably careless, and the trial judge thought this a deficiency. But the California Supreme Court decided otherwise. The deceased's history and the hospital's conduct were proved by lay testimony. The hospital's knowledge was also proved by lay testimony that the hospital staff was told of the deceased's history. What remained was whether these facts warranted the label "unreasonably careless assignment of a room." Although part of the jargon of the law, the phrase is used in everyday speech with the same meaning as it takes in the law. Nothing before the jury was beyond their unaided comprehension; the jury possessed the necessary facts; and so the plaintiff had a prima facie case.

How do you identify or recognize an issue in connection with which it will be proper to call an expert to the stand?

Take, for example, a "spleen-out" case where the main issue is the amount of damages. The plaintiff's attorney will call an expert who will testify that the spleen plays a vital, though as yet unidentified, role in the body's immunological system. The expert will testify that without a spleen this little boy has a life expectancy of a great big question mark, and the case is worth at least half a million dollars. The defendant's attorney will call an expert with equal credentials to testify that the spleen is left over from the days when we were fishes — it is a vestigial organ like the appendix, is of no significance whatsoever, the little boy is no worse off now than he was before he was run over.

On an issue like that, expert witnesses are necessary because the jury is incapable of resolving the question of damages, which turns upon some assessment of the importance of the spleen.

But take a different kind of case. Suppose you have a two-lane highway, and in the middle of the night, two cars approach each other on the highway traveling in opposite directions. Each car is driven by a lone driver, and there are no bystanders. Suddenly, there is a head-on collision. When the smoke clears, one car is over here, and the other is over there. There are skid marks and debris on the highway and two dead drivers. One estate sues the other estate. Once you decide on which side of the road the collision occurred, you know which driver had gone on the wrong side of the road, and you know who's in the right and who's in the wrong. These are the facts of a case that came up in the U.S. district court in North Dakota in 1954.[4]

The estate on the plaintiff's side of the table called an expert in accident reconstruction. Nobody would argue his credentials. The expert undertook to tell the jury that based upon his analysis of the skid marks, the debris, where the cars ended up, etc., the collision occurred in the northbound lane, which means, of course, that the driver who was heading south had gone over on the wrong side of the road. Immediately, defense counsel leaped to his feet and protested, "Objection, not a proper subject for expert testimony." "Objection overruled," said the federal judge, "the expert may testify."[5]

The facts of that federal case are also the facts of a New York State case.[6] The accident reconstruction expert was called. The objection was made, "This is not a proper subject for expert testimony," and the trial judge overruled the objection. The trial judge's overruling of the objection was reversed, however, by the appellate court.

The federal judge, who made his decision back in 1954, was working against the background of a fair number of federal decisions articulating the rule later codified in Federal Rule 702, which is followed in those states that enacted the Federal Rules of Evidence.[7] It is a relaxed kind of rule, which opens the door quite wide to the receipt of expert testimony. The federal rule might be stated as follows: "If the expert's testimony will help the jury, it's admissible." In that highway collision case, obviously it is going to help the jury to have the expert explain to them how he figures out the force vectors and the like.

---

[4]Ern v. Consolidated Freightways, 120 F. Supp. 289 (D.N.D. 1954).

[5]*Id.* These statements are characterizations of the events that transpired at trial and are not direct quotations. This style will appear throughout this chapter.

[6]Stafford v. Mussers Potato Chips, Inc. 39 A.D.2d 831, 333 N.Y.2d 139 (1972).

[7]The Federal Rules of Evidence did not become effective until 1975. Rule 702 states: "If scientific, technical, or other specialized knowledge will assist the trier-of-fact to understand the evidence or to determine a fact in issue, a witness qualified as an expert by knowledge, skill, experience, training, or education, may testify thereto in the form of an opinion or otherwise."

The so-called New York rule is more demanding. It is a stringent rule that closes the door considerably to the receipt of expert testimony. Under the New York rule, the expert may not testify merely because his opinion will help the jury, but only when his opinion is *necessary* to the jury. That is a very different test from the federal rule. The lawyer who wants to keep the expert off the stand will argue that perhaps it will be helpful to the jury to have the expert give his opinion, but it is not necessary or essential. The lawyer will argue that lay jurors can manage to figure the matter out for themselves.

The ramifications of the difference between the federal rule and the New York rule can be illustrated further with two cases.

Imagine, in the first case, that you are a federal judge. The standard is that the expert may testify if it will help jury. You have been presiding for some weeks over a serious and highly publicized criminal case.

The prosecution's principal witness has testified in essence that the defendant is guilty. He knows this to be so because of his own knowledge, because he saw the defendant do what was alledged in the indictment. This prosecution witness has been cross-examined for days and he has not budged one bit from his testimony.

The defendant has taken the stand and has insisted that he did not do it, and that the prosecution witness is lying. The defendant has been cross-examined extensively and he has not budged one bit from his testimony.

There is corroborating evidence on both sides, but it is about equal in weight and balances out. What the jury ultimately has to do is assess the credibility of the prosecution witness and the defendant. If they believe the former, the verdict is guilty. If they believe the latter, the verdict is not guilty.

You are now at rebuttal. You are resting comfortably in the robing room at about quarter to ten in the morning, ready to go onto the bench at ten o'clock, having your cup of coffee, your cigar, your morning brandy, or whatever it is you need to wake you, when there is a knock on the door. Counsel on both sides walk in with the court reporter. The defense counselor makes the following application:

"Your Honor, of course, understands that this case boils down to a matter of the jury assessing the credibility of those two witnesses. In that connection, Your Honor, we have an expert outside whom we propose to put on the stand this morning. We are raising with you the question whether you will overrule us if we put that expert on the stand. The expert is a psychiatrist, but this is no ordinary psychiatrist. This expert is the immediate past president of the American Psychiatric Association and is a professor of psychiatry at the Cornell Medical School. He has just been appointed professor of medicine at the Harvard Medical School and chief of psychiatry at Massachusetts General Hospital. He has studied medicine at Johns Hopkins and psychiatry in Vienna and Zurich. He is unquestionably the preeminent American psychiatrist. This man has never clinically examined the prosecution witness, but he has observed him on the stand. He knows the facts of the witness's life. The witness is a professional writer. The psychiatrist has read virtually every word this witness has ever published. He is willing to take the stand and state, as his professional opinion, that the prosecution witness is suffering from a personality disorder, characterized by a tendency to make false accusations and tell lies.

"Your Honor, I see that you're laughing. With all deference," says defense counsel, "I remind Your Honor that it's not your job to assess the credibility of the witness. It is your job simply to rule upon my application. May I call the witness to the stand?"

Government counsel, of course, says, "This is the first time in the history of Anglo-Saxon jurisprudence that such a thing has ever been suggested."

What is your ruling? May the witness testify? May the witness not testify? All that you need to know is that the test, in a federal court, is whether the expert will help the jury. Invariably, when I have put this question to groups of people, both the professionally sophisticated and otherwise, a very large majority says, "I will not allow the witness to testify." But defense counsel has a valid point. Our job is simply to apply the federal rule, which is a very relaxed one with respect to the propriety of the expert testifying.

That is a real case, and it shows how far judges can go in applying the federal rule. The psychiatrist was named Carl Binger.

The judge was named Henry Goddard. The witness about whom the psychiatrist was going to testify was named Whitaker Chambers. And the case, of course, is *United States v. Hiss*.[8]

The judge ruled quite properly on the basis of federal law that the psychiatrist could testify. If ever you have to argue for the propriety of calling an expert, the case is far beyond anything you are likely to encounter.

Dr. Binger did testify, and his cross-examination was one of the bloodiest scenes ever played out in an American courtroom. It would have been much better for Alger Hiss if the judge had said, "I will not allow this man to testify," because of the boomerang effect. The prosecution so cut up Dr. Binger that it could not help but have an effect on how the jury assessed the rest of the case. This, of course, was the second trial, the one in which the jury found Alger Hiss guilty.[9]

Now, let's look at a New York case, *Kulak v. Nationwide Mutual Insurance Co.*[10] Mrs. Kulak is the victim of an automobile accident. She sues her tortfeasor, who has automobile insurance. These are not the exact numbers but this is essentially what happens. A day or so before the jury is to be picked, plaintiff's counsel goes to defense counsel, who really is the insurance company's lawyer, and says: "Look, John, liability in this case is absolutely clear, and short of a miracle, you can't win on liability." "Agreed," says the defense counsel. Plaintiff's counsel continues, "And the specials are thus and so, and the pain and suffering obvious. Look at the deformed arm and all the rest of it. It seems to me that the jury verdict here is going to be in the range of a quarter of a million dollars. You've got a $100,000 policy. Pay me $90,000, take back $10,000 to the claims adjuster, and the game is over." Defense counsel says, "No. Let's go to trial."

They go to trial. Was the plaintiff's assessment of liability correct? Absolutely, as the jury resolves the case against the defendant. Was the plaintiff's view of damages correct? Absolutely, the verdict was for one-quarter of a million dollars.

---

[8]88 F. Supp. 559 (S.D.N.Y.), *aff'd*, 201 F.2d 372 (2d Cir. 1950), *cert. denied*, 340 U.S. 948 (1951).

[9]*See* United States v. Hiss, 107 F. Supp. 128 (S.D.N.Y. 1952), *aff'd*, 201 F.2d 372 (2d Cir.), *cert. denied*, 345 U.S. 942 (1953).

[10]40 N.Y.2d 140, 351 N.E.2d 735, 386 N.Y.S.2d 87 (1976).

What does defense counsel do? He says, "Win some, lose some." He pays out $100,000, puts the policy on the table, and walks away, leaving the plaintiff $150,000 short. The defendant has no assets, except for the insurance policy, which has been placed on the table. Does that mean the plaintiff can do nothing to collect the additional $150,000. Of course not, because the defendant does have an additional asset: He has his own claim against *his* insurance company for unreasonable refusal to settle, and the claim is assignable.

The defendant assigns to the plaintiff the defendant's claim against his own insurance company, takes a general release, and then goes home. The plaintiff brings a second lawsuit, not against the tortfeasor but against the tortfeasor's insurance company, seeking to collect the additional $150,000.

What is the substantive rule? No lawyer or insurance company has a crystal ball. There is no legal obligation to predict accurately what the outcome of the case will be, but there is a legal obligation to act reasonably. So the question is: Did the insurance company act reasonably when it turned down the plaintiff's proposal of the $90,000 settlement? That is what the jury in the second trial must decide.

In that second trial, the plaintiff calls two experts. The first expert states, "I am experienced in this field of work." Everybody agrees that he is experienced. There is no question about his credentials or his expertise. The expert continues, "And in this field of work, this is how you assess the likely size of the verdict." The first expert tells the story in that second trial about the formula for predicting the amount of the jury verdict in that type of case.

Then, the second expert takes the stand and says to the jury, "Working with the formula the first expert gave us, and feeding in the numbers from the first trial, what the specials were and what the lost earnings were and so on, you come out with the following answer." In short, he indicates that what the defense counsel did was *not* reasonable because he should have expected a verdict in the range of a quarter of a million dollars.

The highest court of New York reverses on the ground that while it was proper for the first expert to testify, it was not proper for the second expert to testify.

The reasoning of the New York Court of Appeals is as follows: The man or woman in the street, our juror, cannot possibly know what these formulas are. The rule is that the expert may testify if it is necessary to the jury, and, obviously, the first expert's testimony was necessary to the jury. But once the jury had the formula of the first expert, it was a matter of elementary school arithmetic to feed in the numbers and do whatever calculations were necessary to come out with an answer. It is helpful to have the second expert do the arithmetic on the blackboard. But since it is not essential, the second expert should not have been allowed to testify. Hence, the verdict is reversed and we send it back for a new trial.

## §13.2  Getting the Expert Into Court

Having identified an issue on which an expert may testify — and, of course, having identified an appropriate expert — the lawyer preparing for trial faces a very practical question: How do you secure the appearance of the expert in court?

Most of the time this is not a problem. Experts are paid. It is their time. The attorney makes the arrangements to pay the expert, and he or she comes to court. There is nothing shameful about it. The expert often is a "house expert," someone whom we have used before. Many lawyers have a "stable" of experts — for example, ten or fifteen doctors, who are indeed doctors in the sense that they have licenses to practice medicine, but these are doctors who prefer to be in court. They are very good at it; they enjoy it. They look like Spencer Tracy; they make an infallible impression upon the jury. In the normal situation, you just call up somebody, you work things out financially, and the expert appears in court.

But suppose you can't work it out? Let us suppose, for example, that you are a lawyer practicing for a public interest law firm. You need an expert, and you do not have the money required. What can you do?

The rules of professional responsibility have blocked one avenue that would otherwise be logical to pursue. The expert has just told you that he will be glad to come to court to testify and that his opinion is helpful to your side of the case, but he has to be paid and his fee will be $500. You say: "Doctor, I'm afraid we don't have the $500."

The expert says, "Well, in that case, good luck to you, but I guess I'm not going to be there in court."

You say, "Doctor, don't hang up. We don't have the $500, but tell me, are you by any chance a gambling man?"

The doctor may well respond, "Now that you mention it, I like to go to Las Vegas every weekend."

"Well, Doctor, I make no promises, of course, but if we win this case, there will be a pot of gold at the end of the rainbow, and ten percent of that pot of gold will be yours."

"Well," says the doctor, "that's a different story. It's a gamble, like you say, and we may lose. But if we do win, I've got ten percent of the pot of gold. You've got a deal."

Do you have a deal? Yes, you do. Are you also in trouble? Yes, you are. Disciplinary Rule 7-109(C) states that the retaining of an expert on a contingent basis is an unprofessional act.[11] The reason is this: If you permit lawyers to retain experts on a contingent basis, that will encourage litigation. Of course, we allow lawyers to be retained on a contingent basis precisely because it will encourage litigation. That is the whole idea. If you are cynical, you say the whole idea is to permit lawyers to earn a living. If you are not cynical, you say that the idea is to permit poor people to come to court and get their problems decided. Yet we say that an expert may not be retained on a contingent basis because that would encourage litigation.[12]

---

[11]Model Code of Professional Responsibility DR 7-109(C) (1981).

[12]An argument can be made that the real point of Disciplinary Rule 7-109(C) is that it discriminates between rich litigants and poor litigants. Rich litigants can retain an expert. Poor litigants may not be able to retain an expert because they do not have the money and are actively forbidden to retain the expert on a contingent basis. The U.S. district judge before whom this argument was raised agreed with it, and declared Disciplinary Rule 7-109(C) unconstitutional under the equal protection clause. Person v. Association of the Bar of the City of New York, 414 F. Supp. 139 (E.D.N.Y. 1976). Judge Duling, however, was reversed on appeal, 554 F.2d 534 (2d Cir.), *cert. denied*, 434 U.S. 924 (1977). *Person* is the only appellate decision to consider the constitutionality of Disciplinary Rule 7-109(C).

For trial lawyers, this is not an issue of merely theoretical, academic, or general interest. One of the reasons you have so much trouble getting an expert if you are without resources is that an expert is in a different position from an ordinary witness. That different position might be phrased as follows: The ordinary or lay witness — for example, the bystander who happens to see the two cars collide — has an *obligation* of citizenship to come to court and give the judge and jury his perceptions. That obligation is invoked or triggered merely by serving upon John Q. Bystander a subpoena and tendering a ministerial witness fee.

The common law, however, has said that an expert witness is in a very different position. The expert witness has an opinion. The common law traditionally regards the expert witness's opinion as his private property. He may give it away, he may sell it, but it may not be compelled. The perceptions of John Q. Bystander may be compelled, but the expert witness's opinion may not be compelled.[13]

For example, you are a young attorney, and your first case is a spleen-out case with no issue of liability. The question is simply the amount of damages, which in turn becomes the question, what is the significance of the spleen? You go to the public library, and you discover that on the faculty of the New York University Medical School is a man who won the Nobel Prize about fifteen years ago for work on the physiology of the spleen. His view is that the spleen does play a vital role in the body's immunological system and significantly affects life expectancy.

You call him up and ask, "Will you come to court, Doctor?" "No," he replies, and since you can't ethically propose a contingent contract, you say to yourself, "I'll serve him with a subpoena, give him a subway token, and then he will have to come to court and tell me about the work for which he won the Nobel Prize in medicine." Of course, he won't come to court until you dare to ask the judge to hold him in contempt or have him arrested. The judge will have none of it.

---

[13]*See, e.g.,* Hull v. Plume, 131 N.J.L. 511, 37 A.2d 53 (1944) (witness may not be compelled to give expert testimony unless he has voluntarily contracted to do so).

But the traditional and well-settled view of this situation may be in the process of changing. The harbinger of this potential change is *Kaufman v. Edelstein*,[14] a decision that arose out of the decade-long government antitrust case (which was ultimately dropped by the government) against International Business Machines Corp.

The controversy in the IBM litigation boils down to matters of opinion. Do they have monopoly power? Are they too big? That is what you try in an antitrust case. About the third or fourth year of trial, the government hears about three men, and when they hear about these three men, the little hairs on the back of their necks stand up. These three men are not professors in economics but do have graduate degrees in economics or business administration. They are business people who, as a part of their own business activities, have made a lengthy study of the computer industry in order to better advise their own clients. Significantly, each of them has come to the conclusion that it would inure to the economical health of the computer industry to break up IBM.

The government goes to them and says, "Will you testify?" "No."

"Why? Do you want to be paid? Name your price. It doesn't matter."

These three men say, "No matter what you pay us we're not going to court because first, it's inconvenient; second, it's undignified; third, it's a lawyer's kettle of fish; and fourth, we just don't want to be in the position of helping the government in this case, even though we are on record that it would work to the economic well-being of the computer industry to break up IBM."

The government causes an ordinary witness subpoena to be served upon each prospective witness. And all of them move to quash the subpoena.

To everybody's amazement, Judge David Edelstein denies the motions. He says, "No. They're going to have to come testify."

---

[14]Kaufman v. Edelstein, 539 F.2d 811 (2d Cir. 1976). *Accord* Carter-Wallace, Inc. v. Otte, 474 F.2d 529 (2d Cir. 1972), *cert. denied*, 412 U.S. 929 (1973).

The government files a notice of appeal and simultaneously moves in the Second Circuit for an extraordinary writ in the nature of a mandamus.

The panel that decided the case was made up of three judges as experienced and distinguished as any three judges in the United States, Henry Friendly, Murray Gurfein, and William Mulligan — men of vast experience as practicing lawyers, and as good as judges ever get to be. They unanimously affirmed Judge Edelstein, not on procedural grounds, but on the merits of the question.

The following is a fair summary of the opinion written by Judge Friendly. The old common law idea that an expert's opinion is his private property, to give away, sell or withhold as he wished, must yield to the reality of modern litigation. With ever increasing frequency, litigation these days turns upon the testimony of experts. It follows, then, that to say to an expert, "You can withhold your opinion at will," is as much as to say to an expert, "You may obstruct justice whenever you please to do so."[15] It is time to equate the status of the expert witness to the status of the ordinary witness. If the ordinary witness has an obligation of citizenship to give the jury his perceptions, then the expert witness has some kind of obligation of citizenship to give his opinions to the judge or jury. Therefore, the testimony of these men is compellable. Of course, the client has to pay something more than the ministerial witness fee for the testimony.[16] It was finally agreed what the compensation would be, and the three men did testify.

*Kaufman v. Edelstein* may well become an important case, ultimately leading to a reformulated rule. An expert witness may be compellable, subject only to the parties agreeing on the amount

---

[15]Pointing out the enormous range of expert knowledge in modern life, the court argued that "[t]o clothe all such expert testimony with privilege [against testifying] would be to seal off too much evidence important to the just determination of disputes." 539 F.2d at 821.

[16]The circuit court handled the issue of payment very sensibly, saying in effect, "We're not going to talk about that at this time; we're going to leave it to the witnesses and the government to work out. If they can't work it out, then come back to us." I am informed, unofficially, that the amount of the witness fee was never the problem.

of compensation, and if they cannot agree, the judge will decide upon reasonable compensation. Putting that aside, you can get an expert to court the same way you get an ordinary witness to court, by serving him or her with a subpoena.

It is possible, on the other hand, that twenty years from now, *Kaufman v. Edelstein* will be nothing more than a historical curiosity. It will be understood that *Kaufman v. Edelstein* is not the precedent of general application. As courts like to put it, "it must be limited to its facts," which means *Kaufman v. Edelstein* is authoritative only the next time the government sues IBM, the case is being tried by Judge Edelstein and the three men, one of whom is named Kaufman, decline to come and testify as experts. But, the former scenario is more likely — that *Kaufman v. Edelstein* will be the precursor of a new prevailing rule.[17]

## §13.3 Qualifying the Expert

There has been a revolution in the development of the law of evidence with respect to matters that come up on the direct examination of an expert, at least in the federal courts and in those states that follow the Federal Rules of Evidence.

You begin the direct examination of any kind of an expert, in any kind of case, by qualifying the expert: asking the questions designed to show that the witness is an expert by reason of education, experience, independent work, or whatever it may be.

Few lawyers take sufficient advantage of the opportunity for advocacy by qualifying the expert. Going through it mechanically is a grave mistake of advocacy as well as a technical mistake. It is based upon a partial view of what you're doing when you qualify the expert.

When you qualify an expert, you are talking to the judge,

---

[17]The experts in Kaufman v. Edelstein had already done the work preliminary to arriving at an opinion, so all that was required of them was to come to court and *repeat* the opinion. What do you do when you've got experts whose expertise makes it possible for them to do the work that will lead to an opinion, but they have not yet done the work? Is there any way of compelling them to do the work, so as to get them to court with their opinions? On that, Kaufman v. Edelstein is absolutely silent.

saying something like, "Your Honor, doesn't this witness possess expertise beyond that of the man or woman in the street?," hence making it proper for this witness to give his opinion under the expert witness exception to the non-opinion rule.

It takes very little to qualify as an expert in that sense. The expert need not be a Nobel Prize winner. If the issue is an issue of medicine, all you need do is show that this person has a license to practice medicine. In fact, in many jurisdictions a license is not necessary — that the witness is a graduate of a medical school will suffice. That he has not yet practiced, that he's yet to win a Nobel Prize in medicine, goes to the *weight* of his opinions, not to the competence of the testimony, and the weight of his opinions is not for the judge to worry about.

An expert does not need a Ph.D. in automotive mechanics from M.I.T. in order to testify on how the braking system of an automobile operates. A mechanic from the gas station down the road that has been doing this kind of work for thirty years will be allowed to give his opinion. Whether the jury buys the opinion is a different story. But it is almost impossible to fail to persuade the judge to allow the witness to give his opinion, which perhaps is why lawyers don't work very hard at it. They sleepwalk their way through.

Talking to the judge, however, is only a part of what's going on. Simultaneously, you are talking to the jury, something like, "Ladies and gentlemen, listen to this expert's credentials. Have you ever heard anything so impressive in your life?"

By the end of the case you will be arguing to the jury that it ought to *accept* your expert's opinion. Never forget that the one thing the jury cannot become is a physician or an economist or an engineer. They cannot master the substance of the discipline involved. They have got to assess credibility by using other things accessible to them, such as qualifications.

There is no one right way to do it, obviously. Everything depends upon the expert, the feel of the courtroom, the judge, the opponent. Generally, when the expert's credentials are impressive, you would want to build them up carefully and end at a high point. Let's suppose you have a Nobel Prize winner. You might begin with the high school where he began, and then have him talk about coming to the United States and learning English before he could go to work as a biochemist, and have him tell of all those years of long nights in the laboratory, working, working, cranking, cranking, publishing, publishing. And then:

"Have you received any professional recognition from your colleagues in the field of medicine?"

"Oh, well — ."

"Come on, Doctor Elko."

"Well, I guess so. A couple of years ago, I won the Nobel Prize."

Of course that's the point at which to end your qualifying, because you've come to the climax. Sometimes it's nice to wrap it up in a pink ribbon. It draws the line to show that the first part of the direct is over. You won't do it with every case, but sometimes you might consider it.

Turning to the judge, after Dr. Elko has announced that he won the Nobel Prize a few years ago, you say to the judge something like, "Your Honor, I ask the court to declare Dr. Elko an expert in the field of physiology."

All you're doing is saying to the judge, "Your Honor, with respect to that first thing that's going on, whether the expert can give his opinion, have I done it? Of course you've done it, so the judge says, "Yes." And the jury hears it as the judge certifying that your expert is an expert. The judge's authority begins to be associated with your expert's authority. Since the judge is the ultimate figure in the courtroom, it's a very nice phenomenon to have working for you.

The other side, of course, doesn't want the jury to hear about those credentials, assuming that the credentials are of any substance. As the opponent, what can you do to keep that from the jury? The instant Dr. Elko's name is called, you say, "Judge, let's save time. There's no need to spend a half hour reviewing Dr. Elko's credentials. I am perfectly prepared here and now to stipulate that Dr. Elko is an expert and entitled to give his opinion under the expert witness exception to the non-opinion rule." You would deliberately say it in jargon so that the jury does not know what you are stipulating. Now, as the proponent, what do you say? The opponent is only stipulating as to the expert's credentials, *not* to his credibility. The proponent would ask the adversary, "Are you prepared to stipulate the *credibility* of Dr. Elko?"

"Of course not."

"In that case, your Honor," say you, as the proponent, "I decline the concession, and I assert a right to put Dr. Elko's credentials before the jury."

The judge may well say, "Wait a minute. I run my court and when there's a chance to save time, I save time. I refuse to let you develop the credentials. You must accept the concession and proceed directly to the substantive part of the direct." This problem has been addressed by a federal court, which ruled that it is a reversible error for the trial judge to insist that the proponent accept the concession, and for the trial judge to refuse to allow the proponent to develop the credentials.[18] Unstated in the decision, but obviously implicit, is that the judge can put a reasonable limit on the time you spend on the credentials.

## §13.4 Opinion on an Ultimate Issue

Years ago, a day would come in the course of Evidence when the professor said, "Ladies and gentlemen, the cases are legion in all jurisdictions that even though everything else is proper for the receipt of the expert's opinion, if the opinion deals with an ultimate issue, the opinion is not admissible. You can't have an opinion on an ultimate issue."

An ultimate issue, the professor would admit, is difficult to define. "You know it when it comes along," the professor might say. "The only way I can characterize it is this: An ultimate issue is a factual question which, once answered, decides the case. It *is* the ball game. And if you look at it that way, you will recognize what it is." In the head-on collision case with which we started, the ultimate issue was, on which side of the road did the collision occur? Once you answer that question, the case is over, at least with respect to liability. There is nothing else to talk about.

---

[18]Murphy v. National R.R. Passenger Corp., 547 F.2d 816 (4th Cir. 1977).

The professor was right. You can't define it, but you can recognize it when you see it. The cases *were* legion in all jurisdictions holding that an opinion on an ultimate issue was inadmissible. But those cases are now almost universally regarded as outmoded. Perhaps there are jurisdictions in which the courts have not yet overruled those old cases, but if you raise the question, surely that will be the court's decision. The contemporary view is that an opinion on an ultimate issue is admissible.[19]

We will look at one federal and one New York example. The defendant in the federal case was charged with maintaining premises for the purpose of taking bets on horses without having paid the necessary tax.[20] The defendant concedes that the apartment in question was his apartment. He concedes that he did not pay the tax. The only issue is whether he was maintaining that apartment as a bookie joint. And on that issue, the prosecution's evidence consists of a few reels of tape, recordings of what was being said over the defendant's telephone lines for a period of some weeks. Those recordings were made pursuant to lawful wiretaps. The only difficulty is that the conversations are in a language totally opaque to the outsider. As far as the jury is concerned, these tapes might as well be *Oedipus Rex* in the original Attic Greek.

The government offers to call to the stand an expert, a revenue agent who spent his life running around the bookie joints. He has no personal knowledge of this case. He will testify solely as an expert to this effect: "I listened to these tapes, and I tell you that what you hear is the language of placing bets on horses." Once that opinion comes in, the case is over — the defendant loses. If you keep the expert testimony out, the defendant wins.

Defense counsel, remembering those old cases that the law school professor told him about, leaps up and says, "I object. It's an ultimate issue." And the judge says, "You're right. It's an ultimate issue, but your objection is overruled. An opinion on an ultimate issue is admissible."

---

[19]Fed. R. Evid. 704.
[20]United States v. Masson, 582 F.2d 961 (5th Cir. 1973).

Our New York example comes from the highest court of the state. The claim is that the product was designed in such a way as to be unsafe and that the state of the art at the time the product was designed permitted the design of a safer product. The state of the art is the ultimate issue.[21]

An expert, whose credentials are not being questioned, testified that the product was not as safely designed as the state of the art would allow. Twenty-five years ago, it would have been startling to suggest that such an issue was admissible. But the New York Court of Appeals — working not with the Federal Rules of Evidence, but with common law evidence — rules that the testimony is perfectly proper although it speaks to an ultimate issue.

The lawyer must distinguish always the expert who testifies on an ultimate issue, which is proper, from the expert who says to the jury, "The plaintiff should win this case," or "The defendant should win this case." That is *never* proper. No expert may ever tell the jury what the verdict *should* be[22] because the verdict involves an application of the law (as explained by the judge to the jury) to the facts. Applying the law is exclusively the responsibility of the jury; no expert is competent to testify to that.[23]

## §13.5 Certainty of the Expert Opinion

The courts have answered the question, "How certain must the expert be?," in a manner consistent with common sense and in a manner philosophers and scientists have told us to be the nature of the universe in which we live. To explore this

---

[21]Lancaster Side & Block Co. v. Northern Propane Gas Co., 75 A.D.2d 55, 427 N.Y.S.2d 1009 (1980).

[22]H. Liebenson, You, The Expert Witness 44-45 (1972).

[23]An unreported criminal case from Arkansas illustrates the point. The prosecutor called a deputy sheriff. The witness testified that as an expert criminal investigator, he investigated the allegations of the indictment and found them to be true. The judge overruled defense counsel's objection to the testimony, reasoning that an expert now can testify to an ultimate issue. The Supreme Court of Arkansas reversed the ensuing conviction, noting that the subject of the testimony was not an ultimate issue. Rather, this was the case of an expert telling the jury what the verdict should be.

question, we will refer to the physician as the expert witness. But everything we say about the physician is transferable to the economist, the engineer, or other expert witness.

Medicine is less than an exact science. Medicine may rest upon some exact sciences, such as anatomy and biochemistry, but when you put it all together, as any doctor will tell you in an honest moment, what you have is not quite a science but more nearly an art. It is highly probable that when you do certain things, other things will happen, but it is by no means 100 percent certain.

What does the law require as the requisite degree of certainty? Obviously, experts must have *some* degree of conviction in their opinions, so certainty has to be more than zero. On the other hand 100 percent certainty really results only from a definition. For example, two plus two equals four because we define four as the sum of two and two. In the world of litigation, you will never have an expert who can be 100 percent certain.

Just about every court that has been called upon to decide the question has held that the requisite degree of conviction must exceed fifty percent. The verbal equivalent of fifty percent would be, "Maybe yes, maybe no — it's about equally weighted on either side." But the certainty most courts seem to want is more like seventy-five percent, which is expressed in the word "probable" — more than possible (because anything is possible), but less than certain.

Recognizing this general rule, most practicing lawyers who interrogate experts, especially physicians, have a certain locution, a formula they recite to ask the expert for an opinion. In New York, in both the state and the federal court, the formula heard day in and day out when a physician is on the stand goes something like this: "Doctor, do you have an opinion that you can give us with a fair degree of medical certainty?" The lawyer, in effect, is saying to the judge, "I know the rules. This expert is going to give us an opinion in accordance with the rule that requires it to be about seventy-five percent on the scale."

The lawyer and the judge know all about the formula, but the lawyer must make sure, in preparing the expert, that the expert understands it as well. A nonlawyer might not distinguish carefully between "probable" and "possible," as was the case in

*Ward v. Kovaks.*[24] The case involved a young, attractive woman in her early twenties. She was earning a fairly good salary as an executive assistant in New York City, and she decided to take her two-week vacation at Fire Island, a swinger's paradise off the south shore of Long Island. She spent her two weeks on the beach at Fire Island swinging, and in the course of a swinging session, she cut her finger. It was more than you would put a bandage on and forget about, but it was not severe enough to require a trip to the hospital. She was treated by a local physician.

She woke up that night and the finger had swollen enormously; the hand was throbbing and the pain was murderous. She realized that she was in trouble and managed to get to a hospital, where she was diagnosed as having a fulminating streptococcus infection. That means, in layman's terms, that the streptococci had gotten out of control; the situation was life-endangering.

The hospital used heroic measures, controlled the infection, and ultimately cured her. However, she was left with a permanently disabled, terribly disfigured hand. She couldn't work at her job any more, and she claimed that her condition was due to the doctor's malpractice.

We're in court. The doctor says that he did not commit malpractice, and that this fulminating infection resulted because the woman's bloodstream was full of LSD. The defense calls as an expert witness a laboratory physician. He doesn't treat patients; he's a scientist, and he's been working on the effects of LSD on the body's system. He has not been properly prepared. He takes the stand and says, "In my opinion, though we're working on this, when you have LSD in the bloodstream in the quantity that the plaintiff did, your ability to resist bacterial invasion is substantially reduced. That's the reason for this fulminating infection: her own ingestion of LSD."

The plaintiff's lawyer senses that the doctor has not been prepared on the significance to lawyers of certain magic words. The cross-examination goes this way. "Really," he says, "Doctor, you're not sure, are you? No, of course you can't be sure."

---

[24]55 A.D.2d 391, 390 N.Y.S.2d 931 (1977).

"It's possible."

"Of course, it's possible." And he sits down, figuring as soon as the doctor leaves the stand he's going to move to strike.

On re-direct: "When it's possible, it's probable?"

"That's right."

Re-cross: "When you say it's probable, it's possible."

"That's right." Back and forth they go, each one feeding the magic word to the doctor and the doctor totally unaware there is a difference. The court concluded that the expert really meant to say *probable;* hence, the motion to strike the expert's testimony was properly denied. We learn from this that the requisite degree of conviction is *probability,* or seventy-five percent if you want to use numbers, but no particular formula is required. It's handy to have the formula. It saves a lot of trouble. But if you don't have the formula, what the court must do is look at the expert's testimony as a whole and in the context of the case and decide whether it was the fair intention of the expert to say *probable.*

## §13.6 Permissible Bases of Expert Testimony

The Federal Rules of Evidence — in response to the question, upon what may an expert rely? — give an answer that amounts to the most radical position taken in the entire codification. Yet the answer given by the Federal Rules is the law not only in jurisdictions following the rules but increasingly in non-federal-rule jurisdictions as well, including New York.

The common law's answer to the question — what we might call the background rule, which used to be followed in all jurisdictions — is that an expert's opinion had to rest upon data in the case.[25] The same thing can be said several different ways. Everything upon which the expert relies must be supported by evidence. Or, there must be enough proof from which a reasonable juror could find the fact to be so, with respect to everything upon which the expert relies. Or, if the expert says, "Here's my opinion, and I rest it upon A, B and C," A, B and

---

[25]3 Weinstein's Evidence ¶703[01] (1981).

C must be in evidence. If the expert says, "Here's my opinion, and I rest upon A, B, C, D, E and F," and the first three are in evidence, and the latter three are not in evidence, an objection to the opinion will be sustained.

The reasoning went like this: Ultimately, the expert's opinion goes to the jury because it will help them or (in jurisdictions that follow the New York rule on receipt of expert testimony) because it will be necessary to them.[26] Therefore, the opinion must rest exclusively upon the evidence in the case, because it is the evidence in the case that the jury is trying to understand. If the opinion of the expert goes beyond the evidence in the case, the opinion is immaterial. It has nothing to do with the jury's work, so we don't let the jury hear it.

A case from New York, before that state joined the march toward the modern rule, shows how the common law rule worked.[27] The expert witness in the case was a physician, a general practitioner; the issue was the condition known as fibrosis. The doctor testifies that he examined the elderly plaintiff. "One of the things I did," he says, "was to feel the back of her neck, and the neck muscles were in spasms." That's Fact A, evidence that the muscles were in spasms. "Next, I looked down her throat and I saw red patches." There's Fact B.

"I found nothing else remarkable. And on the basis of A and B, I could not arrive at a diagnosis. So what I did was send her out to three specialists, a neurologist for a nerve workup, a hemotologist for blood chemistry work and a roentgenologist, for certain X-rays. They did their work and sent me their reports. After I read their reports, I was able to arrive at a diagnosis."

Now, the proponent is going to ask what his diagnosis is. This diagnosis rests upon five pieces of data: A, spastic muscles, in evidence; B, red patches, in evidence; and C, what the neurologist found, D, what the hematologist found, and E, what the roentgenologist found, not in evidence. Those specialists have not testified, and their reports are plainly hearsay.

"Objection," says the opponent, and the objection is

---

[26]See §13.1.
[27]Sirico v. Cotto, 324 N.Y.S.2d 483 (N.Y. City Civ. Ct. 1971).

sustained. The expert cannot give his opinion because three-fifths of the basis of the opinion is not in evidence.

A considerable body of scholarly criticism of that rule developed. The critics argued, first that the rule is very expensive. The proponent who wants to prove that general practitioner's diagnosis is going to have to call not only the general practitioner but the three specialists. Moreover, should not the rule of evidence be congruent with the practice of the discipline represented by the witness? In practicing medicine, after all, it is taken for granted that the general practitioner receives and relies upon the reports of the specialists.

The critics carried the day, and the second sentence of Rule 703 of the Federal Rules of Evidence states: "If of a type reasonably relied upon by experts in the particular field in forming opinions or inferences upon the subject, the facts or data need not be admissible in evidence."

Reasonable is the word and that is the only limit or standard that we have. It is understood to be a statement of two factors. First, is it customary in the expert's field to rely on this information? If it is customary, then the judge has a check or balance function — the judge has to decide that the "custom" is a reasonable one.

Q. Doctor, did you send the patient out to the neurologist, the hematologist, the roentgenologist?

A. Yes.

We assume they're not going to testify.

Q. Doctor, after reading their reports and taking into account the two findings you made upon clinical examination, were you able to arrive at a diagnosis?

A. Yes.

Then you would establish with the doctor that it is customary in the field of medicine for the general practitioner or the family doctor to rely upon the reports received from specialists. The judge would rule that it is reasonable for the general practitioner to follow that custom. And the doctor would give his opinion, even though three-fifths of the material upon which the opinion rests is not in evidence.

New York's highest court adoped this rule by fiat. The ruling came in a criminal case. The defense is insanity; it is now rebuttal. The prosecution calls a psychiatrist whose opinion is that the defendant was sane at the time in question.

"Dr. Psychiatrist, upon what do you rely?"

He says, "I rely on A in evidence, B in evidence, and C in evidence." But the doctor also says: "I also rely upon a statement I was given by the defendant's girlfriend about their intimate relation." This statement is not in evidence and is unknown to the jury. Although the girlfriend had testified about a different phase of the case, she had not been asked anything about the statement or about her personal relations with the defendant.

The statement itself cannot go into evidence. Nevertheless, the New York Court of Appeals holds that the psychiatrist's opinion is admissible.[28] Since the rule to be followed in the second sentence of Federal Rule of Evidence 703 makes a lot of sense, the court says, it is adopted for New York. Granted, the girlfriend's statement was not in evidence and was unknown to the jury, but it is customary for psychiatrists to rely upon such statements about people's personal affairs. The court saw nothing unreasonable about it; therefore, the expert's opinion was admissible.[29]

---

[28]People v. Sugden, 35 N.Y.2d 453, 456, 323 N.E.2d 169, 171, 363 N.Y.S.2d 923, 925 (1974).

[29]How far will a judge let the proponent of the expert witness go? In a private antitrust suit brought in federal court, the plaintiff claimed that the defendants monopolized the business of selling golfing equipment at retail. The plaintiff called an economist to testify that, in his opinion, there was a monopoly in this line of commerce. The following came out on cross-examination:

Q. Mr. Economist, on what do you rely?
A. Well, I rely principally upon what I was told by somebody I met at a cocktail party. I don't know his name. But I met him at the cocktail party, and he said he's a retailer in the field and he told me about the way things were. And that is what I relied upon.

That is over the line, the judge said — it is neither customary nor reasonable.

## §13.7 Eliciting the Expert's Opinion

The approach of Rule 703 of the Federal Rules of Evidence, opening the door to opinions resting upon things not in evidence, is particularly troublesome because of the tack taken by Rule 705. Rule 705 addresses the traditional method of eliciting expert opinion, the hypothetical question.

The problem of eliciting the expert's opinion first presented itself to common law lawyers and common law judges when the universally applied rule was that the opinion had to rest entirely upon data supported by evidence. The mechanical problem was how to elicit the opinion in a way that the judge and the opponent could be certain that everything was supported by evidence in the record. The resolution of that mechanical problem was the hypothetical question, used in all but the rare case in which an expert had personal knowledge of the underlying facts.

Consider again Dr. Elko, our Nobel Prize-winning expert on spleens. He has a Ph.D. in chemistry but is not a medical doctor. "Dr. Elko, I'm going to ask you to assume certain things. A little boy, eight years old, as a result of being hit by a car at a school crossing is taken to the hospital." Is there evidence of that? Yes.

"At the hospital, he is diagnosed as having a ruptured spleen. The surgeon removes the spleen in an uneventful splenectomy." Is there evidence? Yes.

"The little boy makes an eventful recovery except for a small scar of no cosmetic significance. He is now fine; of course, he has no spleen." Is there evidence of that? Yes.

"Doctor, assuming those to be the facts, do you have an opinion which you can give us with a reasonable degree of physiological certainty as to the significance to that little boy of the fact that he no longer has a spleen?"

"Yes."

"What is that opinion?"

And you're in business. Of course, no lawyer worth his salt would dream of asking Dr. Elko that hypothetical in such a pedestrian manner. The questions above are satisfactory for the record, but they do nothing for the jury. Every lawyer of any experience knows that the hypothetical question is a wonderful way of summing up to the jury without really summing up. An effective personal injury lawyer would spend at least half an hour asking that hypothetical question.

There is no requirement that everything in the hypothetical be relevant to the opinion so long as, under the old rule, everything is supported by evidence. "Doctor, I'm going to ask you to assume certain facts. When Johnny got up that morning, Doctor, the sun was out, birds were chirping in the trees. Doctor, he came down to the kitchen at 7:35; you know what he said to his mother, Doctor? 'What's for breakfast.' "

And on and on. By the time the hypothetical is over, the jury is weeping, and we're weeping too.

The scholar says, "This is not the purpose the hypothetical was intended to serve. We don't want jurors weeping in the jury box." Because hypothetical questions were asked in ways that struck many scholars as undignified, a movement arose some years ago to do away with them. The movement bore fruit, which can be observed in Rule 705, which reads, "The expert may testify in terms of opinion or inference and give his reasons therefor without prior disclosure of the underlying facts or data . . . . "

The rule does not do away with the hypothetical question for good and all, but it does permit the proponent to elicit the expert's opinion on direct examination without asking a hypothetical question. Advocates may still ask hypothetical questions if they wish to, but they need not. After qualifying the expert, the lawyer may simply say, "Now, Doctor, give us your opinion," without any preliminary specification of the facts upon which the opinion is based. On cross-examination, the opponent may ask questions designed to explore, illuminate, and identify the facts upon which the opinion is based.[30]

The combination of Rules 703 and 705 requires the cross-examiner to walk through a mine field. Rule 705 eliminates the need for a hypothetical question. The proponent can put the expert physician on the stand, qualify him, and ask, "Doctor, what

---

[30]The second sentence of Rule 705 states: "The expert may in any event be required to disclose the underlying facts or data on cross-examination."

is your opinion? What is the diagnosis?" "Well, my diagnosis is thus and so." The proponent sits down. The opponent can use cross-examination to question the data upon which the physician relies, but the opponent does not know what those data are, so he is treading his way through a mine field. And even if some of the data are unsupported by evidence, that makes no difference under Rule 703, so long as they are the kind of data upon which experts in the field reasonably rely. For someone brought up in the tradition of the adversarial trial, in which everything introduced by one side is subject to cross-examination by the other side, this is very unsettling.[31]

---

[31]We return to the problem of cross-examining the expert in §15.6.

# CHAPTER 14

# Objections

## §14.1 Preconditions

The usual occasion for an objection is the other side's violation of some rule of evidence. The violation in itself, however, is a wholly insufficient reason to object. We are not in court to vindicate the law of evidence. Good trial lawyers will object only if the violation of the rule actually hurts them. When it does not hurt — and most of the time, it does not — there is simply no point in objecting. That is why a trial between two good lawyers goes by so quickly and quietly. Neither lawyer objects without good reason, and so there are very few objections.

Common sense suggests a third precondition. We should not make an objection unless we are reasonably confident that the judge will sustain it. The objection, after all, draws the jury's attention to the question. It tells them that the answer will be something special. If the objection is overruled, we shall only have emphasized the opponent's evidence, and that is to our disadvantage. If the objection to a question is sustained, on the other hand, most jurors will not speculate on what the answer would have been. We must therefore try to predict the judge's ruling in each instance. Doing so calls for a good knowledge of the law of evidence; but even that is rarely enough, as no two judges will rule on every objection in the same way. We shall also need to tap the grapevine for information about the inclinations of our own particular judge.

## §14.2 General and Specific Objections

There are two distinct types of objections, both of which have been part of the law for a long time. The first is a general objection, "general" because it does not indicate to the judge the ground upon which the objection is made. "I object!" "Objection, Your Honor!" An inarticulate noise from the throat may sometimes be taken as a general objection, as may the mere act of coming to one's feet. The second type is the specific objection. In however artless a manner, it tells the judge the ground of the objection. "I object — hearsay!" "It gives an opinion." "He's leading, Your Honor."

The law prefers specific objections over general objections. Federal Rule of Evidence 103 tells us that a general objection will not preserve the point for appeal,[1] which amounts to saying that the judge is free to ignore it. A general objection, then, is just about the same as no objection at all.

All the same, from the viewpoint of a working trial lawyer, a general objection can still be very useful. Suppose, for example, that the other side has done something wrong. The harpoon is in, and it hurts. We know the ground of the objection. "Objection!" we say, and we take a deep breath to state the ground. But before we can get it out, the judge says, "Sustained!" When that happens, we sit down at once. We do not say another word. If we give the ground of the objection after the judge has sustained, the judge will take it as our saying that he did something

---

[1]Fed. R. Evid. 103(a) states:

"Error may not be predicated upon a ruling which admits or excludes evidence unless a substantial right of the party is affected, and

"(1) *Objection.* In case the ruling is one admitting evidence, a timely objection or motion to strike appears of record, stating the specific ground of objection, if the specific ground was not apparent from the context . . . ."

right. Judges do not like lawyers telling them that. And, because all judges like to think that they have an elfin sense of humor, it will come out something like this:

Q. What happened then?
A. Well, my wife said to me . . .
Counsel: Objection!
The Court: Sustained.
Counsel: Right, Your Honor. That's hearsay.
The Court: Oh. On that ground, overruled.

That is not the only way to say too much. Many lawyers will object to a question, state the ground, and immediately launch into an argument why the question is improper. Such arguments should not usually be necessary, because we will already have raised the tough issues in the motion *in limine*.[2] When the arguments are necessary, they should be made out of the jury's hearing.

No one can carry the law of evidence in front of his mind all of the time, but the computer between our ears has it all stored away. With experience, we develop a litigator's ear. It detects discords, rather like a musician's ear does. When the other side does something wrong, an alarm goes off. But sometimes the ground of the objection is not on the tip of the tongue. The harpoon is in, and it hurts. We are on our feet saying, "Objection!" We know that there is a perfectly valid ground for the objection, but it takes us a few seconds to figure out what that ground is. The general objection gives us those few seconds. The judge looks up; he directs us to make it a specific objection; and during that time the wheels spin. It sounds something like this:

Q. What happened then?
A. Well, my wife said to me . . .
Counsel: Objection!

---

[2]See §4.5.

The Court: On what ground?

Counsel: Well, Your Honor, we all . . . Ah, it's hearsay, right?

The Court: Sustained.

But sometimes, the wheels spin and nothing comes out.

Q. What happened then?

A. Well, my wife said to me . . .

Counsel: Objection!

The Court: On what ground?

Counsel: Yes, Your Honor. Well, we all know . . .

The Court: Counselor, didn't you hear me? What's the ground of your objection?

It happens to all of us. One possibility is to deal with the judge as we would with the jury: simply to tell the truth. It is amazing what the truth can accomplish.

Q. What happened then?

A. Well, my wife said to me . . .

Counsel: Objection!

The Court: On what ground?

Counsel: Ah . . . Your Honor, I don't know.

The Court: Well, I do! Sustained!

That will work only once in a trial. But the problem may come up more often. For the second and subsequent occasions, we need a set of locutions: statements that sound like the ground of an objection, but really are not. If we say these with enough conviction, they will often carry the judge. Every lawyer must develop his or her own repertoire, and over time they become cherished tools in the kit. One example here will suffice.

Q. What happened then?

A. Well, my wife said to me . . .

Counsel: Objection!

The Court: On what ground?

Counsel: Your Honor, he can't do that!

The Court: Right! Sustained.

## §14.3 Purposes of Objections

The authorities tell us that objections are to serve three purposes. First, objections keep improper evidence from the jury. Second, they give the trial judge an opportunity to correct any error. Third, they preserve the point for appeal.

In addition to those in the authorities, there are four other purposes that objections can serve. Two of them are always perfectly proper. One, in my own view, is always unethical; we take it up last. The remaining purpose edges close to the boundaries of professional responsibility. There are no fixed rules telling us whether it is ethical, that being something for every lawyer to decide in view of the particular circumstances. Litigation, like basketball, is not in theory a body contact sport. But in basketball, when we put ten giants on a small floor and have them run down that floor at thirty miles per hour to stop short under a basket, there is bound to be some contact with elbows and knees. It is unavoidable. Some of that happens in the courtroom as well, and it complicates the ethical decisions.

The objection of questionable propriety is one made to interrupt the opponent. The trial is almost over, let us say. We have done a good job, to be sure, but the other lawyer has been superb. Now he is summing up, and his summation has the jury hypnotized. He has them in the palm of his hand. Before our eyes, we see our case going out the window. We can sit back and let it happen, or we can interrupt — not because he has done something wrong, but only to break the spell and upset his rhythm. Whether or not to do that is an ethical decision. But if we decide to do it, we must do it so that it works. There is an old saying: If you are going to shoot at a king, you must kill him. It does no good merely to say, "Objection." He will not miss a beat. Instead we must make a speech, as loudly and vigorously as we can. What we say in the speech makes no difference at all.

> Objection! Your Honor, didn't we learn in law school —
> I know I learned in law school, and I'm sure Mr. Smith
> learned in law school — didn't you, Mr. Smith, didn't you
> learn it in law school? Your Honor, even Mr. Smith must
> have learned in law school that . . .

And on we go, filling time that way, until the judge finally breaks in. "What are you talking about? Sit down! Whatever you're saying, it's overruled!"

We say, "Thank you, Your Honor," and we sit down. The opponent turns back to the jury. "Where was I?" he says — exactly what we wanted him to say.

The objection is within the letter of the rules; it is not something we can be disbarred for doing. Many lawyers nonetheless feel that the tactic hits below the belt, and they choose never to use it. Again, that must be an individual decision based upon the particular circumstances.

Even lawyers who forgo the tactic will want to guard against its being used against them. The best defensive method is one borrowed from people in the theater. It is not completely reliable, but it works most of the time. Theater people use it when a play is interrupted — for example, when a member of the audience faints or becomes sick. Occasionally someone in the audience has a heart attack and dies right there in his seat. An actor or actress with any professional pride will try to hold the audience, so that even though the play must pause, it can continue where it left off after the victim has been carried away.

It is we, now, who are summing up to the jury. We have them hypnotized; they are in the palm of our hand. The other lawyer jumps up. He starts to rant and rave. And this is what we learn from the theater people: the instant he begins to talk, we freeze. We do not move. We do not even move our eyes. If we are looking at Juror No. 7 at the moment of interruption, we keep our eyes on him. The other lawyer raves on, hoping that we will protest. He wants us to say, "Your Honor, this is an outrage! I'm going to the bar association with this!" — because that will break the spell we have cast over the jury. But we do not respond. We hold the freeze and remain silent. When the judge finally sits him down, we do not acknowledge the interruption in any way. We do not say, "Let me see; where was I?" or, "Before I was so outrageously interrupted . . ." We just pick it up where we left off, or as nearly as we can remember, and at the same emotional level. Usually that will work to hold the jury.

One purpose of objections that is always permissible is to speak with the judge. Recall our example of a motion *in limine*, asking for an advance ruling on whether a particular witness could testify, "I didn't see the light, but my wife cried out, 'My God, the light is red!' " We change the facts a little; this time it is the other side who is calling that witness. The judge, let us say, declined to rule in advance. And now the witness is on the stand. It is almost five o'clock in the afternoon. The carbon dioxide level is approaching the lethal. The judge is not asleep on the bench — the judge is never asleep on the bench — but neither is the judge firing on all cylinders.

Q. Did you get into the car?
A. Yes.
Q. Did anybody get in with you?
A. Yes.
Q. Who was that?
A. My wife.

About three questions from now, the crucial question will come: "What color was the light?" We know it; the other side knows it; but the judge does not know it. If he sustains the objection, as we hope, it can still happen in either of two ways. We want it to sound like this:

Q. What color was the light?
Counsel: Objection!
The Court: Sustained!

But if the judge is slow in responding, it will come out this way instead:

Q. What color was the light?
Counsel: Objection!
A. My wife said the light was red.
The Court: Sustained.

We want the objection to be sustained quickly, before the witness answers. And so we want the judge to pay attention. To alert him, we make an objection — not for a ruling, but simply to bring the judge awake. Most jurisdictions have a formula for it. In New York, for example, it sounds like this:

Q. Did you get into the car?
A. Yes.
Q. Did anybody get it with you?
A. Yes.
Q. Who was that?
A. My wife.
Counsel: Objection, Your Honor. We're on dangerous ground here.

It is a tactful way of saying, "Pay attention, Judge. We're coming up to that matter raised by the motion *in limine*. Kindly be on top of it, so you can make your ruling on the beat." The judge's ruling on this objection will always be the same: "Thank you, Counselor." There is no ethical problem at all.

Sometimes we are a little slow at getting an objection out; or the judge is slow in ruling; or the question sounds fine, but when the answer comes, it is for some reason inadmissible. Whatever the cause, the jury hears the answer before the objection is sustained. We must then make a motion to strike the testimony, and couple it with a request that the judge instruct the jury to disregard the answer. The jury will still remember what they heard. But at the very least, the motion to strike will prevent the opponent from referring to that testimony in the summation.

The third purpose of objections that we consider here is to signal something to the witness. Ordinarily it too is perfectly ethical. For example, the witness has begun to testify to things that he sincerely believes to be true, but which he did not himself observe. We make our objection to the judge, but it is really for the witness's ears: "Objection, Your Honor. The witness is not telling us what he himself saw. He is telling us what he believes is true, based upon what he saw." The ruling is unimportant. All that matters is that the witness hear the objection.

The final kind of objection is sometimes made, but I can conceive of no situation in which it would be ethical. It is an objection for the purpose of talking to the jury, in order to tell them something that they are not entitled to know. No reputable lawyer will ever have occasion to use it.

# CHAPTER 15

# Cross-Examination: The Technology and the Art

## §15.1 The Scope of Cross-Examination

Suppose that a witness is testifying — any kind of witness in any kind of case. On direct examination, the witness testifies to facts *A*, *B*, and *C*. Direct examination ends. Then comes cross-examination. The cross-examiner may always go into facts *A*, *B*, and *C*, the subject matter of the direct examination. May the cross-examination go beyond facts *A*, *B*, and *C*? There are two possibilities.

Under the first possibility, assuming that the witness is competent and that the new facts are material, the cross-examiner may go beyond facts *A*, *B*, and *C* to facts *X*, *Y*, and *Z*. This is called the wide-open rule, or sometimes the English rule, because our cousins across the water try cases in accordance with it. A small minority of the American states follow it as well.

The other possibility: When the witness has testified on direct examination to facts *A*, *B*, and *C*, then that is the limit of the scope of the cross-examination. The witness may be competent to testify to facts *X*, *Y*, and *Z*, and those facts may be material to the case,

---

Portions of this chapter are drawn from "The Art of Cross-Examination," by Irving Younger, a monograph published by the American Bar Association Section of Litigation. © 1976 American Bar Association. Used with permission.

but the cross-examiner will have to call the witness as part of his own case, and elicit X, Y, and Z on direct examination. This is the restrictive rule, sometimes called the American rule to distinguish it from the English rule. This is the rule followed in a large majority of the American state courts, and in the federal courts as well.[1]

The American rule notwithstanding, a lawyer who cross-examines on the topics gone into on direct examination will frequently manage to go beyond those topics. One way is simply to do it. One may, within the bounds of responsibility, go on to X, Y, and Z, leaving it to the adversary to raise the objection. The form of the objection: that the examination is beyond the proper scope of cross, because it exceeds the scope of the direct.

Suppose that the judge sustains the objection. You might then say something like this: "Your Honor, even though in this jurisdiction we follow the prevailing American rule, the restrictive rule, would Your Honor exercise your discretion and permit me to go on to facts X, Y, and Z?" No appellate court will fault the judge for doing so. Alternatively, you might say, "Your Honor, I realize I have exceeded A, B, and C, and that I'm going on to X, Y, and Z. I could elicit facts X, Y, and Z by calling this man back to the witness stand as my witness the day after tomorrow. But why inconvenience the witness? Your Honor, for these purposes, let's assume that I, not my adversary, called him to the stand. He is my witness; it is direct examination."

Observe the sequence. We have direct examination on A, B, and C; cross on A, B, and C. Now the cross-examiner goes on to X, Y, and Z. The witness is his, meaning that this is now direct examination. In consequence, no leading questions are allowed.[2] The proponent comes back with re-direct on A, B, and C, but cross on X, Y, and Z. After that, there is re-cross on A, B, and C, and re-direct on X, Y, and Z. It is just a matter of plaiting the braid, not difficult if it is worked through slowly and carefully.

---

[1]"Cross-examination should be limited to the subject matter of the direct examination and matters affecting the credibility of the witness. The court may, in the exercise of discretion, permit inquiry into additional matters as if on direct examination." Fed. R. Evid. 611(b).

[2]See §11.2.

The chief consequence of where one stands in the sequence, for each fact, has to do with the form of the questions allowed: With exceptions, there may be no leading questions on direct or re-direct. On cross or re-cross, leading questions are freely permitted.

## §15.2 Modes of Impeachment: The First Group

Cross-examination is merely the name for one stage of a witness's testimony: his examination by any lawyer other than the one who called him. It follows that cross-examination need not always be unfriendly. To the contrary, a lawyer in a civil case may find himself cross-examining his own client. Suppose, for example, that we represent the defendant. The plaintiff's lawyer calls our client to the stand. The plaintiff's lawyer is then the proponent of our client, and we are the opponent.[3] When we ask the client questions, it will be thus be cross-examination, though it will obviously be friendly. Cross-examination can also be neutral in tone. The other side might call a witness who has no stake in the controversy one way or the other. We too were planning to call that witness. If the other side does not bring out all of the facts on direct examination, we might conduct a cross-examination in order to fill the gaps.

Those are the exceptions, to be sure. Cross-examination is much more often destructive in purpose. On cross-examination we are usually trying to impeach or discredit the witness — to persuade the jury that the witness is not worth believing.

All of the miscellaneous rules dealing with cross-examination to impeach or discredit a witness coalesce into nine categories. Not every jurisdiction permits all nine categories, and, as a matter of tactics, a lawyer will rarely use all of them, but the nine pigeonholes are exhaustive. They represent the universe of possible impeachment. For the sake of convenience, these pigeonholes may be divided into three subclasses. We will consider them as a group of four, then a second group of four, and finally, by itself, the ninth.

---

[3]See §11.1.

Although they may not think in these terms, trial lawyers use the first four modes of impeachment every single time they are in court. They learned about these first four modes of impeachment, perhaps abstractly and imperfectly, in an evidence course in law school. They are based on the elements of competence — the eligibility of a human being to take the witness stand.

What does it take for a human being to take the witness stand today? We put aside incompetence by reason of status, the dead man's statutes, spousal incompetence, the incompetence of a juror to testify in that very trial;[4] we need to consider the great mass of proposed witnesses.

Four elements must be present.[5] The first requirement of competence is that the person take the oath or some substitute for the oath. "I swear to tell the truth," or "I affirm to tell the truth," or "I promise to tell the truth," or "As one grandfather to another, Your Honor, I will tell the truth," or something like that. If he says that he will not take the oath or some substitute for the oath, he is not competent. He may go to jail for contempt, but he may not take the stand to testify.

What is the second requirement? You ask, "What did you see or hear or smell or touch or taste?" The witness must have perceived — through one or more of his five senses — something which relates to the transaction that forms the subject matter of the lawsuit. The second requirement is perception. We call the witness to the stand. He takes the oath. "Sir, did you see the accident?" "No, I did not." "Where were you?" "I was in Europe." What happens now? "Well," the judge says, "thank you for your assistance; you may go home, sir." He is an incompetent witness; he perceived nothing.

The third element of competence requires that we move from time past — when the transaction that forms the subject matter of this lawsuit occurred — to time present in the courtroom. In other words, we must establish memory, recollection; we must bridge the temporal gap. The witness must remember something of what he perceived concerning the transaction that is the sub-

---

[4]See §§8.2-8.7.
[5]See §8.8.

ject matter of the lawsuit. We have satisfied two requirements: The witness took the oath, and the witness saw the accident. "What do you remember seeing?" "Nothing." "Go home. You are incompetent." He has failed to satisfy the third requirement.

Finally, the witness must satisfy a fourth requirement. The witness must be able to get across to the jury or the judge the substance of what he perceived and now remembers about the transaction in question. The witness must be able to communicate in some rational fashion what he remembers perceiving — typically, in the English language, or in a foreign language if that is necessary. He can write it out if he is unable to speak, or he can use the international sign language. The only requirement is that the mode of communication be rational.

**Oath.** At trial, the most frequently raised question of competence concerns the capacity of a witness to take the oath. Almost every trial lawyer has been involved in a trial in which a child has been called to the witness stand — an eight-year-old, a nine-year-old, a ten-year-old. What does the lawyer do? If tactically appropriate, he raises a question concerning the competence of the witness. Mechanically, the child can raise his or her right hand and say, "Yes, I swear." To judge the witness's competence, however, we must look more deeply into the question; it is necessary to determine whether the witness has sufficient maturity to understand the nature and significance of the oath. The judge must make this determination because competence is a question of law. Generally, the judge will conduct a voir dire, usually in the robing room. Sometimes, the judge will voir dire the witness in open court, but probably not in the presence of the jury, if there is a jury. The judge will say: "Sonny, how old are you?" "Eight, sir." "Do you go to Sunday School?" "Yes, sir." "You know what happens if you tell a lie?" The judge then decides whether this witness has sufficient maturity to understand the nature and significance of the oath. And that is an either/or proposition. The witness knowingly can take the oath or he cannot. If the former, the witness is competent, with respect to that first element; if the latter, the witness is incompetent.

The competence of a witness is rarely challenged on grounds of perception, recollection, or communication. If a witness's competence were challenged on these grounds, however, the trial judge would decide the question of competence by the same procedures used to test a witness's capacity to take the oath.

We all know that no human being perceives everything, that no human being remembers everything, and that few human beings are supremely eloquent. If a question is raised concerning the competence of a witness, the judge will take out his handy judicial thermometer, calibrated from zero to 100, and he will take the witness's temperature with respect to perception, recollection, or communication. No one will score 100. Occasionally, a witness will score zero. If a witness scores zero, the judge will say, "You are incompetent: You perceived nothing, you remembered nothing, or you can communicate nothing. Go home." That is very rare.

Usually, when there is a bona fide question of competence, the thermometer reading will be low, but more than zero. Of course, we are quantifying what cannot be quantified. To make it easy, we will assume that the question raised concerns the degree to which the witness remembers. The judge uses his handy thermometer and gets a reading of five on a scale of 100. If the witness gets any perceptible reading on the thermometer, anything more than zero, no matter how low, the court will usually conclude that the witness is competent. The witness may testify; the court will leave it to the cross-examiner to bring out the extent to which the witness did not perceive, does not remember, or cannot communicate.

When the judge rules that the witness may testify, the subject of the inquiry changes from competence, a question of law, to credibility, a question of fact for the jury to decide. Although the judge has ruled that the witness is competent, the jury is free to conclude that a witness who rates only five out of 100 on the memory scale should not be believed and that his testimony is not worth crediting. The jury is perfectly free to reject that testimony in its entirety. In doing so, the jury is not overruling the judge; it is simply deciding a different question.

We have now established the basis for the first four categories of impeachment. We take the four elements of competence, turn them around, and use them destructively. Tactically, of course, we may not want to use some, or all, of them. We are working out a checklist of all the possibilities; these are the first four. Take the oath, for instance, and turn it around. Cross-examination: "Sir, you just took an oath to tell the truth?" "Yes." "When was the last time you went to church or synagogue?" Is that the kind of cross-examination that you need to know about and will want to use? Well, yes and no. It is included because it is the first item on the checklist. Will you ever use such a question on cross-examination? Not if you are in your right mind, because it is greasy kid's stuff. You may have used it when you were a youngster at the bar. But nowadays you never would; it is embarrassing. If that is the only kind of question you have to ask on cross-examination, you will not ask it.

As a matter of fact, Rule 610 of the Federal Rules of Evidence prohibits you from impeaching a witness by asking questions about religious belief or practice. This first pigeonhole is not available in the federal courts. The drafters of the Federal Rules excluded it because it is greasy kid's stuff. You should not do it, so they put it right in the rule.

**Perception.** Perception, the second requirement of competence, provides the second pigeonhole of impeachment. A witness's competence could be challenged when he is sworn, but the judge will find the witness competent if the question is raised at that stage. Consequently, we wait for cross-examination. Assume that the witness has testified on direct examination that he saw the automobile accident and that it took place in front of the Cloisters in Fort Tryon Park in Upper Manhattan. On cross-examination: "Mr. Witness, where were you when the accident occurred?" "I was at Thirty-Fourth Street and Fifth Avenue."

What should the cross-examiner do now? Of course, he should stop and sit down. It may be difficult for a trial lawyer of any age to overcome his congenital inability to stop, sit down, and be quiet, but he must attempt to do so. The witness has testified that he saw an accident at the northern tip of the island when he was standing three miles to the south.

The cross-examiner should stop and argue in summation that the witness was three miles away. What will the average trial lawyer do? He will be unable to overcome the temptation; he will go on to the next question: "Then how could you see the accident if you were three miles away?" And every time he fails and succumbs to the temptation, the answer to the question will be: "Well, I was on top of the Empire State Building with high-powered binoculars, and I saw it through the binoculars."

**Recollection.** The third requirement of competence — recollection or memory — provides a very useful mode of impeachment. All experienced trial lawyers will have used it, but perhaps without knowing the right label for what they were doing. An example from the criminal field will demonstrate the use of recollection impeachment.

We will assume that you are a defense lawyer in the *Rosenberg* case; what was alleged was a conspiracy to steal the secret of the atom bomb and send it behind the Kremlin wall. One of the overt acts charged in the Rosenberg indictment was that one of the conspirators registered at the Waldorf-Astoria Hotel in New York City on a particular day.

The prosecutor calls a witness for direct examination. "Who are you, sir?" "I'm the desk clerk at the Waldorf-Astoria." "Were you on duty on January 1, 1949?" "Yes." And now we start to play the game. What does the prosecutor say? He says: "Mr. Witness, look around this courtroom and tell us, yes or no, whether you see in court somebody who registered on that day."

First the witness takes off his glasses and spends thirty seconds polishing them. The tension builds. Now the witness starts. He begins with the judge. No, it is not the judge. Then he starts with the people in the jury box, runs right down the line, and surveys all twelve of them. No, it is none of the jurors. He starts working across those chairs in the well of the court. Finally, the witness gets up to that special chair where the defendant sits, and he says. "Ah! That's the person I registered that day." The prosecutor sits down; he has proved that devastating overt act.

As the defense lawyer, you may use the three modes of impeachment we have developed. Will you impeach by asking him when he last went to church? Of course not. Are you going to impeach by asking him whether he really saw the person register? No, he is not lying. So, how might you cross-examine?

Q. The Waldorf-Astoria is a big hotel, isn't it?

A. Yes.

Q. How long had you been a desk clerk before the day in question?

A. Nine years.

Q. How many days a week do you work?

A. Five.

Q. How many weeks a year?

A. Forty-eight.

Q. And how many people a day do you register?

A. About two hundred and fifty.

Q. So, in the nine years before this date, by my arithmetic, you had registered 1,212,917 people? Correct?

A. Correct.

Q. Now, have you been working since then?

A. Yes.

Q. Right up until today?

A. Yes.

Q. So in the time since, you have registered another 2,412,813, correct?

A. Correct.

And now what do you do? Stop. Sit down. And what will you argue in summation? He cannot possibly remember one person out of four million.

Will you stop? No. Will you sit down? No. Instead, you will ask the next question: "Then, how come, Mr. Bigshot, you can remember this one person out of four million?" And every time you ask that question, you will get the answer: "Well, he walked up to me, and he put a gun to my head, and he said to me, 'If you don't register me, I'll kill you.' So I remembered."

**Communication.** The fourth element of competence is communication. This mode of impeachment is not used very frequently. But when you are able to impeach through communication, the impeachment is devastating.

Assume that you are in court. Your opponent calls a witness. You will have to cross-examine that witness. You watch the witness. Every meter is on. Your tentacles are out; you are picking up the radar, the emanations, the impressions; you are operating for those few minutes or few hours at a degree of concentration and sensitivity unknown to practitioners in other branches of the profession or other professions. At once, you size up the witness. He has the intelligence of an earthworm and the morals of a scorpion. He talks. You listen to the direct examination. Suddenly, in the middle of his testimony on direct examination, there comes the word that clinks: "antidisestablishmentarianism."

On cross-examination, you use the fourth mode of impeachment: communication.

Q. Mr. Witness, you used the word, "antidisestablishmentarianism"?

A. Yes.

Q. What does it mean?

A. I don't know.

Q. Here is a yellow pad. Write it down.

A. I can't.

Q. You mean, you don't know how to spell it?

A. No.

Q. When is the first time in your life you ever heard that word?

A. When the district attorney told me what to say on the witness stand.

You sit down. What will you argue in summation? "That's no witness, that's a human tape recorder, just repeating what the district attorney programmed into him before this trial started."

## §15.3 Collateral Issue and Good-Faith Basis

The first four modes of impeachment, considered in the preceding section, are related: They involve the reverse use of the elements of competence. The middle group of four, considered in the next section, share certain characteristics that are unlike those of the first group.

**Collateral/Not Collateral.** One characteristic of the middle group of four is that we impeach the witness by asking a question that has nothing directly to do with the subject matter of the testimony given on direct examination. Every experienced trial lawyer has impeached a witness in this manner, and this category of impeachment ties into one aspect of the art of cross-examination: A cross-examiner will never want the witness to repeat on cross-examination what he said on direct.[6]

Assume that we have a case about the traffic light — who had the light? The witness has testified on direct examination that the traffic light was green. We wish to impeach the witness. We ask him this question: "Sir, is it not a fact that you beat your wife last night?" This has nothing to do with the issues of the case or with the witness's testimony on direct examination.

Assume for the sake of argument that the question is proper because it fits one of the middle group of four modes of impeachment. The witness says, "Yes, I did it." You leave the subject and go on to something else; you will argue in summation what wife-beating suggests about the credibility of the witness. But suppose the witness denies it. He says, "No, I did not beat my wife." The issue is joined. What happens when a witness denies the impeaching information and says no to the impeaching question? Will we be permitted, as part of our case, to introduce evidence tending to show that the denial was false?

The question can be argued both ways. We argue for the introduction of further evidence because it bears upon credibility. In most trials, credibility is the ball game: It is what the jury has to decide. It is worth spending the time to develop further evidence to show that the denial was false. We may also argue against its admission. This is a trial about a traffic light, not wife-beating. Further evidence of wife-beating would waste the court's time.

The question we have raised concerns the collateral/not collateral distinction, which has confused lawyers and judges for

---

[6]See §15.8.

generations. The collateral/not collateral distinction does not relate to the propriety of the impeaching question, which is determined by reference to the nine pigeonholes of impeachment. If an objection is made to an impeachment question, you should take the question and run it along the nine pigeonholes. If the question fits one of the pigeonholes, it is proper insofar as the law of evidence is concerned. If it does not fit one of the pigeonholes, it is improper.

The collateral/not collateral distinction, on the other hand, applies only to further evidence that may be elicited. If the issue is not collateral, we may call the next-door neighbor who heard the wife-beating going on, to prove that the denial of the impeaching question was false. If the issue is collateral, we may ask the question if it fits into one of the pigeonholes, but we may not go beyond the witness's answer if he denies it. If the issue is collateral, we may not call the other witnesses to testify that he really did beat his wife.

Whether or not an issue is collateral depends upon the pigeonhole that the cross-examiner uses to test the proposition. We must consider each of the pigeonholes to determine whether the issues they raise are collateral or not.

**Good-Faith Basis.** The second common feature of the second group of impeachment techniques concerns the cross-examiner's good-faith basis for asking the impeachment question. Assume that the witness has testified on direct examination that the traffic light was green. The question is, "Mr. Witness, is it not a fact that you commit sodomy every night with a parrot?" Now what? First, they peel the jurors off the back wall. Then, His Honor gestures to the cross-examiner; he would like to speak to you. You trot up to the side bar. His Honor looks at you, and he says: "What the hell are you doing?" What is your response? Well, if you were younger, you might simply bat your baby blue eyes at the judge and say, "Well, Your Honor, I'm just testing credibility." If that were a sufficient answer, there would be no limit to your power to poison the jury, except to the extent that you have a diseased imagination. If the question fits one of the pigeonholes, you could make up anything. The answer would be irrelevant as long as the jury heard the question. Although the question fits one of the categories, it is improper because there must be a limit on your ability to poison the jury by asking hair-raising questions of that kind.

The law requires that the cross-examiner must have a good-faith basis for asking the question. The contours of a good-faith basis will vary with the circumstances, and the circumstances are, of course, infinite. When the judge calls you to the side bar after you ask the parrot question, and asks you what you are doing, your response should be, "Your Honor, it fits the third category, and I have a good-faith basis for asking the question." The judge may then ask for a representation as to what your good-faith basis is. You know how to answer that: "Well, Judge, here is the parrot. Ask him." Whether you have a good-faith basis is a law school question; the answer depends upon the degree to which the parrot is articulate.

The collateral/not collateral issue and the good-faith basis requirement provide a framework for examining the four modes of impeachment in the middle group.

## §15.4 Modes of Impeachment: The Second Group

**Bias, Prejudice, Interest, Corruption.** The first category of the middle group encompasses four labels. Together they consitute one pigeonhole.

What is bias? An irrational predisposition in favor.

What is prejudice? An irrational predisposition against.

What is interest? A stake in the outcome.

What is corruption? Bribery.

The labels themselves tell you what you need to know. In every jurisdiction, you may impeach a witness by showing that he is biased, prejudiced, interested or corrupt. You have an absolute right to do so; if the judge curtails cross-examination involving this particular mode of impeachment, there is a likelihood of reversal on appeal. This type of impeachment can be accomplished very delicately; when you have the ammunition, it is dynamite with the jury.

Assume that the witness, an elderly woman, has testified in support of the defendant's alibi in a criminal case. You are the prosecutor. The woman has testified that the defendant was with her in the movies at the time the bank was robbed. You stand up. You have a good-faith basis, of course, and you ultimately say, "Well, madam, you are the defendant's mother, aren't you?" "Yes, I am."

Not one question more is necessary; even a beginner could recognize it. No jury is going to believe that woman's testimony. She is the defendant's mother. You have used the first pigeonhole of this middle group of four: bias or interest. The woman has an irrational predisposition in favor of her son and an emotional stake in the outcome.

Prejudice is similar. Assume that you represent a black person. You are cross-examining a witness who has testified against him. You have a good-faith basis and ask the question, "Sir, you are a member of the Ku Klux Klan, are you not?" "Yes." Sit down. You have shown prejudice.

Finally, we may impeach by establishing corruption: "Sir, you have been bribed to give your testimony in this case, haven't you?" There had better be a good-faith basis for that one. And assuming that there is, you have won the case once you have asked that question. In more humdrum terms, assume that you are cross-examining a physician in a personal injury case. "Doctor, what are you getting paid for your testimony here?" "I'm not getting paid for my testimony; I'm getting paid for my time." You fence around, and ultimately it comes out. If it is a really big sum, the jurors tend to be a little bit disturbed, and there you have it.

We should consider whether these questions are collateral or not: "You're his mother, aren't you?" "No, I'm not." "You're a life member of the Ku Klux Klan?" "No, I'm not." "You have been bribed to give your testimony?" "No, I haven't." You will be permitted to call other witnesses to testify that, yes, she is his mother; yes, he is a life member of the Ku Klux Klan; and, yes, he has been bribed. The issues are not collateral. The law recognizes that the impeaching value of questions that fit into the first pigeonhole of the middle group of four is very high; the impact on the jury is enormous. The time spent in testing the truth of the answers to these questions is well spent.

**Prior Convictions.** Impeachment by showing that the witness has been convicted of a crime is probably the most controversial issue in the law of evidence in recent years.

In its original form, impeachment by proof of conviction allowed a cross-examiner to impeach any witness in any kind of case by showing that he had been convicted of a crime, however defined in the jurisdiction. To be impeached, the witness must have been convicted on the basis of a guilty plea or after trial. A mere indictment or an arrest was insufficient. And the offense must have been a crime — a misdemeanor or felony, not a traffic infraction or the like, and not a juvenile delinquincy adjudication. The impeaching material would be the conviction itself, not the underlying crime.[7]

This mode of impeachment has become controversial with respect to a specific kind of witness: the defendant in a criminal case. The privilege against self-incrimination guarantees that a defendant need not take the stand. The defendant may, however, decide to take the stand for his own reasons. In its original form, the law provided that once a defendant decided to testify, he became a witness like any other, subject to the same techniques of impeachment.

Q. The fact is, Mr. Witness, that you have been in trouble before, haven't you?

A. Well, now that you mention it, yes.

Q. You were convicted last year of statutory rape, right?

A. Well, yes.

Q. And the year before that of selling heroin to junior-high school students, right?

A. Yes.

Q. And the year before that of kidnapping?

A. Yes.

---

[7]*See, e.g.,* People v. Burgess, 50 A.D. 1036, 377 N.Y.S.2d 724 (3d Dept. 1975) (reversal where proecutor delved into underlying facts of defendant's prior conviction and alluded to same in summation).

Q. And the year before that of bank robbery?
A. Yes.

And what is happening all the time? We have demonstrated beyond a doubt that the defendant is a hardened criminal. At the same time, we profess to believe the fundamental principle of Anglo-Saxon criminal law requiring that the defendant's guilt or innocence be determined solely on the basis of evidence tending to show that he did or did not do the acts charged in an indictment. The indictment says that he robbed a bank. The only evidence that the jury may consider is the evidence that shows that he did or did not rob the bank. He cannot be convicted merely because he did not cry at his mother's funeral. He cannot be convicted merely because he has been a bad boy all these years.

Assume that the defendant takes the stand, and the jury hears about these convictions. The judge will address the jury:

> Ladies and gentlemen, you have heard about these hair-raising convictions. I nearly fell out of my chair when I heard them myself. I know that as good citizens you probably reacted in the same way, but you must put that reaction to the side. Those convictions are before you only to the extent that they may help you assess the credibility of the defendant on the witness stand. You may not consider those convictions as tending to show that the defendant deserves to be convicted. You must convict or acquit the defendant on the basis of evidence tending to prove that he robbed the bank. You must not convict him merely because he has led a bad life with five prior serious convictions.

The judge will instruct the jury in such terms. He can do so until he is blue in the face. Of course, they will not understand what he is talking about. The instruction is a pious fiction that we pretend to believe in order to get our work done. The jury sits there and they do their best to listen, but when they get in the jury room, they say: "Did you hear those convictions? They ought to lock that guy up and throw away the key to protect the rest of us."

This subject has become controversial as we have confronted the realities beneath the layer of fiction and as our concern with providing the defendant a fair trial has grown. A number of solutions have been proposed; they are the subject of experiments in several jurisdictions. In some jurisdictions, only specific types of convictions may now be used to impeach the defendant. In other jurisdictions, only recent convictions may be used.

An important limitation on impeachment by use of prior convictions was established by the Court of Appeals for the District of Columbia Circuit in *Luck v. United States*.[8] Finding that the relevant statute allowed the trial judge to exercise his discretion in determining whether prior convictions should be presented to the jury, the court of appeals held that a defendant is entitled to a hearing. At that hearing, the defendant takes the stand and gives testimony. The district attorney shows the criminal record to the judge, who exercises his discretion. Conviction by conviction, the judge must weigh possible prejudice against relevance to the issue of credibility.

Although the *Luck* doctrine began as a rule for the District of Columbia, it has been adopted by other courts, including the New York Court of Appeals.[9] It also appears in modified form, together with other kinds of restrictions, as Rule 609 of the Federal Rules of Evidence. Rule 609 is a complex rule and it contains several important limitations on the right of a prosecutor to impeach a defendant by use of prior convictions.[10]

---

[8]348 F.2d 763 (D.C. Cir. 1965).

[9]People v. Sandoval, 34 N.Y.2d 371, 314 N.E.2d 413, 357 N.Y.S.2d 849 (1974).

[10]   (a) *General rule.* For the purpose of attacking the credibility of a witness, evidence that he has been convicted of a crime shall be admitted if elicited from him or established by public record during cross-examination but only if the crime (1) was punishable by death or imprisonment in excess of one year under the law under which he was convicted, and the court determines that the probative value of admitting this evidence outweighs its prejudicial effect to the defendant, or (2) involved dishonesty or false statement, regardless of the punishment.

   (b) *Time limit.* Evidence of a conviction under this rule is not admissible if a period of more than ten years has elapsed since

One other case should be noted. In *State v. Santiago*,[11] the Supreme Court of Hawaii squarely held that the use of prior convictions to impeach a defendant who takes the stand on his own behalf violates due process. Impeachment by prior convictions is not permitted in a criminal court in Hawaii. Although *Santiago* is binding precedent only in Hawaii, it is a constitutional decision by a supreme court; it has a certain precedential value. All defense lawyers should have it as part of their armory, and they should pull it out when the occasion arises.

The Federal Rules of Evidence do not so much as mention any of the impeachment modes we have discussed down to this one, except to disallow the questioning of a witness about his religious beliefs.[12] It is understood that these modes of impeachment are part of the law of evidence in the federal courts, just as they are part of the law of evidence everywhere else. But impeachment by prior convictions is more controversial. There is a provision for it in the Federal Rules, as there are cases and statutes and rules on it in all the states.

Federal Rule of Evidence 609 adopts the *Luck* doctrine in modified form, together with other kinds of restrictions. In a nutshell, the rule tells the trial judge to weigh the prejudicial effect of each prior conviction against the relationship of the conviction to credibility.

While the rule was under consideration, on one side were those who argued for unlimited use of convictions to impeach; on the other side were those who urged strict limits. To secure

the date of the conviction or of the release of the witness from the confinement imposed for that conviction, whichever is the later date, unless the court determines, in the interests of justice, that the probative value of the conviction supported by specific facts and circumstances substantially outweighs its prejudicial effect. However, evidence of a conviction more than 10 years old as calculated herein, is not admissible unless the proponent gives to the adverse party sufficient advance written notice of intent to use such evidence to provide the adverse party with a fair opportunity to contest the use of such evidence . . . .

Fed. R. Evid. 609.
[11]492 P.2d 657 (Ha. 1971).
[12]Fed. R. Evid. 610. See §15.2.

the votes of both sides, something was given to each. Exception was piled upon qualification to please Marcus and qualification upon exception to please Lucius, until Rule 609 had been tortured into a mockery of the form one expects of a statutory rule of evidence. In symbols, the first two paragraphs of Rule 609 read thusly: A is the rule if either B and C are the facts or D is the fact; but A is not the rule if E is the fact, unless F is the fact, in which case A is the rule, but only if G is the fact.

Simplicity is a great and underrated virtue, in whose name I dare to hope that Congress will someday amend Rule 609 along these lines: Any witness may be impeached with convictions, subject to the judge's discretion under Rule 403.

The collateral/not collateral issue with respect to prior convictions is easy. It will never arise as a practical matter. When you ask the witness whether he has been convicted of a crime, he knows that you have the record of conviction. There is no point in denying it, so he will not deny it. If the witness denies the conviction, however, it is not collateral. You may prove the conviction by other evidence, but you will be limited in your proof to the most efficient evidence available: the certified or exemplified judgment of conviction.

**Prior Bad Acts.** A witness may also be impeached by questions relating to prior bad acts, which are defined as acts of an immoral, criminal, or vicious nature. Acts for which the witness was actually acquitted may not be used. Rather, this mode of impeachment brings out acts for which he was never prosecuted, or never arrested. One special instance may seem to be an exception, but it is really consistent with the rule. Suppose that a prior conviction took the form of a juvenile adjudication, and for that reason is not admissible as a conviction.[13] The underlying facts of the offense may be admissible nonetheless, as bad acts.[14]

For example, assume that the witness has testified on direct examination that the traffic light was green. "Mr. Witness, did you

---

[13]Fed. R. Evid. 609(d).

[14]*See, e.g.*, People v. Cook, 37 N.Y.2d 591, 338 N.E.2d 619, 376 N.Y.S.2d 110 (1975) (where defendant improperly impeached with youthful offender adjudication, cross-examination should be confined to underlying facts).

beat your wife last night?" "Do you commit sodomy with a parrot?" These acts did not lead to a criminal conviction, but they are acts of an immoral, criminal, or vicious nature. In most courts, you will be permitted to question the witness about any one of them on the theory that it has a bearing on credibility. You must, however, have a good-faith basis for asking the question.[15]

A majority of the jurisdictions, but not all of them, allow this mode of impeachment. More precisely, the various jurisdictions follow no fewer than six different rules: (1) Bad act impeachment is permissible; (2) It is permissible, but only with respect to conduct bearing directly upon credibility; (3) It is permissible, but only with respect to conduct evincing such extraordinary wickedness as would likely render the witness insensible to the obligations of an oath; (4) It is permissible, but only if the witness is someone other than the defendant in a criminal case; (5) It is permissible in the discretion of the trial judge; (6) It is not permissible at all. There is no general rule.

Before the adoption of the Federal Rules of Evidence, the federal jurisdiction did not permit bad act impeachment. To understand the evolution of Rule 608(b), which does allow it, we must begin with a New York case, *People v. Sorge*.[16] The defendant was charged with performing an abortion. She took the stand and testified on her own behalf, whereupon the district attorney sought to discredit her by asking whether she had committed other abortions. The New York Court of Appeals held that such impeachment is permissible, subject to the trial judge's discretion to limit it — a melding of the first and fifth rules above.

Prior to adoption of the Federal Rules, the leading federal case on the issue was *United States v. Provoo*.[17] The defendant was charged with treason. His testimony on direct examination mentioned that he had been confined and hospitalized at various times during his Army career. On cross-examination, he was impeached with questions asking whether the confinements had been for homosexuality. The U.S. Court of Appeals for the Sec-

---

[15]See §15.3.
[16]301 N.Y. 198, 93 N.E.2d 637 (1950).
[17]215 F.2d 531 (2d Cir. 1954).

ond Circuit explicitly declined to follow *Sorge*. Instead, it found that prior bad acts are not a proper subject for impeachment. But the opinion went on to say that questions about specific acts of misconduct *will* be proper so long as the acts involve misconduct bearing upon credibility. *Provoo* thus laid down two conflicting rules: no bad act impeachment, and bad act impeachment only when the act bears upon credibility. The opinion did not say which rule applies, and neither does any subsequent Second Circuit Opinion.

The Federal Rules of Evidence pick up the second of the two *Provoo* rules and carry it into general federal law: The acts brought out must bear on credibility.[18] There is no exception for defendants. Like any other witness, a defendant who testifies is subject to bad act impeachment.

Although Rule 608(b) is unequivocal, it leaves open three troublesome questions. First: What kind of act proves untruthfulness? Second: Suppose that a defendant takes the stand and is impeached with some prior, unprosecuted criminal act suggesting untruthfulness. What is he to do? Should he answer the question, and perhaps convict himself of that other crime? Or should he plead the privilege against self-incrimination and pray that the jury in this case will not be affected? Third: How is a trial judge to weigh the defendant's right to testify in his own behalf against the prejudice inherent in bad act impeachment?

A possible solution to the third problem lies in *People v. Sandoval*,[19] a New York case. *Sandoval* adopted the federal *Luck* rule. *Luck* applies not to bad acts, but to impeachment by prior conviction. The rule of that case permits a hearing at which the judge reviews each prior conviction to determine whether it is a proper subject for impeachment. For each conviction, the judge weighs its bearing on credibility against prejudice to the defendant. But in New York, *Sandoval* sanctioned the application of this procedure

---

[18]"Specific instances of the conduct of a witness, for the purpose of attacking or supporting his credibility, . . . may, however, in the discretion of the court, if probative of truthfulness or untruthfulness, be inquired into on cross-examination of the witness (1) concerning his character for truthfulness or untruthfulness . . . ." Fed. R. Evid. 608(b).

[19]34 N.Y.2d 371, 314 N.E.2d 413, 357 N.Y.S.2d 849 (1974).

beyond prior convictions, to bad act impeachment as well. It is hard to quarrel with this.

Despite the untempered language of Rule 608(b), there is room enough in the Federal Rules, taking them as a system, to warrant the qualification of bad act impeachment along the lines of *Sandoval*. Rule 102 commands that the rules "shall be construed to secure fairness in administration . . . ." Rule 403 allows the exclusion of relevant evidence "if its probative value is substantially outweighed by the danger of unfair prejudice . . . ." Moreover, Rule 609(a) codifies the *Luck* doctrine by authorizing the court to forbid the use of certain kinds of convictions for impeachment unless "the probative value of admitting this evidence outweighs its prejudicial effect to the defendant . . . ." If balancing of this sort is permitted under the Federal Rules with respect to prior convictions, it should be permitted, *a fortiori*, with respect to bad acts.

In those jurisdictions that allow impeachment by bad acts, the issue is collateral. You may ask the question, but you must take the witness's answer; you may not call other witnesses to testify that the primary witness beat his wife or committed sodomy with a parrot. Although the question relates sufficiently to credibility to render the question permissible, the relationship is so slight that we will not listen to independent evidence to show that the denial was false.

As a matter of tactics, it is sometimes possible to characterize bad acts as bias or prejudice, thus shifting the impeachment question from this third pigeonhole of the second group to the first pigeonhole. Because issues raised in impeachment by bias or prejudice are not collateral, the shift will make it permissible to disprove the witness's denial.

**Prior Inconsistent Statement.** Impeachment by prior inconsistent statement is the most frequently used mode of impeachment and, perhaps, the simplest. Most trial lawyers are aware of this form of impeachment, but many are unable to use this fourth mode of impeachment crisply and eloquently.

Suppose that the witness says on direct examination that the light was green. We now put before the jury a prior statement by the witness in which he said that the light was red. The impeachment value is obvious: The witness talks out of both sides of his mouth. He is not worth believing; he says one thing today, he said something else yesterday. This mode of impeachment is very common, and it can be very potent.

In most jurisdictions, there is a preliminary requirement to be met before you can impeach with a prior inconsistent statement: You must lay a foundation for the statement. In order to understand the foundation requirement, it is necessary to understand its historical background. As with most of the law of evidence, this mode of impeachment was invented by our English cousins, who passed it along to us. Impeachment by prior inconsistent statement goes back at least to the seventeenth century. Assume that we are in an English court. We are barristers now, not American lawyers. By definition, a barrister is a gentleman or a gentlewoman. To this very day, an English barrister is immune to a suit for malpractice because he is not a professional person doing a professional job but a gentleman or a gentlewoman doing a favor.

Of course, a gentleman doing a favor feels embarrassment when he is about to confront a witness with a prior inconsistent statement. Here is a witness who, right now and in front of this jury and this judge, is about to be proved a bold-faced liar. Decency demands that you do something to minimize the embarrassment.

What the barrister does is to give the witness a chance to think up a lie, to get out of this lie and explain it away. We give him the chance to lie by laying the foundation. It may be done in either of two ways. If the prior inconsistent statement was oral, you direct the witness's attention to the time, place, and circumstances of the making of the prior inconsistent statement. When you have done that, you have laid the foundation; you have directed his mind to that prior statement and given him time to think up whatever explanation can be thought up about it. Assume that the witness, on direct examination, says that the traffic light was green. Our investigation reveals that he previously said that the light was red. We lay the foundation:

> Q. Mr. Witness, remember last week when you went to the local bar and grill?
>
> A. Yes.
>
> Q. You talked to the bartender?
>
> A. Yes.
>
> Q. You talked about this accident.
>
> A. Yes.

You have laid the foundation. And now you can ask the impeaching question: "Didn't you say to the bartender that the light was red?" If he admits that he said it, sit down. If he denies that he said it, the question is whether the issue is collateral or not.

If the prior inconsistent statement is in writing, we lay the foundation in a somewhat different way. In most jurisdictions, we must go back to the rule in *Queen Caroline's* case.[20] When the prior inconsistent statement is in writing, we must show the statement to the witness and give the witness a chance to read the statement to himself. Again, we focus his mind on the statement and give him a chance to think up any explanation that is possible. Once we have complied with the rule in *Queen Caroline's* case, we have laid the foundation. The witness has testified on direct examination that the light was green.

> Q. Mr. Witness, do you have a mother?
>
> A. Yes.
>
> Q. Do you write to her from time to time?
>
> A. Yeah.
>
> Q. I hand you a piece of paper. What's that?
>
> A. Well, that's a letter I wrote to my mother.
>
> Q. Read it to yourself.

He reads it. The letter says that the light was red. "Is it not a fact, Mr. Witness . . . ." We may proceed to ask whatever ques-

---

[20] 2 Brod. & B. 284, 129 Eng. Rep. 976 (1820).

tions we want about the content of that document; we have laid the foundation.[21]

The Federal Rules of Evidence, for all practical purposes, do away with the requirement of the foundation because we are not barristers. We are not gentlemen! We are trial lawyers. We do not want to give the witness a chance to dream up a lie to explain away the first lie. We want to demonstrate before the jury that he is a bold-faced liar. We can best accomplish this result by confronting him with the lie without any preliminaries. Under the Federal Rules, we may do so.[22]

Assume that you have established the foundation perfectly. The judge is extremely pleased with you. "Mr. Witness, did you go to the bar?" "Did you talk to the bartender about this case?" "Didn't you say to the bartender that the light was red?" "No, I did not." He denies the prior inconsistent statement. The issue is whether the matter is collateral. Will we be permitted, as part of our case, to call the bartender to say, "Yes, he did say the light was red." Will we permitted to call any other witness who will say, "Yes, I heard the fellow make the prior inconsistent statement"? We struggled with this problem in law school; we read an English case called *Attorney General Hitchcock.*[23] You may not recall it because you may not have understood it. If you went back and read it today, you would not understand it. If you read

---

[21]It is the asking of the foundation questions that lays the foundation, not the witness's answers. Once the witness has heard the questions — once the witness is on notice that he or she is about to be called a liar — the foundation is laid whether the witness answers or not. Occasionally a court will miss this point. In *People v. Gunne,* 65 Mich. App. 216, 237 N.W.2d 256 (1975), for example, the witness, invoking her privilege against self-incrimination, declined to answer the foundation questions. The Court of Appeals of Michigan held, quite wrongly, that as a result the foundation had not been laid, and that the prior inconsistent statement was therefore inadmissible. *But see id.* at 221, 237 N.W.2d at 258 (Kelly, J., dissenting) ("[T]he foundation is laid when the prosecutor asks the foundational questions, and the witness cannot nullify that foundation by refusing to answer . . . .")

[22]"In examining a witness concerning a prior statement made by him, whether written or not, the statement need not be shown nor its contents disclosed to him at that time, but on request the same shall be shown or disclosed to opposing counsel." Fed. R. Evid. 613(a).

[23]1 Ex. 91, 154 Eng. Rep. 38 (1847).

it every day of your life until you died, you still would not understand it; there is no meaning to it. The case is important only because it states what seems to be the prevailing rule with respect to the collateral/not collateral distinction: If the witness denies the prior inconsistent statement, the issue may or may not be collateral. Sometimes you may call another witness to prove the prior statement; sometimes you will not be able to do so. The real question is, when will it be collateral, and when will it not be collateral? The answer is simple: When it is important, it is not collateral. When it is unimportant, it is collateral. Ten thousand cases add up to that.

Suppose that the witness says on direct examination that the light was green. "Did you go to the bar and talk to the bartender about this case?" "Didn't you say the light was red?" "No, I did not." Will we be permitted to call the bartender? Surely. That is important; it is close to the heart of the case. The principal issue concerns the color of the light.

A slightly different case will demonstrate the distinction. The witness on direct examination says the light was green. We are ready to impeach.

Q. Mr. Witness, you were standing on the street corner, and you saw the light?

A. Yes.

Q. How did you come to be on the street corner?

A. I was on my way home.

Q. What were you going to do at home?

A. Have lunch.

Q. What were you going to have for lunch?

A. Cream cheese and jelly sandwich.

Q. Did you go to the bar last week?

A. Yeah.

Q. Did you talk to the bartender?

A. Yes.

Q. About this episode?

A. Yes.

Q. Didn't you say to the bartender that you were going to have a peanut butter sandwich?

A. No.

Will we be allowed to call the bartender to say that he really said he was going home to have a peanut butter sandwich? No, it is not important. That takes care of a lot of cases.

## §15.5 Modes of Impeachment: Reputation for Veracity

The last of our nine modes of impeachment differs from the first eight in that it is not used on cross-examination of the witness. Instead, the lawyer who seeks to impeach calls, as part of the lawyer's own case, another witness whose testimony consists of this ninth mode.

We shall call the primary witness, whose credibility is under attack, W-1. The witness whom we shall call to help impeach W-1 will be W-2. The judges of England, who invented the preceding eight modes of impeachment, concluded that in addition to everything else, it would be very useful for the jury to know whether, in general, W-1 is a liar. The judges of England then had to address the technical question, how does one put evidence before the jury to show that, in general, W-1 is a liar?

There are three possibilities. First, call another witness, W-2, who will testify to specific instances of lying on the part of W-1. Second, call another witness, W-2, who will testify that in his opinion, W-1 is a liar. Third, call another witness, W-2, who will tell us what the gossip is about W-1. When people talk over the back fence, what do they say about W-1? Does what they say add up to the gossip that he is a liar, or not?

The judges of England, like the judges of America today, were reluctant to call things by their plain and simple names. Instead of referring to gossip, they spoke of reputation — reputation for lack of veracity, reputation for not telling the truth, reputation for being a liar.

Of the three possibilities — specific instances, opinion, and gossip or reputation — to the judges of England the only one that had real probative force was gossip. That provided the common law rule. The ninth and last way of attacking the credibility of a witness is to call another witness who testifies, in substance, that the reputation of W-1 is that of a liar. We can call W-2 a reputation witness. Because the impact of his testimony on the jury will be slight, this mode of impeachment is seldom used, but to call the witness is permissible in all jurisdictions.

The Federal Rules permit W-2 to testify as to W-1's reputation. But the draftsmen realized that we do not live in England in the seventeenth century. No one has a reputation any more. We are all strangers to one another. When W-2 takes the stand and testifies as to W-1's reputation as a liar, he has been coached to speak in those terms. What he really means, of course, is that in W-2's own opinion, W-1 is a liar. The Federal Rules make it possible for W-2 to say what he really means. He may speak of W-1's reputation, but if he wishes, he can omit that and simply say, "In my opinion, W-1 is a liar."[24]

## §15.6 Impeaching the Expert Witness*

Always remind yourself as you plan the cross-examination of the opposing side's expert that an expert is, to begin with, a witness like any other: Any mode proper for the impeachment of an ordinary witness is proper for the impeachment of an expert. Most of the time, there is nothing that you can do. But one time out of a hundred, there will be something that you can do.

------

[24]"The credibility of a witness may be attacked or supported by evidence in the form of opinion or reputation, but subject to these limitations: (1) the evidence may refer only to character for truthfulness or untruthfulness . . . ." Fed R. Evid. 608(a).

*Portions of this section are drawn from "A Practical Approach to the Use of Expert Testimony," by Irving Younger, which appeared in the Cleveland State Law Review, vol. 31, no. 1 (1982). © Cleveland State Law Review. Used with permission.

For purposes of this first item on your checklist, forget that he's an expert. He's just John Q. Bystander.[25]

There are, in addition to the usual methods of impeachment, two special methods of impeachment available only with respect to experts. They are available in the federal court, and they are available in all states that follow federal practice. There may be a few states that permit only one of these two. But, by and large, all states permit both. For an example of these methods, consider *Ruth v. Fenchel*,[26] which is little more than an essay on these two

---

[25]I had the experience, when serving as a trial judge, of seeing many times over a Spencer Tracy-like plaintiff's expert, Dr. Smith. Dr. Smith was awfully impressive to jurors seeing him just one time. When asked for his opinion — which was always that the plaintiff had been destroyed by the accident — he would turn to the jurors, cross his legs, look at them with his clear blue eyes, and there was nothing that those jurors would refuse him. He just emanated the fatherly role.

Twenty times I had him in my court and twenty times defense counsel was absolutely feckless on cross-examination. In the twenty-first case, I'm sitting there minding my own business. Dr. Smith tells his usual story. Defense counsel gets up like a tiger, and his first question is, "Dr. Smith, have you ever been convicted of a crime?"

And I start getting ready to say, "Counselor, you can't ask that question without a good-faith basis." But before I can open my mouth, Dr. Smith, who has been told he must be candid about everything, replies, "Yes, I have been."

Q. Was that in federal court or state court?
A. Federal court.
Q. Was it a felony or a misdemeanor?
A. It was a felony.
Q. What felony was it?
A. Income tax evasion.
Q. Were you found guilty after trial, or did you plead guilty?
A. I pleaded guilty.
Q. What was your sentence?
A. A year in jail.
Q. Did you serve it?
A. Yes.

Twenty defense lawyers let that doctor present himself to the jury as if he were Spencer Tracy. Only the twenty-first remembered that an expert is a witness like any other. If you have the ammunition, you can impeach him as you can an ordinary witness.

[26]21 N.J. 171, 121 A.2d 373 (1956).

modes of impeachment and all of their ramifications. It was decided by the New Jersey Supreme Court, and the author of the opinion is William J. Brennan, Jr., now a Supreme Court justice.

The two methods of impeachment, when trial lawyers get together to talk shop, are usually described together as "impeachment out of treatise." By "treatise" we mean any printed source: a textbook, a treatise, an article in a journal, or whatever it may be.

To demonstrate this, let's take an absolutely absurd example. Assume that the witness is a physician who has testified on direct examination that, in his opinion, the appendix is on the left side of the body. We all know that this is wrong: In all but a vanishingly small minority of people, the appendix is on the right side of the body. Suppose this physician wrote a textbook on anatomy, and on page 100 it says, "The appendix is on the right side of the body." Can we use it? Certainly. Is there anything unusual about it? No. This witness has just said something different from what he said in his textbook. So it's impeachment of the witness by a prior inconsistent statement.

If you have an ordinary witness, may you impeach him with somebody else's inconsistent statement? *A* on the stand says one thing, *Z* says something else. Can you tag *A* with *Z*'s contradictory statement? No, you cannot — it is not permitted by the rules on impeaching an ordinary witness. But when the witness is not ordinary, when the witness is an expert, there are circumstances in which you can impeach him with what somebody else said.

There are two ways of doing it. The first method of impeaching out of a book has been around the longest. There are cases in every jurisdiction permitting it. The cross-examination proceeds something as follows — not necessarily in these words, but retaining the essence as stated here:

Q. Doctor, do you see what I have in my hand?

A. Yes.

Q. This is *Gray's Anatomy,* isn't it?

A. Yes.

Q. Is this a standard reference work in anatomy, Doctor?

A. Yes.

Q. Doctor, did you consult this book in the course of getting ready to testify in this case?

If he says yes, we have him. The precondition of this mode of impeachment is that the expert acknowledge having relied upon the book, consulted it, looked at it — any such words — for purposes of testifying in the case.

If he does say yes, he did consult the book, then as a matter of technique you are well advised to ask him no more questions. Instead, turn to the judge and say, "Your Honor, may I read to the jury from page 100?" The judge will say yes. And you read to the jury the contradictory passage: "I read from page 100 of *Gray's Anatomy,* quote, 'the appendix is on the right side,' close quote." Slam the book shut and sit down.

Needless to say, that affirmative answer to your question, "Did you consult or rely upon this book?" — is not often forthcoming. The doctor is not a fool; he has been prepared to testify; he has been alerted to the fact that he may be impeached out of the book. Did he consult it? Chances are, he will say he did not.

That brings us to the second of the two modes of impeachment available with respect to an expert. Again, every jurisdiction will allow it. The threshold question here is not whether the witness consulted the book, but in essence goes something like this:

Q. Doctor, do you see this book that I have in my hand?
A. Yes.
Q. *Gray's Anatomy,* isn't it?
A. Yes.
Q. Do doctors generally regard this as the bible of anatomy?

That is the threshold question. Instead, it could be, "Do doctors generally regard this as a standard work in the field?" Or, "Do doctors generally accept this work as authoritative?"

Here we digress to a matter of technique. A lawyer really trying the case would come at the threshold question more indirectly:

Q. Doctor, you have your office on Main Street downtown, don't you?

A. Well, yes, I do.

Q. That office consists of a receiving room where you talk to patients, then an inner examination room where you examine people on an examining table?

A. That's right.

Q. And, Doctor, in the outer office where you talk to patients, you've got a desk?

A. Sure.

Q. You sit behind that desk, and the patient sits on the other side?

A. That's right.

Q. To your right, Doctor, as you sit behind the desk, there's a little bookcase, isn't there?

A. That's right. How did you know?

Q. I ask the questions here, Doctor. In that bookcase, do you have certain books?

A. Yes, I do.

Q. Doctor, is this one of those books?

Then, when you ask whether the book is authoritative, he must answer yes. Otherwise he is telling the jury and the public at large that he keeps outmoded, unauthoritative books in his office. (How did you know he had that book there? You sent your investigator to his office the day before, pretending to be a patient. And while the doctor was doing other things, the investigator examined the books in the bookcase. You then went looking for the book the investigator saw.)

We have the witness saying, "Yes, that book is authoritative." Again, you proceed just as before. "Your Honor, may I read to the jury from page 100?" Read the contradictory passage, slam the book shut, and sit down.

**The Hearsay Issue.** These modes of impeaching expert witnesses raise a question. On direct examination, the doctor said that the appendix is on the left side of the body. We have read to the jury from a book that the appendix is on the right side of the body. Is there now evidence before the jury upon which the jury may properly conclude that the appendix is on the right side of the body? In other words, is the contradictory material from the book admissible to prove the truth of what it asserts? Or is it admissible merely to impeach the expert, to show that the expert does not know what he is talking about?

The common law analysis is that the statement from the book does not come in to prove the truth of what it asserts. It comes in solely as bearing upon the credibility of the expert you are impeaching. You have no hearsay problem, but neither do you have any affirmative evidence that the appendix is on the right side of the body. And if you have the burden either of going forward or of proof with respect to that issue, you will, by common law, be required to call your own expert to testify that the appendix is on the right side of the body.

That is the common law analysis. Under the Federal Rules, all kinds of marvelous things are available to you. The place to look is Federal Rule 803(18)[27] or your state rule equivalent if your state has enacted the Federal Rules. There are four possibilities under 803(18). Not all of them are universally noted by lawyers, and potentialy each of them is very useful.

First you can impeach the other side's expert in the manner that we have described. Under 803(18), when you read from page 100 that the appendix is on the right side of the body, you are doing two things simultaneously. First, what you are doing in common law is impeaching the expert. The out-of-court statement comes in as affecting the expert's credibility. But simultaneously, it comes in to prove the truth of what it asserts, so that at the end of the cross-examination, you have not only discredited the other side's expert, bu tyou have also put affirm-

---

[27]Rule 803 states exceptions to the hearsay rule. Number (18) refers to learned treatises: "To the extent called to the attention of an expert witness upon cross-examination or relied upon by him in direct examination, statements contained in published treatises, periodicals, or pamphlets on a subject of history, medicine, or other science or art, established as a reliable authority by the testimony or admission of the witness or by other expert testimony or by judicial notice. . . ."

ative evidence before the jury that the appendix is on the right side of the body.

Second, you call your own expert, and under 803(18), you can use a treatise affirmatively. You say to your own expert, "Doctor, is this book authoritative?" Your expert says yes, and you may now read to the jury whatever is relevant. It comes in to prove the truth of what it asserts; you have your expert's live opinion supported by the material in the book.

The third situation is rare, but one can imagine a case in which it would happen. You are not cross-examining the other side's expert and you do not have an expert yourself, but the book is sufficiently well known that the judge will take judicial notice that the book is authoritative. You may then read to the jury what you want and it comes in to prove the truth of what it asserts. It may lack a certain sex appeal, but this method takes the place of a living witness.

The fourth situation is implicit in the rule. For example, you would like to be able to call Dr. Elko, the Nobel Prize winner, but for one reason or another, you cannot. He's sick, or maybe he's dead — for whatever reason, you can't get him to come to court. He won the Nobel Prize for an article, one paragraph of which states the matter with which you are concerned as clearly as it can be stated. If only you could get that to the jury to prove the truth of what it asserts, you would be in business. The other side is not calling an expert, so you can't use the first method. You are not calling an expert so you can't use the second one. And the article is not so well known that the judge would take judicial notice of its authoritative nature.

You call an expert, not a physiologist, not a physician, but a *medical librarian* whose testimony (not in these words, of course) adds up to, "I don't even know what a spleen is. I'm not a doctor. I don't know anything about it. But I do know about the literature of medicine, and I do know that this is the thing you look at when you want to learn about the physiology of the spleen." Your expert testifies, not to the underlying fact, but to the authoritativeness of the treatise. You may now read to the jury whatever you want from the treatise and it comes in to prove the truth of what it asserts.

You can get some sex appeal out of this fourth method. If the librarian is prepared properly, the librarian will say, "This is what you look at, because the author of it won the Nobel Prize for this article." The jury now starts to pay attention. Your reading from the article is almost as good as having the Nobel Prize winner on the stand — all under 803(18).

**Preparing Your Expert for Cross-Examination.** You must also prepare your own expert to meet this kind of cross-examination. You must always work on the assumption that the other lawyer knows as much as you do, that the other lawyer has worked through the literature and knows what in the literature contradicts your expert's opinion.

First, you have to do whatever you can to persuade the expert that you understand there will be contradictions in the literature. Nothing is unanimous. Everybody disagrees on everything of any importance. Experts who are not familiar with how lawyers operate are reluctant to tell you that. They are afraid that you are going to cry or lose heart in the case or send them home. Make sure that your expert tells you what in the literature differs from or contradicts his opinion. Then you work with the expert on getting ready to meet it.

Next, suggest that when the other lawyer pulls out a book or journal, your witness should very politely say, "Just a minute, Counsel. May I see the book?" So long as the witness asks politely, the lawyer will automatically hand him the book, or the judge will say, "Give him the book."

Your expert takes a second or two to look at the book. What is he looking for? Literally every day, major discoveries are being made. New editions come off the presses very frequently. What your expert is doing when he looks at the book is checking to be sure that it is the current edition. Perhaps the book is *Jones on Recombinant DNA*, fifth edition, but the sixth edition came out last month.

If it is the current edition, no harm is done and we proceed. If it is not the current edition, the expert simply gives the book back and says, "What's the question?"

The lawyer says, "My question, Doctor, is whether that book, *Jones on Recombinant DNA*, is authoritative?"

"No." That should be it, just, "No." The lawyer, nonplussed, will say, "What do you mean? How come? How dare you say that it is not authoritative?"

And your expert, in the gentlest manner possible, should respond, "Well, you see, Counselor, no doctor, just as no lawyer, would look at anything other than the most recent edition. If it is not the most recent edition, it is not authoritative. And, Counselor, that book you have in your hand is outmoded. It is not the most recent edition." Your expert has taught opposing counsel something in the jury's presence. That's a wonderful way to enhance your own expert's credibility.

In the face of an up-to-date book that contradicts your expert, you must prepare an appropriate re-direct examination. You have to work it out in advance. Your re-direct might go like this:

Q. Doctor, on direct examination, you said that your opinion was *A, B, C*?

A. That's right.

Q. And we hear on cross-examination that the treatise says *X, Y, Z*?

A. That's right.

Q. Do you wish to change the testimony you gave on direct?

A. No.

Q. Do you wish to correct your statement that the book is authoritative?

A. Absolutely not.

Q. Doctor, I think you had better explain that to the jury.

Then you get out of the way and sit down. If you've prepared him, he will know how to explain it, and the explanation should go something like this:

The book is perfectly authoritative. But, you see, books have to be written about the typical or the usual case. That book is a perfectly accurate description of what you will usually find. But every once in a while, maybe one time out of a million, you get the unusual, the unique case; and that is what we have here. It is extraordinary and that is why it is beyond what the author of the book wrote about.

The expert's explanation is intuitively persuasive. It is consistent with the juror's sense of the way the world works. Obviously, books cannot be written about the exceptions; they have to be written about what the authors *usually* find. Moreover, this explanation lets the juror think, "I'm on jury duty, but not on an ordinary case. This is one for the books. I mean, they'll be talking about this forever, and I'm on the jury."

## §15.7 The Art of Cross-Examination: In General

We have seen what the law of evidence permits and what it does not permit us to do on cross-examination. We will now consider the art of cross-examination — the how to do it.

Most trial lawyers have vivid recollections of their first cross-examinations, regardless of how long ago they may have taken place. Probably, you wanted the ground to open beneath you so that you could sink in, have the ground close up around you, and never be heard from again. If it was a criminal case, your client would go to jail for a long, long time because of your cross-examination. If it was a civil case, your client would pay out a lot of money because of your cross-examination. More importantly, you had exposed yourself to public scorn. You had embarrassed yourself. The feeling is awful and every one of us has experienced it, because cross-examination is far and away the most difficult part of the art of being a trial lawyer.

No part of trial advocacy is easy, but cross-examination is almost impossibly difficult. At any one time there are probably fewer than ten brilliant cross-examiners in the country. Many trial lawyers can do a brilliant direct examination, opening, or summation; many others are brilliant in preparing a case. Cross-examination, however, is something special. It is subtle and difficult and complex beyond description. A reasonably effective cross-examiner must have a thorough mastery of the law of evidence and the law of procedure. He must also have a thorough mastery of the law of trial advocacy or trial techniques.

Technical mastery is the easiest requirement to meet. It is available for anyone who wants it; you need only go to the library and study, and you will learn it.

The second quality that goes to make a good cross-examiner is experience. There are no Mozarts among trial lawyers. Nobody is born a brilliant cross-examiner; it takes experience. My measure of the minimum experience necessary is twenty-five jury trials. The nature of the case or the court is unimportant. You must have twenty-five jury trials as part of your experience before you have your sea legs, before you know what you are doing. And, of course, the more the better.

The third quality that goes to make a good cross-examiner is talent. Although it is unfashionable, anti-egalitarian, and elitist to speak this way these days, talent is also the rarest of the qualities necessary for a good cross-examiner. Either you have it or you do not. If you have it, it is because God gave it to you; if you do not have it, there is no way to acquire it. If you have the talent, you can acquire the technical mastery and develop the experience; you will be a Clarence Darrow.

There are very few Clarence Darrows. Even without talent, however, anyone can be a reasonably effective cross-examiner if he has technical mastery and experience. And reasonably effective cross-examination is all we need. When a lawyer walks into most courtrooms and conducts a reasonably effective cross-examination, he may not equal Clarence Darrow or Max Steuer, but the bell rings in the courthouse. People come from all corners to watch a lawyer who can conduct a reasonably effective cross-examination.

**Preparation.** Imagine that we have before us an intelligent layperson who has no experience with the trial process. We say to that intelligent, thinking layperson, "Based upon movies and television, whatever you have been able to find out about trial work, give us your idea of how a trial lawyer goes about preparing a trial." The answer would be something like this: "Well, you walk into court and you conduct a direct examination of your witnesses. Then you cross-examine the other side's witnesses, and you find out whatever you can find out. As the trial moves along, your mind is working, of course, and you fit the pieces together. Finally, at the end, you sum up. You stand up to the jury with your theory of the case, your defense, your account of what it is that happened."

If any trial lawyers think this is the right way to do it, they ought to hand in their shingles. It is time to go to dental school if that is how they think a trial lawyer goes about preparing a case for trial. It is absolutely backwards.

How does a trial lawyer prepare a case for trial? If he has one minute, one day, one week, one month, or one year to prepare the case, he must take that time and put everything else out of his mind. He will think of nothing except that case; he will work on nothing except that case. He must live, breathe, eat, and sleep that case to the exclusion of everything else. I daresay there are lawyers who stop reading the newspaper when it comes time to prepare a case for trial. Some lawyers stop answering the mail and stop taking telephone calls, because these things are distracting.

A trial lawyer must concentrate on his case to a degree unknown to practitioners in other branches of the profession. To what end? To the end that nothing at trial should come as a surprise. Everything must be considered, prepared, and planned for in advance. Of course, it is not a perfect world. You are never able to prepare a case to the point where absolutely everything that occurs in the courtroom has been considered in advance, but if more than ten percent of what occurs has not been planned in advance, you have not done your job. To the extent of ninety percent or more, everything must be determined, considered, and worked out before that trial starts.

A trial lawyer should be able to sum up to the jury before the trial starts. He must know what he would say. If he were to deliver his pretrial summation and tape-record it, and then record the summation he actually delivers after the day or week or month of trial, the summation he finally delivers should be in large part the summation he could have delivered before the trial started.

Among other things, you should know before the trial starts what you will say to the jury in summation about the credibility of the other side's witness. This is the key to effective cross-examination: You should cross-examine only to the extent necessary to secure the ammunition you will need to support the argument you have already thought out. If that argument rests upon information that comes out on direct examination, what is your cross-examination? None. You have no questions. You should sit down.

It seems to be part of the young lawyer's personality that he is afraid to say, "No questions on cross-examination." He thinks that his client will feel that he is not earning his fee, or that the judge will look down at him and say, "You are afraid. You can't be a trial lawyer if you are afraid. You've got to do something." Not at all. The mark of the master is to do as little as possible. The courage to stand up and say, "No questions," when there is nothing to be gained by cross-examination, is the mark of supreme mastery.

**Arguing Lack of Credibility.** It is not possible to give a cookbook collection of recipes for the kinds of arguments that will persuade a jury that a witness is not credible. But there are three touchstones that characterize the good jury argument. These touchstones will not guarantee success. Sometimes, maybe a lot of the time, you will not be able to come up with the right argument. But when you do come up with the right argument, it will always correspond to these three touchstones.

First, the argument must be simple; the simple argument carries the day with the jury. The master's argument has the kind of simplicity that a twelve-year-old can understand. It is very difficult for lawyers to acquire the knack of being simple. In law school, we had three years of intensive work — distorting the English language, learning to use complicated words instead of simple words, and turning our backs on the simple sentence. As a result, how do we write and talk? Every clause must have its own subordinate clause. Every subordinate clause must have a qualification. Every qualification must have an exception, and the exception must itself have a qualification that relates back to the beginning of the sentence. Around and around we go. Nobody knows what we are talking about except ourselves; sometimes we don't know either. You must rid yourself of that faculty; if you are going to try cases, you must learn how to be simple.

Second, the argument must be tactful. Trial lawyers sometimes lose sight of the obvious fact that trials are microcosms of human nature. We must make an argument about the credibility of the other side's witness. The witness is not a character we read about in an opinion or a novel. This witness is a human being; he was here in the flesh. He took the witness stand and, under oath, he gave certain testimony. We now argue to the jury that they should not believe him because he did not know what he was talking about or he did not remember or he did not tell the truth — whatever it may be. That is a very harsh thing to ask people to do. In effect, we are asking the jury to conclude that a human being whom they met, in a manner of speaking, just yesterday or last week, is not worth believing. Juries are very reluctant to accept such a harsh argument. It is an argument with the bark on. You do not want to make that kind of argument. You must take the bark off.

We will take an example that we have used before.[28] You are the prosecutor; you are concerned with the defense's alibi. The alibi witness is the mother of the defendant. "He was in the movies with me," says she. How are you going to cross-examine? Probably just one question: "You are his mother, aren't you?" And you sit down. Now it is time to sum up to the jury. You cannot tell the jury that she is a liar. That argument is not tactful. It comes across as being too hard. The bark is too overwhelming. You cannot ask the jury outright to conclude that this lovely old lady is a liar.

How should you handle it? Your argument should be light and tactful:

> Ladies and gentlemen, the defense's alibi rests on the testimony of Mrs. Jones. Now you heard the cross-examination? She freely admitted that she is the defendant's mother.

---

[28]See §15.4.

You shrug and move on. That shrug tells the whole story. You need not say anything else. When the jury retires, they will conclude that the woman is a liar. But you must leave it to the jury to take that last step; if you take the step for them, they will not go along.

Finally, a trial lawyer must respect the jury's intelligence. Juries are extraordinary. As G. K. Chesterton said, "You take twelve people, lock them in a room, and the Holy Ghost descends." The jury becomes something special, a unique organism. Collectively, the jury remembers every word of testimony, understands every issue in the case, understands every legal argument, and finds the best, most humane resolution of the case. The jury always comes up with the right answer.

## §15.8 The Art of Cross-Examination: The Ten Commandments

We have noted a central concept of the art of cross-examination. We should cross-examine only to the extent necessary to get the ammunition we need for our summation. Not often, however, are we in a position of saying, "No questions, Your Honor." Most of the time we will have to stand up to cross-examine. Now, our job is to avoid embarrassing ourselves.

Specific advice on the subject of cross-examination can be reduced to ten commandments. A word of confession, however: The number is really smaller than ten. Only six or seven of the commandments are truly distinct, but the number ten adds a certain literary ring.

These commandments are simple and easy to remember. Yet they are almost impossible for trial lawyers to obey. I cannot express how powerfully I wish to preach them. They are infallible. Every time a lawyer violates any one of them, he will want the ground to open up beneath his feet. There is one exception, of course: A Clarence Darrow may violate these rules to his heart's content. The rest of us must not.

**I. Be Brief.** Be brief, short, succinct. There are two reasons. First, the chances are excellent that any lawyer cross-examining any witness is doing a poor job of it. The shorter the time that he spends, the less damage he is likely to do.

The second reason for succinctness follows from the premise that any trial, even the simplest, is an extremely complicated experience for the jury. To the lawyer who has spent days and weeks preparing the case, the facts have become second nature — but they are not second nature to the jury. It takes the jury an hour just to figure out which party is the plaintiff and which is the defendant, and which lawyer represents whom.

The jury hears the facts at trial for the first time, and hears them only once. Moreover, the jurors must grasp this complex constellation of information through their ears. Most of us take in the bulk of our information through our eyes, which is a much more efficient method. A trial lawyer must remember the very low ceiling on the jurors' ability to absorb information aurally. Once the jurors reach their point of saturation, they not only stop soaking up new information, but they disgorge whatever they might have already acquired, and in the end remember nothing.

A lawyer, then, must help the jurors to remember the information that the lawyer brings out on cross-examination. The jurors cannot possibly take the information into account in their deliberation if they are unable to remember it. The lawyer must keep it brief because otherwise the jury will simply not absorb it. Unless he is Clarence Darrow, a lawyer should never make more than three points on cross-examination. Two points are better than three, and one is best of all.

Recall our previous example, in which the defendant's mother testified on direct examination in support of her son's alibi: "He was in the movies with me."[29] Our cross-examination consisted of only one question: "You are his mother, aren't you?" And in summation, we tactfully argued only one point — that she is his mother and therefore should not be believed. We make that point and no others because we can be confident that the jury will remember it. And that brings them halfway to accepting the point.

---

[29]See §§15.4, 15.7.

**II. Use Plain Words.** We have noted the importance of using plain words in connection with jury selection[30] and the opening statement.[31] It deserves mention on every possible occasion.

Good trial lawyers do use a special language, but it is a language of simplicity, not complexity. One mark of the master is the use of the two-cent word instead of the half-dollar word. In five and one-half years as a trial judge in New York City, I must have presided over 500 car accident cases, yet not once did I hear a lawyer use the word "car." The questions were always put like this: "What did you then do with respect to the operation and control of your motor vehicle?" To many nonlawyers, "vehicle" is a fancy word. It sounds rather like something to do with the sidecar on a motorcycle. If the jurors are busy wondering how a motorcycle suddenly got into the case, they are not listening to the testimony; and if they are not listening, they cannot be persuaded. The solution is to use short questions and plain words.

**III. Use Only Leading Questions.** With exceptions, the law of evidence forbids leading questions on direct examination: The lawyer may not ask questions that suggest the answer.[32] The lawyer is not under oath, and can report no personal perceptions of the transaction in question; the lawyer is not competent to testify;[33] the law of evidence, therefore, does not allow the lawyer to put words in his witness's mouth. But the law of evidence says nothing about the form of questions on cross-examination.

Not only are leading questions perfectly permissible on cross-examination, but on cross-examination we must ask nothing *but* leading questions. Our whole aim on cross-examination is to grab the witness by the collar and take him where we want him to go. We make him say what we want him to say. And we do that by putting words in his mouth with leading questions.

It should offend our very souls to hear a cross-examining lawyer ask, "What happened next?" Thinking that he has to do

---

[30]See §3.6.
[31]See §5.2.
[32]See §11.2.
[33]See §8.8.

something, the lawyer says, "There are a couple of points from your direct testimony I would like to clear up. Did you really see it? Did it really happen that way?" It shows that a lawyer has not the faintest idea of what to do on cross-examination. Nothing is worse than allowing the witness to repeat his story in his own words. We must make the witness say what we want him to say.

Q. It was two o'clock in the afternoon, wasn't it?
A. Yes.
Q. It was a warm day?
A. Yes.
Q. The sun was shining?
A. Yes.
Q. You were standing there on the corner?
A. Yes.
Q. And then the octopus came up out of the manhole, right?
A. Right.

We must say it for him. We want to set his automatic pilot on "yes." Let him say "Yes, yes, yes," right down the line.

**IV. Be Prepared.** On cross-examination, we never ask a question to which we do not already know the answer. Again, we must be well enough prepared that even before the trial begins, we know what we shall say in summation about the credibility of the other side's witnesses.[34] We cross-examine only to bring out the information we need for that summation. Cross-examination is not a fishing expedition; it is not a deposition; it is not the time to conduct the investigation we should have done before trial. If we do not know what the answer will be, we do not ask the question.

There are two exceptions. First, we occasionally do not care about the answer at all; it is the question we want the jury to hear. In that event we need not know the answer in advance.

---

[34]See §15.7.

But we must be certain that any answer the witness might give will suit us. Second, it may happen that we wish to ask the witness an important question, one to which we do not know the answer. It is a sign of inadequate preparation; it should not happen. But when it does happen, a skilled cross-examiner may be able to interpose a series of apparently innocuous questions designed merely to advance his own knowledge. From the answers to those, he determines what the answer to the important question will be, and then decides whether or not to ask it. If we attempt this gambit, it is essential that the jury not understand what we are doing. We must keep open the option of forgoing the important question, in the event that the answer promises to be unfavorable.

**V. Listen.** Too often, lawyers do not listen to the answers that the witness gives. The reason is stage fright. The lawyer may be young or old, but his stage fright never disappears. His heart pounds on the way to the lectern, and he concentrates on remembering the first question. "What is your name?" He thinks, "Hey, I got it out! And I'm still going! Let's see; what's the next question?" He asks aloud, "Where do you live?" And on it goes. The lawyer is too worried about his own thought processes to listen to the answers. Witnesses sometimes say the most extraordinary things, and lawyers blithely sail on because they are not listening.

An anecdote illustrates the point. It is not literally true, but it has the truth of poetry. The story comes not from the world of trials, but from the world of almost-trials — from that unforgettable period when the whole nation watched a Senate committee inquire into the Watergate affair. It was a Greek tragedy come to life. There was a catharsis, a purification; the whole nation was wedded together, watching those senators at work. Yet none of those senators knew how to ask a question. Principally they seemed concerned with making the right appearance on television.

The rules allowed each senator fifteen minutes to cross-examine the witness, and the questioning proceeded from one senator to the next, across the room. The person to watch was the senator who would cross-examine next. He would be combing his glorious white hair, lining up his chin at the right angle with the camera. Finally the camera would come to him. He would glance at the questions written out by his staff, and in all his glory he would ask:

Q. Did you then enter the oval office?

A. Yes.

Q. What did you see?

A. Well, I walked into the oval office and there was the president, naked as a baboon, prancing around on all fours with the Gemstone file in his mouth.

Q. And when did you next see the president?

We must listen to the answers.

**VI. Do Not Quarrel.** Every once in a while, luck is with us. We ask a question, and the answer is contradictory, absurd, patently false, irrational, crazy, lunatic. The master stops. He sits down. Once he has that answer, he is finished. But most trial lawyers have a congenital inability to sit down. They want to argue with the witness. "How dare you say such a thing? How can that possibly agree with what you said a moment ago?" We must avoid doing that. It is bad style and bad craftsmanship. In short, it is inelegant. And if we give the witness the chance, he will inevitably explain away the inconsistency. The advantage of the crazy answer will be lost.

An anecdote from the Nuremburg trials offers a good example of the danger of quarreling with a witness. When the trials were getting under way, the British government sent Sir John Wheeler Bennett — not a lawyer, but a distinguished specialist in modern European diplomatic history — to observe the proceedings and to set down his impressions for posterity. It was probably not in his formal report, but Bennett once told me his impression of the four prosecuting teams. Robert Jackson, the American, was frequently brilliant but occasionally unprepared; when he was unprepared, he got into trouble. The British prosecutor was ineffective on the whole, but when Jackson stumbled, the Englishman would move in and bail him out. The Frenchman, said Bennett, was totally charming and totally incompetent.

To Bennett, the Russian was the best of all. He was like a Russian heavy tank, fifty tons of steel clanking forward, unstoppable by anything on earth. Hermann Goering was on the witness stand. The Russian would say, "Hermann Goering, I hand you a document. Does it bear your signature? Did you read it before signing it? Do you now confess yourself to be a fascist beast?" Goering would say, "No, I do not." The Russian would do it again with another document. For three days, he handed documents to Goering, asking, "Do you now confess yourself to be a fascist beast?"

That question — "Do you now confess yourself to be a fascist beast?" — is a perfect instance of quarreling with the witness. Every time we are tempted to ask a question with that ring, we must suppress it.

**VII. Avoid Repetition.** Never allow the witness to repeat on cross-examination what he said on direct examination. If the jurors hear the testimony once, they may or may not believe it. If they hear it twice, they will probably believe it. If they hear it three times, they will certainly believe it.

The key to effective impeachment lies in asking questions that have nothing to do with the direct examination. Rather than invite the witness to tell the jury yet again how the accident occurred, we ask instead, "You were bribed to give your testimony, weren't you?" "Have you been convicted of a crime?" "Did you beat your wife last night?"

**VIII. Do Not Allow the Witness to Explain.** A trial lawyer must never permit the witness to explain anything on cross-examination. If the witness's answer is irrational, inconsistent, or absurd, we stop and sit down; we then have the foundation for the point we need to make in summation. If we allow the witness to explain his answer, an explanation will always be forthcoming. It will always diminish the impact of the answer. Only a virtuoso may depart from this commandment.

**IX. Limit Questioning.** Every day, all over the country, lawyers walk out of courtrooms thinking, "My God, if only I had stopped when I said to myself, 'Stop.' If only I had not yielded to the temptation to ask that one question too many!" The one question too many will always blow up in that lawyer's face.

There is a classic apocryphal tale to illustrate the one-question-too-many problem. The case is a criminal prosecution for first-degree assault. The prosecution's theory is that the defendant and the victim got into a fight, in the course of which the defendant put his teeth around the victim's nose and bit it off. It is horrible, but possible. The teeth are sharp; the jaws are strong; and most of the nose is only cartilage. One can bite it off.

The prosecution depends upon the testimony of an eyewitness. The defense lawyer cross-examines:

Q. Where were the defendant and the victim when the fight broke out?
A. In the middle of a field.
Q. Where were you?
A. On the edge of the field.
Q. What were you doing?
A. Bird-watching.
Q. Where were the birds?
A. In the trees.
Q. Where were the trees?
A. At the edge of the field.
Q. You were looking at the birds?
A. Yes.
Q. So your back was to the people fighting?
A. Yes.

We stop. We sit down. We have challenged the witness's perception.[35] In summation, we shall argue that the witness could not possibly have seen what happened, not with his back to the victim and the defendant. But we do not stop. We do not sit down. We ask that one question too many:

---

[35]See §15.2.

Q. If your back was to them, then how can you say that the defendant bit off the victim's nose?

A. Well, I saw him spit it out.

**X. Save for Summation.** Save the ultimate point for summation. We will have the opportunity to invoke this commandment only on those rare occasions when everything works. We have prepared; we have conceived an argument that is simple and tactful and respects the jury's intelligence,[36] and will ultimately persuade them. We have worked out an elegant and artistic cross-examination, buttressed by brief leading questions. The argument is overwhelming, but there remains one element to be added to the picture. We are reasonably confident that it can be established with one additional question. As we ask it, we know what is happening, but the jury does not know; the jury does not understand the significance of that question. And we sit down, because that is how we want it to be. The jury will pay attention from then on. They will wonder about that question for the rest of the trial. If they wonder about it, they will remember it; and if they remember it, we are halfway toward persuading them.

The temptation is to explain it all on cross-examination, by asking the witness a question that invites him to explain. That will always be the one question too many. It will erode the force of the impeachment. We must save it. Later, when we stand up for summation, we can say, "Ladies and gentlemen, do you remember my cross-examination of . . . ? Do you remember the one question I asked him? Did you understand what I was driving at? Then let me tell you what I was driving at." Now, you give them the whole story. They walk into the jury room and they can talk of nothing except that cross-examination.

**A Word of Advice.** Effective cross-examination requires experience. I have suggested that twenty-five jury trials represent the minimum experience necessary. That, of course, takes time. But there is a way to condense the process of acquiring the experience, and it can be helpful even to a mature trial lawyer who already has the experience.

---

[36]See §15.7.

In a word, read. Not law; there is too much law as it is, and most of it is better unread. But there is a small library of books, perhaps 200 in English, about trial lawyers, trial judges, and trials. These books are not great literature, but they are commendable as sources of vicarious experience. We can relive *Triangle Shirtwaist* with Max Steuer;[37] or, with Sir Edward Carson at the height of his powers, we can cross-examine Oscar Wilde. F. Lee Bailey's books teach. So do Louis Nizer's.

Trial lawyering raises recurring problems. If Edward Bennet Williams once had a certain problem and solved it, and we can relive it with him by reading about it, we have made his solution a part of our armory. We can stand up in court, confronted with the very same problem, and use the very same device that the great master used. If it worked for him, it may just work for us as well.

---

[37]See §9.3.

# CHAPTER 16

# Character and Other Problems of Proof

## §16.1 Character and Credibility

In the last chapter, we were concerned with the witness's credibility. We now expand the discussion to look also at his character. Despite some indications in judicial opinions and rules of evidence that might suggest otherwise, the words "credibility" and "character" have quite different meanings.

"Credibility" means in the law what it means in ordinary speech: believability. Applied to a witness in the courtroom, credibility refers simply to whether the witness appears, in the eyes of the jury, to be telling the truth. When we impeach a witness using any of the nine modes,[1] or accredit him in any of the three ways we will discuss later in this chapter,[2] we are operating on his credibility — tearing it down or building it up, respectively.

The word "character" in ordinary usage has a broader reach than "credibility." Credibility is one component of character, as the latter term is commonly used, but it is one component only.

The Federal Rules of Evidence use the word "character" in no fewer than three different ways. In Rule 103(b), "character"

---

[1]See §§15.2, 15.4, 15.5.
[2]See §16.4.

means "type" or "nature."[3] In Rule 405(a), it means a quality of personality.[4] And in Rule 608(a), it means credibility, the appearance of telling the truth.[5] The first of these usages is not to our point here, and we set it aside. The second and third usages, however, bespeak a looseness of terminology which, commonplace though it may be, needs correction.

The Federal Rules seem to designate as "character" anything that cannot be photographed. What is worse, "character" is not used consistently in the rules to mean a person's nonphysical qualities. Sometimes the word "credibility" appears. Since credibility is generally taken as an aspect of character, the word is capable of more precise deployment than "character." Yet the Federal Rules slip from "credibility" to "character" without applying any readily discernible system.

Let us imagine a lawyer reading consecutively through the rules. In Rule 104, on preliminary questions, he comes upon the reference, "evidence relevant to . . . credibility."[6] In Rule 404(a)(3), he learns that "character" may be proved in conformity with Rules 607, 608, and 609 — all of which, he finds, speak to "credibility": Rule 607 mentions only who may attack credibility;[7] Rule 608 deals with attacking or supporting credibility with evidence of "character;"[8] and Rule 609 speaks of otherwise attacking credibility.[9] Rule 405, meanwhile, has taught the reader that "character"

---

[3]"The court may add any other or further statement which shows the character of the evidence . . . ." Fed. R. Evid. 103(b).

[4]"In all cases in which evidence of character or a trait of character of a person is admissible, proof may be made by testimony as to reputation or by testimony in the form of an opinion. . . ." Fed. R. Evid. 405(a).

[5]"[E]vidence of truthful character is admissible only after the character of the witness for truthfulness has been attacked . . . ." Fed. R. Evid. 608(a)(2).

[6]". . . This rule does not limit the right of a party to introduce before the jury evidence relevant to weight or credibility." Fed. R. Evid. 104(e).

[7]"The credibility of a witness may be attacked by any party . . . ." Fed. R. Evid. 607. See §16.5.

[8]"The credibility of a witness may be attacked or supported by evidence in the form of opinion or reputation, but subject to these limitations: (1) the evidence may refer only to character for truthfulness or untruthfulness . . . ." Fed. R. Evid. 608(a). See §§15.5, 16.4.

[9]"For the purpose of attacking the credibility of a witness, evidence that he has been convicted of a crime shall be admitted . . . ." Fed. R. Evid. 609(a). See §15.4.

may be proved by reputation, by opinion, and occasionally by specific instances of conduct, the congruence of all of which with Rules 608 and 609 is not immediately obvious. In Rule 610 the reader finds "credibility" again,[10] and in Rule 803(21), "character" again,[11] although it is plain that, at least in part, the same things are meant.

With intense application, the dedicated lawyer or judge no doubt will master the difficulty. But why should such application be required? With respect to "character" and "credibility," the following maxim would make life much simpler:

- Use the word "credibility" to mean, and only to mean, the jury's determination of the extent to which a witness seems to be telling the truth.

- Use the word "character" to mean, and only to mean, evidence tending to show that the defendant in a criminal case has led a good life (or a bad life), in consequence of which the defendant should be acquitted (or convicted).[12]

- Since "credibility" and "character" mean two different things, they should not be used interchangeably or as if the one were part of the other.

- Anything that is not credibility or character should be called by some other name and treated merely as an ordinary fact to be proved.

Maintaining the distinction between character and credibility may be of little moment to those who value substance over form; but to those who understand the professional competence of a lawyer to extend chiefly to matters of form, it is an issue worth

---

[10]"Evidence of the beliefs or opinions of a witness on matters of religion is not admissible for the purpose of showing that by reason of their nature his credibility is impaired or enhanced." Fed. R. Evid. 610. See §15.2.

[11]"The following are not excluded by the hearsay rule, even though the declarant is available as a witness: . . . (21) Reputation as to character. Reputation of a person's character among his associates or in the community." Fed. R. Evid. 803.

[12]But see §15.4.

making clear. If a good carpenter cares for his tools, a good lawyer is prudent with words. What else do lawyers know but language?

## §16.2 The Character Witness

When lawyers offer evidence, they seek to prove something by that evidence. The evidence, then, must have some logical connection with the thing that the lawyer seeks to prove. If it has that logical connection, we say that the evidence is relevant. If the thing sought to be proved further has some bearing upon an issue in the lawsuit, we say that the evidence is material.[13]

The central principle of the modern law of evidence is that all material evidence ought to be admitted, unless there is some good reason to exclude it. One good reason might be the rule against hearsay; another might arise from a matter of privilege. The balance of this chapter deals with two sorts of evidence which are material but which, for reasons derived from other policy considerations, will not always be admissible.

The first instance is encountered in criminal practice. At common law — in England, the United States, and other countries that trace their legal tradition back to England — a defendant's guilt or innocence must be determined solely upon the basis of evidence tending to show that the defendant did or did not do the thing charged in the indictment. Nothing else counts; that is the genius of Anglo-Saxon criminal law. That the defendant has led a bad life, has committed other crimes, has engaged in other sorts of antisocial behavior — all of that is simply beside the point at common law. The prosecution may not say to the judge or jury, "The defendant is a bad man; therefore he deserves to be convicted." We summarize the principle this way: Character is never in issue in a criminal case.

The English judges who invented that rule, and from whom we inherit it, went on to consider another aspect of what happens in a criminal trial. The defendant is protected by a presump-

---

[13]See §8.1.

tion of innocence. The prosecution must prove guilt beyond a reasonable doubt. But despite these great safeguards of the law, one's sense of what actually happens in a criminal courtroom is rather different. It is not unduly cynical to say that most jurors take it for granted that the police do not arrest people at random, that cases of mistaken identity are very rare, and that if the defendant has been arrested and charged with a crime, then there is very good reason to believe that the defendant did something and deserves to be convicted. Perhaps in most cases tried in the criminal courts, the presumption in practice is turned around. The jury's attitude is, "We'll acquit him if he shows us that he's innocent; but otherwise, we'll convict him."

The judges of England some centuries ago recognized this imbalance: that, in fact, the cards are stacked against the defendant in a criminal case. This is troubling, because our loyalty is to the great principle of the presumption of innocence. The judges of England saw that to redress the balance, to make it a little fairer, the defendant would have to be given something additional. And so they added a qualification to the rule that the defendant's character is never in issue. The prosecution may never argue that the defendant is a bad man and therefore deserves to be convicted. But, said the judges of England, the defendant, if he wishes, may say in substance to the jury, "I am a good man, and therefore, I deserve to be acquitted." Thus, the complete statement of the rule on character goes something like this: Character is never in issue in a criminal case — unless and until the defendant puts his character in issue. It is the defendant's option. He may put his character in issue, but he is not obliged to do so.

There remains the technical problem of how the defendant puts his character in issue. Although there is a great deal of confusion about this, there need not be; it is very simple and very clear. There is only one way in which a defendant can put his character in issue. That is by calling a special kind of witness called a character witness. The effect of the character witness's testimony is to put the defendant's character in issue.

Recall that the defendant's credibility is a wholly separate matter from his character.[14] The two operate independently of one another. The defendant's credibility is in issue when he himself takes the stand and becomes a witness. His character is in issue when he calls a character witness. Mathematically, there are four possible combinations of these events. (1) The defendant's credibility is in issue, but not his character, when he takes the stand but does not call a character witness. (2) The defendant's character is in issue, but not his credibility, when he calls a character witness but does not take the stand. (3) Both his credibility and his character are in issue when he both takes the stand and calls a character witness. (4) Neither his credibility nor his character is in issue when he neither takes the stand nor calls a character witness. The two, in short, are independent variables and must be analyzed separately.

When the defendant does call a character witness, what does the witness testify to? The judges of England solved this technical problem. It will not do simply to say that the character witness testifies as to character; that is not informative enough. A character witness will tell the jury, in effect, that the defendant has led a good life. There are three possible ways to do that.

The first way is by specific instances of virtuous conduct on the part of the defendant: "I remember such-and-such an occasion when he helped an old lady across the street. And there was another time when he got a cat down out of a tree."

Second is the witness's own opinion: "In my opinion," says the character witness from the stand, "he is a very good man."

Third is gossip about the defendant — except that, instead of gossip, we call it reputation.

(These three possibilities parallel the three possible kinds of testimony for impeaching a witness by proving that he is a liar.[15] The similarity can be misleading, however. We deal here with building up character, while to impeach a witness is to attack his credibility. The two are different matters.)

Of the three possibilities, the judges of England said that only one has real probative force: gossip or reputation. At common

---

[14]See §16.1.
[15]See §15.5.

law, therefore, and in most of the states to this day, the character witness, when he takes the stand, testifies to gossip in the community concerning the defendant. The testimony can refer to any traits of personality that speak well of the defendant, and among those defense counsel will be given a good deal of latitude. That the defendant is a peaceful, honest, law-abiding citizen will apply in just about every case. But defense counsel can also select other personality traits appropriate to the charge. If the charge is drunk driving, defense counsel might ask the character witness, "What reputation does the defendant have in the community for being a peaceful, honest, sober citizen?" Or, if the charge is assault — the defendant is accused of having lost his temper and beat up someone — "What is the defendant's reputation in the community for being a calm, even-tempered, quiet sort of person?" And so on.

In practice, after the character witness has given his name and address, it sounds something like this:

Q. Sir, do you know the defendant?

A. No, I don't.

It is unimportant whether the character witness actually knows the defendant. But it is important that he answer yes to the next question:

Q. Do you know *about* the defendant? Have you heard of him?

A. Oh, yes, I have.

Q. In what connection have you heard of him?

A. We are members of the same lodge [or whatever].

Q. Do you know people who know the defendant?

A. Yes.

Q. And over the years, have you heard those people talk about the defendant?

A. Yes, I have.

Q. As a result of what you've heard, can you tell us that you are familiar with the defendant's reputation for being a peaceful, honest, law-abiding citizen?

A. Yes, I am familiar with it.

Q. What is that reputation?

A. It is excellent.

The whole thing takes thirty seconds, but any experienced criminal lawyer will agree that its importance goes far beyond the thirty seconds that it takes. In particular, the identity of the character witness has real impact on the jury. When a solid citizen, a famous person, comes in and stands up for the defendant, juries are impressed. And defense counsel is never restricted to just one character witness. The upper limit lies in the judge's discretion. There are criminal cases in which the numbers of character witnesses have run well into the teens. There are criminal cases in which, beyond any doubt, an acquittal has been secured by the character witnesses.

One more example, this one from a real criminal case. The character witness was Judge Calvert Magruder; the defendant, Alger Hiss.

Q. Judge Magruder, you are the Chief Judge of the United States Circuit Court of Appeals for the First Circuit, are you not?

A. Yes, sir.

Q. And that Circuit has its headquarters where?

A. Boston.

Q. How long have you been on that court?

A. Over ten years.

Q. Prior to being appointed to that court what official positions had you held, say from 1920 on?

A. I was professor at the Harvard Law School from 1920 to 1939. I had leave of absence from that school two years and I was serving in Washington in various capacities; in 1934-35 I was general counsel of the old National Labor Relations Board, and 1938-39 I was general counsel of the Wage and Hour Division of the Department of Labor.

Q. Do you know Alger Hiss?

A. I do.

Q. When did you first meet him?

A. I met him when he was a student at the Harvard Law School, perhaps 1928 or thereabouts.

Q. Before going to Harvard Law School had you lived in Maryland?

A. That was my home.

Q. Will you tell His Honor and the jury the occasions when you met him, if you can, from the time you first met him on, Judge Magruder?

A. I don't recall my first meeting with him but he was prominent as a student at the law school. I do not believe he ever took a course with me but he came from my home state and I got to know him quite well socially and saw a good deal of him and had him in my home and I have since then remained a friend of his.

Q. When you were in Washington did you see him?

A. I did.

Q. Have you been in his home in Washington?

A. I have.

Q. Do you know other people who know Alger Hiss?

A. Yes.

Q. What is his reputation for integrity, loyalty, and veracity?

A. Excellent.

Defense Counsel: You may inquire.

So far we have summarized the common law with respect to the defense calling character witnesses. That is the law that will be followed in most states. It will also be followed in the federal courts, but with one addition. Recognizing that people in our faceless, anonymous society do not really have reputations, and that a character witness who testifies to reputation has been carefully coached to testify that way, the draftsmen of the Federal Rules thought it advisable to write a rule that permits the character witness to testify in accordance with what he really means: that in the witness's own opinion, the defendant is a good man.[16] The character witness may still testify as to reputation, as at common law, but in the federal courts he may also say, "In my opinion, the defendant is a peaceful, honest, law-abiding citizen."

Testimony as to specific instances of virtuous conduct is not permitted at common law. Under the Federal Rules, specific instances will be admissible only in very limited situations.[17]

## §16.3 Impeaching the Character Witness

The criminal defendant has the option of calling a character witness, and thus of putting his character in issue. He is not obliged to; but if he does, then the character witness takes the stand and testifies as summarized in the preceding section. The character witness then becomes subject to impeachment or discrediting just as any other witness. Since it is always the defense who calls the character witness, impeachment will always be in the hands of the prosecutor.

Let us say that W-1 is a character witness called by the defendant. Depending on the jurisdiction, he has testified either in accordance with the common law rule, as to the defendant's reputation as a peaceful, honest, law-abiding citizen,[18] or in accordance with the federal rule, that in the witness's own opinion, the defendant is a peaceful, honest, law-abiding man.[19] That is the end of the direct examination.

The prosecutor then stands up to impeach. He may use any of the nine modes of impeachment discussed in the preceding chapter.[20] Taking them in reverse order, we come first to impeachment by showing reputation for lack of veracity.[21] To impeach

---

[16]"In all cases in which evidence of character or a trait of character of a person is admissible, proof may be made by testimony as to reputation or by testimony in the form of an opinion. . . ." Fed. R. Evid. 405(a).

[17]"In cases in which character or a trait of character of a person is an essential element of a charge, claim, or defense, proof may also be made of specific instances of his conduct." Fed. R. Evid. 405(b).

[18]See §16.2.

[19]Fed. R. Evid. 405(a). See §16.2.

[20]See §§15.2, 15.4, 15.5.

[21]See §15.5.

the character witness using that ninth and last mode of impeachment, the prosecutor calls witness W-2 who testifies that he knows the reputation of character witness W-1 for telling the truth, and that W-1's reputation is terrible.

Continuing to work backwards through the nine modes of impeachment, the nine pigeonholes, we come to the second group of four.[22] The first we meet (it was last, in the original sequence) is impeachment by a prior inconsistent statement:

Q. Mr. Character Witness, didn't you go to the bar last week? Didn't you say to the bartender that the defendant's reputation is in fact perfectly awful?

A. Yes, I did say that.

Bad act impeachment, assuming that the jurisdiction permits it:

Q. Mr. Character Witness, didn't you beat your wife last night?

A. As a matter of fact, I did.

Prior convictions:

Q. Mr. Character Witness, weren't you convicted of perjury last year?

A. Yes, I was.

Bias, prejudice, interest, or corruption:

Q. Mr. Character Witness, aren't you in fact the brother-in-law of the defendant?

A. That's right, I am.

The first four modes of impeachment are the four elements of competence, turned around and used destructively: oath, perception, memory, and communication.[23] Few lawyers nowadays would use the element of the oath, for it amounts to an attack on the witness's religious convictions and is for that reason unseemly. But the element of perception is more interesting. Every witness testifies to what he has perceived, subject to exceptions. The character witness testifies, in the common

[22]See §15.4.
[23]See §15.2.

law jurisdictions, to having perceived the gossip concerning the defendant. In the language of the courtroom, the character witness testifies to the defendant's reputation.

Suppose the defendant was once convicted of a crime. If he takes the stand and thereby puts his credibility in issue, it may be that his prior conviction will come out by way of an attack on his credibility.[24] But if the defendant does not take the stand, his credibility is not in issue. Therefore, he cannot be impeached, and so the jury will not hear about the prior conviction by way of his impeachment.

Assume now that the defendant does not take the stand, but that he does call a character witness. The prosecutor cannot simply ask the character witness, "Sir, was the defendant convicted?" That fits none of the nine modes of impeachment. It is the character witness on the stand whom the prosecutor must seek to impeach, not the defendant. The defendant's conviction speaks only to the defendant's credibility, not to the character witness's credibility.

The prosecutor wants to bring out that prior conviction nonetheless, whether the defendant takes the stand or not. Suppose that he tries to do it, not through impeachment by a prior conviction, but through impeachment by inadequate perception — the character witness's perception. In our taxonomy, the prosecutor switches from the second pigeonhole of the second group to the second of the first group.

It works this way. The character witness says on direct examination that he perceived the gossip about the defendant. If the defendant had a prior conviction, people would talk about it. It would affect his reputation. The questioning might go like this:

Q. Mr. Character Witness, you say you are familiar with the defendant's reputation?

A. Yes, I am.

Q. Have you ever heard that the defendant was convicted of thus-and-so?

---

[24]See §15.4.

If the character witness answers, "No, I never heard of it," he indicates that his perception is less than complete. And if he says, "Yes, I have heard of it," having told the jury on direct that the defendant's reputation is excellent, he is not communicating accurately.

From a tactical standpoint, the prosecutor is aiming not to impeach the character witness, but to make sure that the jury hears of the conviction. Life being what it is, the prosecutor will be seeking within certain limits to poison the jury, and this is a way of going about it. From an analytical standpoint, however, the prosecutor is merely asking a question to impeach the character witness.

Assume that the defendant was never convicted, but merely arrested. A defendant who takes the stand cannot be impeached with an arrest. An arrest does not fit any of the nine pigeonholes. Anybody can be arrested; it can be a mistake or an accident. But suppose now that the character witness is on the stand. The arrest will have entered into the gossip concerning the defendant; it will have affected his reputation. On the theory that he is attacking the character witness's perception as to reputation, the prosecutor asks, "Have you ever heard that the defendant was arrested?" Again, if the character witness answers no, then his familiarity with the gossip — his perception of the defendant's reputation — is limited. If he answers yes, having said on direct that the reputation is excellent, then he is not communicating clearly. More important to the prosecutor, the information about the arrest will have been placed before the jury.

The same principle applies to bad acts.[25] Many of the states do not allow bad act impeachment, and in such a jurisdiction the prosecutor cannot impeach the defendant on the stand by asking, "Did you beat your wife last night?" But if the defendant does beat his wife, and people talk about it, it will affect his reputation. And so, when the defendant calls a character witness, the prosecutor cross-examines the character witness: "Have you ever heard that the defendant beats his wife?"

The prosecutor cannot make up such a question out of whole

---

[25]See §15.4.

cloth. But assuming that he has a good-faith basis for the question,[26] it is permissible in every court in the land, state or federal.[27] With a good-faith basis, the questions can extend to arrests, convictions, or the mere commission of almost any kind of bad act.

This sort of impeachment of a character witness was authorized by the U.S. Supreme Court in *Michelson v. United States*.[28] Therefore it is generally called *Michelson*-type cross-examination. A more recent example is *United States v. Crippen*,[29] a Fifth Circuit case. Crippen was an automobile dealer on trial for perjury in connection with a grand jury investigation of fraud in the industry. He called a number of character witnesses. The first was a nun. She spoke highly of the defendant. On cross-examination, the prosecutor asked whether her opinion would be the same if she knew that the defendant had admitted to turning back odometers on used cars before selling them. Defense counsel objected. He pointed out that in the days when Crippen was turning back odometers, it was not yet a crime to do so. The prohibiting legislation came only later. But the trial judge, having satisfied himself as to the prosecutor's good-faith basis for the question, admitted it. The Fifth Circuit affirmed, citing *Michelson*.

When the defendant has a background likely to raise a problem under *Michelson* — most commonly, when he has been convicted or arrested, or has engaged in bad acts — the defense counsel must be wary not only of the wisdom of putting the defendant on the stand, but also of the wisdom of calling a character witness. That opens the door to *Michelson*-type cross-examination. In the guise of impeaching the character witness, the prosecutor will succeed in putting before the jury all of the adverse information about the defendant himself.

In short, once the defendant has placed his character in issue by calling a character witness, then his character is indeed in

---

[26]See §15.3.

[27]"On cross-examination [of a character witness], inquiry is allowable into relevant specific instances of conduct." Fed. R. Evid. 405(a).

[28]335 U.S. 469 (1948).

[29]570 F.2d 535 (5th Cir. 1978), *cert. denied,* 439 U.S. 1069 (1979).

issue. The prosecutor becomes entitled to say to the jury, in effect, "The defendant is a bad man; therefore he deserves to be convicted."

A prosecutor who is not satisfied with *Michelson* cross-examination may also, as part of his own case on rebuttal, call a bad-character witness. At common law, the bad-character witness would testify that the defendant's reputation for being a peaceful, honest, law-abiding citizen is terrible. Under the Federal Rules, the bad-character witness may say, in addition, "In my opinion, the defendant is a very wicked man indeed."[30] But this kind of testimony is rarely used. The potency of the *Michelson* case, and the sort of impeachment that it authorizes, usually makes the bad-character witness unnecessary.

## §16.4 Accrediting the Witness

The last chapter laid out the nine modes of impeachment — the nine techniques for raising doubts in the minds of the jurors as to a witness's credibility. Here we turn to the other side of the ledger, the matter of accrediting or bolstering the credibility of a witness. Usually it is the proponent who accredits the witness, and he may not do so unless the witness has previously been discredited. Thus, the process is sometimes called rehabilitating the witness. The general method is to ask questions whose purpose is to build up believability. In contrast with the nine ways of discrediting the witness, there are only three modes for accrediting the witness.

The first mode of accrediting the witness is simply to have him explain the damaging testimony he gave when he was being impeached. Because the impeachment almost always occurs on cross-examination, this mode of accrediting is almost always used on re-direct. As a matter of the craft of advocacy, it can be very tricky. The proponent often does not know what the explanation will be, and so by bringing it out the lawyer runs the risk of making a bad situation worse.

---

[30]Fed. R. Evid. 405(a).

Tactical considerations aside, the law of evidence permits us to ask questions inviting the witness to explain, or drawing out the explanation. For example, the witness on direct said that the yellow Plymouth had the red light. Here is the impeaching cross-examination:

Q. You say that the driver of the yellow Plymouth had the red light?

A. Yes.

Q. Now, you're a male — a man — are you not?

A. Yes.

Q. You observe that the driver of the yellow Plymouth is female, a woman?

A. Yes, I see that.

Q. Is it not a fact that on January 1, 1969, you and the driver of the yellow Plymouth were married?

A. Yes, that is so.

The cross-examiner has used the first mode in our second group of four, interest or bias:[31] emotional predisposition in favor of one's wife. Now, re-direct examination by the proponent:

Q. You were married to the driver of the yellow Plymouth on January 1, 1969 — is that correct?

A. Yes.

Q. But it's a fact, isn't it, that you were divorced on January 1, 1975?

A. That is so.

Q. Are you married to her today?

A. No.

That is permissible. It is an instance of accrediting the witness by explanation of the impeaching material.

The second method of accrediting a witness is to call another witness who will testify to the primary witness's reputation for

---

[31]See §15.4.

veracity. Let us say that W-1 has been impeached: The adversary called W-2, who testified that W-1 has a reputation for lack of veracity.[32] Under the Federal Rules, W-2 may also have testified to his own opinion that W-1 is a liar.[33] The proponent of W-1 may now rehabilitate him by calling a third witness, W-3, who testifies that W-1 has the reputation of being a truth-teller. Although it is permissible under the Federal Rules[34] and in all of the states, this method is rarely used.

The third and last method of accrediting a witness is seen quite frequently. Not infrequently, it is misunderstood by lawyers and judges alike. The rule that governs it is called the prior consistent statement rule, or sometimes, the recent fabrication rule. The law in all jurisdictions is the same, and it is settled, so there should be no reason for confusion or misunderstanding.

A prior consistent statement is exactly what the name implies: a prior statement by the witness that is consistent with what he now says on the witness stand. Many lawyers think that a prior consistent statement is always admissible to accredit, to show the jury that the witness has been saying the same thing all along. That is not so. Many other lawyers believe the rule to say that a prior consistent statement is never admissible. That is not so, either. A prior consistent statement is admissible to accredit only in certain circumstances. When those circumstances are present, this third and last way of accrediting a witness becomes available.

Look at *People v. Singer*,[35] a decision by the highest court in New York that would be followed anywhere. The defendant was on trial for homicide. The victim was a woman. Her death grew out of a botched abortion, at a time when abortions were illegal. At trial, the prosecution called a witness named Schneidewind, whose testimony added up to an assertion that Singer was guilty. The defense lawyer then stood up to impeach, and he did a very

---

[32]See §15.5.

[33]Fed. R. Evid. 608(a).

[34]"[E]vidence of truthful character is admissible only after the character of the witness for truthfulness has been attacked by opinion or reputation evidence or otherwise." Fed. R. Evid. 608(a)(2).

[35]300 N.Y. 120, 89 N.E.2d 710 (1949).

good job. It went something like this:

> Q. Schneidewind, at such and such a time, were you not called before the grand jury?
> A. Yes.
> Q. Were you not asked certain questions?
> A. Yes.
> Q. Among those questions, were you not asked, "Is Singer guilty?"
> A. That's right. I was asked that.
> Q. And did you not make the answer, "Singer is not guilty"?
> A. Yes, I said that.

With his first three questions, defense counsel laid the foundation for impeachment with a prior inconsistent statement, the fourth mode of impeachment in our second group of four.[36] Schneidewind's testimony before the grand jury was oral, and so the lawyer directed the witness's attention to the time, place, and circumstances of the prior inconsistent statement. Only then did he elicit the statement. But that is not all defense counsel did. The cross-examination continued along these lines:

> Q. After you testified before the grand jury that Singer was not guilty, didn't you step out into the corridor and have a little conversation with the district attorney?
> A. Yes.
> Q. Didn't the district attorney point out to you that you were an accomplice to this homicide?
> A. Yes, he did.
> Q. And didn't the district attorney point out that you yourself stood to be indicted for murder?
> A. Yes, he said something like that.

---

[36]See §15.4.

Q. Didn't he say that you could go to Sing Sing for twenty years?

A. Yes, I think he did.

Q. And didn't he say that you could help yourself here?

A. Well, maybe he did.

Q. Now, he didn't make any promises, did he? Of course not.

A. No, he didn't make any promises.

Q. But didn't you go back to the grand jury two days later?

A. Yup.

Q. And didn't you then tell the grand jury that Singer was guilty?

A. Yup.

Q. Have you been indicted yourself?

A. No.

This mode of impeachment is not a prior inconsistent statement. Rather, it is impeachment by interest,[37] the first in our second group of four. Considering his own plight, the witness Schneidewind had every reason of self-interest to tailor his testimony to please the prosecution.

The prosecutor stood up for re-direct examination. In effect, it went like this:

Q. Schneidewind, is it not a fact that thirteen months ago, long before either one of your appearances before the grand jury — in fact, on the very day following the abortion — on that day, did you not tell the victim's father that Singer was guilty?

A. I told him that, yes.

That statement to the victim's father is a prior consistent statement: It is prior to Scheidewind's testimony at trial, and it is inconsistent with his testimony at trial.

---

[37]See *id.*

Now we turn to the prior consistent statement rule, also called the recent fabrication rule: When a witness has been impeached in such a fashion as to suggest that his testimony was a fabrication — not a mistake, but a lie — then a prior consistent statement will be admissible, so long as the statement was made at a time preceding the existence of a motive to fabricate.

Under the rule, Schneidewind's statement to the victim's father is admissible to accredit Schneidewind. Both requirements of the rule are satisfied. First, Schneidewind was impeached in such a way as to suggest that he had lied on direct; defense counsel showed that he had earlier, in his grand jury testimony, said the opposite of what he said on direct. For the second requirement, we look to when Schneidewind's motive to fabricate first arose. That would be when Schneidewind was before the grand jury and had his little talk with the district attorney. The statement to the victim's father was made before that time, before the existence of a motive to fabricate; therefore it is admissible. That is the rule in the federal courts and in all of the state courts.

## §16.5 Discrediting One's Own Witness

In the early days of the common law trial, more often than not the status of a prospective witness would render him incompetent to testify.[38] A prospective witness would be incompetent if he were a litigant, or a friend or relative of a litigant, or if he knew anything about the controversy. Who, then, in those days, took the early equivalent of the witness stand and functioned in a manner that we associate with present-day witnesses? How did an early common law trial proceed? At the risk of making too simple what is still in considerable mystery, owing to the unavailability of records, it is possible to sketch broadly some stages in the early history of the common law trial.

Life in England before the Industrial Revolution was simple, but life in any society necessarily engenders disputes. That is human nature. Every society must have some way short of

---

[38]See §8.2.

self-help for resolving those disputes. In England too, 900 or 1000 years ago, there were disputes, and there were mechanisms for resolving them.

One of the early mechanisms was trial by ordeal. The procedure was to take the plaintiff, tie him up, and throw him in the river. If he floated, he won. If he sank, he lost. He also drowned to death, but there was nothing wrong with that; it is perfectly rational, if we are willing to assume a conscious God who misses nothing. Such a God will make sure that the litigant whose cause is just survives the ordeal. Tying up the litigant and throwing him in the river is merely a mechanism by which God can make his will known. It served the further purpose of keeping down calendar congestion.

In due course this procedure struck our cousins across the water as somewhat primitive, and so they evolved in its place trial by combat. Each side chose a champion. The champions fought. And again, God made sure that the gladiator representing the side whose cause was just won the contest.

Eventually trial by combat also came to strike the English as primitive. From it next evolved trial by compurgation — trial by oath-taking. There was a class of professional oath-takers, people who earned their living by taking oaths. They were called compurgators. They did not take oaths to tell the truth, for they knew nothing relevant to the controversy. They simply took the oath. Typically the oath was a very complicated form of words. The judges listened to see whether the compurgators' tongues tripped. If a compurgator made a mistake in reciting those complicated words, God was showing that the side he represented deserved to lose. The cause of that side was unjust.

In trial by combat or compurgation, it makes sense to speak of a moral connection, or moral nexus, between the litigant and his representative, the champion or compurgator whom he chose. If the gladiator lost the contest, or if the compurgator tripped over a word, it was the fault of the litigant who chose him. The litigant, one might say, had a moral responsibility for his representative.

In time the common law trial evolved from the old forms of trial by ordeal, trial by combat, and trial by compurgation to trial by witnesses: witnesses who perceived, remembered, and could communicate.[39] In place of the idea that God would determine which side had the just cause, it fell to a judge or jury to decide which side's witnesses seemed to be telling the truth, and to be making the more sensible presentation.

The plaintiff in a trial by witnesses could no longer call as a witness someone for whom he wished to have a moral responsibility. Instead, he would have to call the person who happened to see the accident, or whatever else underlay the dispute, and who was therefore competent to testify. The plaintiff would prefer to call as his witness the local archbishop; but unfortunately, the archbishop did not see the accident. The person who did see the accident might be the local mob chieftain — someone for whom the plaintiff does not in the least wish to feel morally responsible. Yet it is the mob chieftain whom he must call.

The modern concept of a competent witness leaves no moral nexus whatsoever between litigants and the witnesses they call. Nevertheless, as recently as a quarter-century ago, every American jurisdiction imposed such a relationship between the litigants and their witnesses. Most still do. A witness nowadays is competent only because of the chance circumstance that he happened to see, and can remember, and can communicate something that bears on the transaction giving rise to the lawsuit. But the litigant, by calling the witness to the stand, is nonetheless vouching for him. Of course, the litigant no longer vouches that the witness will fight effectively, or will take the oath without his tongue tripping. Instead, merely by calling him to the stand, the litigant vouches for the witness's credibility. The litigant impliedly represents to court and jury that the witness will tell the truth. The logical consequence is that, having called the witness to the stand, the litigant cannot attack that witness's credibility. That would be flatly inconsistent with vouching for the witness's credibility.

This remains the law today in most of the American states, outmoded and absurd though it may be. The proponent, the lawyer who performs the purely mechanical office of calling the

---

[39]See §8.8.

witness to the stand,[40] thereby vouches for his credibility, and so may not attack it.

There is an exception to the rule, and it has two requirements. First, the witness must testify in such a fashion as to hurt or prejudice the proponent; and second, the hurtful or prejudicial testimony must come as a surprise to the proponent. When both conditions are met, the proponent may attack the credibility of that witness. This is commonly called the surprise-and-prejudice exception to the rule against the proponent attacking the witness's credibility.

The rule does not apply at all, however, in the federal courts. Even before the passage of the Federal Rules of Evidence, the federal courts had begun to recognize that "there is no reason in logic or common sense or fairness why the party who calls [witnesses] should have to vouch for everything they say."[41] Proponents do not choose witnesses because they like them, by and large, but because circumstances have picked them out. That is why Rule 607 makes a great deal of sense. In its entirety, the rule says, simply, "The credibility of a witness may be attacked by any party, including the party calling him." In the federal courts, proponents have not vouched for their witnesses, and they are not stuck with witnesses' testimony in any way at all. The rule represents a path-breaking, pioneering effort that abolished 800 years of common law history. It will likely have a great deal of influence on the states.

## §16.6 Prior Similar Acts

We now take up a second sort of evidence which, although material, is not always admissible. It arises most commonly in criminal work, and that is the context in which we shall examine it here; but there is nothing inherent that limits the issue to criminal cases.

The starting point once again is the genius of Anglo-Saxon

---

[40]See §11.1.

[41]Johnson v. Baltimore & O.R. Co., 208 F.2d 633 (3d Cir. 1952), *cert. denied*, 347 U.S. 943 (1954).

criminal justice: A defendant's guilt or innocence must be determined solely upon the basis of evidence tending to show that he did or did not do the thing charged in this indictment. Nothing else counts — not the defendant's other crimes, nor his generally bad life, nor that he has done the same sort of thing before.

True, facts concerning the defendant's prior misdeeds will come to the jury's attention if the defendant takes the stand and thereby puts his credibility in issue. He can then be impeached by his prior convictions or his bad acts.[42] But the theory, in that event, is that the convictions or bad acts come in only as bearing on the defendant's credibility. They do not authorize the jury to say, "He's a rotten apple, so let's convict him." Again, if the defendant puts his character in issue by calling a character witness,[43] he opens the way for adverse information to come before the jury.[44] But it is the defendant's option to put his character in issue; it is not the prosecution's.

The problem we address here came up for the first time in a celebrated way in an English case that goes back to the early years of this century.[45] It involved George Joseph Smith, one of the great murderers of all time. At the time of the case he was middle-aged, quite big, very handsome, and, it would seem, particularly irresistible to rich ladies. He met and married a rich lady, unimpeded by the fact that he was already married at the time. At Smith's insistence, his wife — at least she thought she was his wife — executed a will, naming Smith as beneficiary.

The very next day, Smith had a bathtub installed in the house. Just four days after that, Smith left a note for the doctor. "Come at once!" the note said. "I think my wife is dead." And indeed she was — dead by drowning in their brand-new bathtub. There were no signs of violence. Smith suggested to Scotland Yard that she must have had a fit while taking her bath. Of course, Smith stood to receive a very large sum of money under the will.

Scotland Yard, ever indefatigable, was suspicious. They kept

---

[42]See §15.4.
[43]See §16.2.
[44]See §16.3.
[45]Rex v. Smith, 84 L.J.K.B. 2153 (Crim. App. 1915).

a keen eye on Smith, and their diligence paid off. Approximately one year later, George Joseph Smith met a different rich lady. He married her. He had her take out a large insurance policy and make him the beneficiary. Smith bought a bathtub. And shortly afterward, the bride was found dead, drowned in the bathtub. The investigation continued. About a year later still, the same thing: rich bride; large insurance policy; new bathtub; bride drowned.

Suppose that we are crown counsel, the prosecutor. It is perfectly obvious that George Joseph Smith is a murderer. But we have some technical problems. We can indict Smith for the first murder. The prosecution must now prove the corpus delicti: that a death occurred and that it occurred by criminal agency. The woman is dead, certainly. But did it happen by criminal agency? There is no bullet in the brain, no knife wound in the heart, no marks of violence whatsoever. It could easily have been the kind of accident that Smith claimed it was — unless, of course, we take into account that the same thing happened two other times. One such death is a tragic accident. Two is an unbelievable coincidence. Three makes George Joseph Smith a damned murderer.

As crown counsel, what do we do? The fast answer is to try Smith for murder number one, and to put in evidence about murders two and three. Then, it is perfectly obvious that murder number one was no accident; it had to have been done deliberately. But as soon as we offer evidence of murders two and three, then Smith's counsel — Marshall Hall, the leading barrister in criminal practice in England at the time — leaps to his feet and he says, "I object! That violates the genius of Anglo-Saxon criminal law. You are seeking to prove my client's guilt by showing that he has done it at other times. You may not do that. You must prove his guilt by evidence bearing upon whether he did or did not do the thing charged in the indictment."

To no one's surprise, the court rejected that argument. Smith did not take the stand; he did not put his credibility in issue; nor, for that matter, did he put his character in issue. He was convicted nonetheless, and he went to the gallows. That could not have been the outcome unless the jury heard the evidence about the deaths of his other wives.

The case of George Joseph Smith stands for an important precedent that is with us to this day and now appears in the Federal Rules of Evidence. The case does not, however, represent a turning back on the rule that the defendant's guilt must be determined solely on the basis of evidence that he did the acts charged in the indictment. That rule, the genius of Anglo-Saxon criminal justice, still stands.

The case of George Joseph Smith stands for a doctrine commonly called the prior similar act rule — although, strictly speaking, it can also apply to subsequent acts. The prosecution may not put before the jury evidence tending to show that the defendant has done the same thing on other occasions, on the theory that he is therefore likely to have done it this time. But, where the evidence of other similar activity has a narrower theory of relevance — something more specific than a generalized proof of guilt — then the evidence of the other similar acts will be admissible. In the case of George Joseph Smith, the narrower theory of relevance was, of course, that the bride's death was not an accident.

A more recent example appeared in a 1973 Fourth Circuit case, *United States v. Woods*.[46] The defendant was a parent, a foster parent, and a babysitter. She took care of a lot of babies. One of those babies, an eight-month-old foster child, was found one morning dead in his crib. The defendant was indicted for murder and tried. It was the prosecution's obligation to prove the corpus delicti: that a death occurred — of which there was no doubt — and that it happened by criminal agency. The defendant claimed that the baby died of natural causes — what pediatricians call sudden infant death syndrome, and laymen call "crib death." The pathologist who conducted the autopsy testified that the baby could indeed have been a victim of crib death, or, on the other hand, he could have been asphyxiated with a pillow. The pathologist could not determine which. He did estimate that there was one chance in four of the death having been from natural causes. Because the prosecution must prove guilt beyond a reasonable doubt — and one chance in four is certainly a rea-

---

[46]484 F.2d 127 (4th Cir. 1973), *cert. denied*, 415 U.S. 979 (1974).

sonable doubt — the case could not have gone to the jury on that evidence alone.

But the prosecution had additional evidence. Over the preceding years, other children in Mrs. Wood's care had suffered episodes of cyanosis — breathing difficulties — a total of twenty reported episodes in nine children. Seven of those children died. One or two dead children, perhaps, could be crib deaths. With seven, and now an eighth, the odds against them all being crib deaths become astronomical. The argument is the same as that in the case of George Joseph Smith: If there are three brides dead in bathtubs, someone is drowning them. Likewise, if there are eight babies dead in their cribs, someone is asphyxiating them.

The trial judge admitted the evidence of the seven prior deaths, and the Fourth Circuit affirmed. "[E]vidence of other offenses," it held, "may be received, if relevant, for any purpose other than to show a mere propensity or disposition on the part of the defendant to commit the crime . . . . " [47]

The Federal Rules of Evidence, in Rule 404(b), reach the same result: "Evidence of other crimes, wrongs, or acts is not admissible to prove the character of a person in order to show that he acted in conformity therewith. It may, however, be admissible for other purposes, such as proof of motive, opportunity, intent, preparation, plan, knowledge, identity, or absence of mistake or accident." Notice that the narrower theories of relevance listed in the rule — motive, opportunity, etc. — are only examples. Much as did the Fourth Circuit in *Woods*, the federal rule allows evidence as to similar acts to prove anything narrower than that the defendant, just because he did it before, did it again this time.

Here is another example. The victim of a rape testifies essentially as follows: "I was raped. The man who did it wore a ski mask, so I have no way of knowing whether it was the defendant sitting here in court. But before he actually committed the act, he went through all sorts of bizarre rituals. Until he did that, he was not in a state to carry out the crime." The witness goes on to describe the rapist's rituals, and they are indeed bizarre.

---

[47]*Id.* at 134.

The next witness is also a victim of a rape, but her rape is not the one for which the defendant is on trial. She testifies: "The man who raped me did not wear a ski mask. I recognize him; it was the defendant sitting here in court. And before he was able to carry out the crime, he went through a bizarre ritual." She describes the ritual. It is the same one that the first victim described.

This second victim is testifying to a criminal act that is not charged in this indictment. Her testimony is admissible nonetheless. It is not admissible to show that the defendant is a bad fellow, and so deserves to be locked up. It is admissible on a narrower theory of relevance: identity. The prior act, owing to its bizarre nature, serves as a kind of trademark, a behavioral fingerprint. It demonstrates that the man on trial for this crime is the same man who committed the other crime. The second witness can identify her rapist as the man on trial, and so it follows logically that he is the same man whom the first victim described.

One last example. Suppose that the defendant is charged with knowing possession of a stolen radio. The prosecution proves, and the defendant admits, that he possessed the radio. The prosecution next proves that the radio was stolen. "Well, I'll admit that it was stolen," the defendant says. "But I didn't know that it was stolen." If he did not know that it was stolen, he did not commit a crime. An element of the crime charged is mens rea, the knowledge that the radio was stolen.

The prosecution must now prove the defendant's knowledge. One way of doing it is this: "We charge the defendant with knowing possession of that stolen radio on Friday. As part of our case, we will put in evidence that on Thursday, the defendant possessed a different stolen radio. And on Wednesday, yet another stolen radio. On Tuesday, another one. And on Monday, yet another one. On each of those four days, he possessed a different stolen radio. Here he is on Friday with a fifth stolen radio — and he says he didn't know it was stolen."

The prosecution can put in the evidence of the prior four stolen radios to prove guilty knowledge. The chances of that many stolen radios coming into the defendant's possession innocently are inconceivable. This is yet another narrower theory of relevance. It is not among the examples listed in Rule 404(b), but the evidence is admissible nonetheless. Again, the listing in the rule is not exhaustive.

Finally, here is an example of a case that is over the line, one in which evidence of the prior similar acts will not be admissible — the sort of evidence an overly enthusiastic prosecutor may seek to offer. The defendant is on trial for bank robbery. The prosecution offers evidence that on three prior occasions in the preceding two years, the defendant robbed banks. Just that; nothing more. The prosecutor will argue for its admission on the theory of prior similar acts.

The correct ruling? The evidence is not admissible. The only possible basis for putting the evidence in is to show that the defendant is a bad man, a professional bank robber, and therefore ought to be locked up. That violates the genius of Anglo-Saxon criminal law. There is no narrower theory of relevance. Unlike the cases of George Joseph Smith and the infant deaths, there is no possibility of accident to exclude; banks are not robbed by accident. There is no claim here, as in the rape case, that the bank robbery was carried out in such a unique fashion as to suggest a kind of signature or fingerprint. To support the receipt in evidence of prior similar acts, the prosecutor must have that narrower theory of relevance. Without it, the evidence is not admissible.

# CHAPTER 17

# Summation

## §17.1 Delivery

It is the beginning and the end of a presentation that make the longest-lasting impressions. Much as jury selection and the opening statement are important because they came first,[1] the summation is important because the jury hears it last. The summation is our final chance to persuade the jurors that they ought to decide the case our way. Indeed, much of what we do during the trial, and especially in cross-examination, is done primarily to bring out the information we shall need for summation.[2]

There is a fairly wide latitude on what we can discuss in summation. Eligible topics include:

- Any issues in the case;
- All evidence in the case;
- All reasonable inferences from the evidence;
- Any argument that is fair;
- Any matters of common knowledge.

---

[1]See §5.1.
[2]See §15.7.

The elements that add up to a good summation are much the same as those that we have already discussed with regard to other stages of the trial. They include careful planning and rehearsal;[3] developing and maintaining a sense of trustworthiness;[4] lucidity;[5] variety;[6] use of plain English;[7] narrative;[8] theme;[9] tact;[10] respect for the jury;[11] and brevity.[12]

We have looked at the special problems of arguing lack of credibility on summation.[13] More generally, the principles above expand into the following advice:[14]

1. Be prepared and rehearsed.
2. Consider carefully ahead of time which arguments to anticipate from the other side. The opponent may not think of a particular argument, and in that event our rebutting it will have been unnecessary. Worse, there is the danger of mentioning an argument that the other side did not plan on making — and which we are then unable to rebut effectively. It is always best to concentrate on arguing our own case. If we spend the entire summation answering the other side, we will lose.

   We may occasionally have a lawyer on the other side who ends his summation with a very old trick. While the jury looks on, the lawyer turns to us and says, "Justice demands that you answer these questions." He then ticks off a list of questions. It is a trap, and we should not fall for it. Instead, we stand up and explain to the

---

[3]See §5.2.
[4]See §1.3.
[5]See §3.6.
[6]See *id.*
[7]See §5.2.
[8]See §5.3.
[9]See §10.1.
[10]See §15.7.
[11]See *id.*
[12]See §15.8.
[13]See §15.7.
[14]The task of criminal defense counsel in persuading the jury to acquit his client is the subject of the Appendix, "Persuading to Acquit: A Dialogue."

jury that they have just witnessed one of the oldest tricks in the book. The adversary, we tell them, wants us to spend all of our time talking about his questions, because he knows that they have nothing to do with the case. We then proceed to argue our own case.

3. Remember that juries decide cases on the equities. Sometimes a jury's decision, based on a feeling of what is right, does not coincide with what the rules of law require. The summation should, accordingly, include an argument on the equities in the case.

4. Avoid flowery language and rhetoric. Most juries will regard it as phony.

5. Ignore the adversary. Juries do not like to see the lawyers engaging in personality conflicts.

6. Always discuss the issues, the evidence, and credibility of the the witness.

7. Remember to argue for the verdict or remedy you seek. We must tell the jurors precisely what we want them to do.

8. By and large, it is unwise to make objections during the adversary's summation.[15]

9. Organize. As Professor Jeans has said, "Whether your target [in summation] is the head or the heart, the key to hitting the bull's eye is organization."[16]

10. Appear to be fair. The importance of seeming to be trustworthy[17] has come up many times in these chapters, and it carries no less weight in the summation.

11. Watch where you stand. The optimum distance is about six to eight feet from a six-person jury, and about eight feet from a twelve-person jury. A closer approach will impinge upon the jurors' personal space. Beyond about sixteen feet, the distance is too great for good communication.

---

[15]See Chapter 14.
[16]J. Jeans, Trial Advocacy §16.7 (1975).
[17]See §1.3.

12. Avoid using a lectern unless the judge insists on it. The lectern is a physical impediment to communication.

13. Do not overuse notes. The ideal summation is carefully organized, but nevertheless sounds spontaneous.[18] It is best, then, to use no notes at all. Next best is to use them sparingly.

14. Speak plain English.

15. Use visual aids during the summation, whenever they may be helpful.

16. Do not misstate evidence.

17. Be explicit, not implicit. Do not depend on the jury's ability to figure out what you mean. Say it plainly.

18. Be tactful.[19]

19. Always respect the jury's intelligence.[20]

## §17.2  Request to Charge

We have already looked at the request to charge as one of the matters that must be taken care of before trial.[21] Usually submitted early in the trial, the request to charge is a piece of paper that tells the judge how we would like him to instruct the jury at the end of the case. Our previous discussion concerned a relatively rare situation. A point of law central to the case was one of first impression in the jurisdiction, and so we requested an instruction on the legal theory most favorable to our side. That is unusual, for there is seldom any real dispute as to the law. Here, we take up the request to charge in its more commonplace application, as it concerns the factual contentions of the parties.

In the language of the appellate opinions, the judge is obliged to "marshal the proof" as part of the charge to the jury. The judge's burden is heaviest in the federal courts, but to one extent or another most judges must summarize three things for the jury:

---

[18]See §5.2.
[19]See §15.7.
[20]See *id.*
[21]See §4.4.

(1) the factual contentions of the parties; (2) the witnesses' testimony; and (3) how the witnesses' testimony relates to the factual contentions of the parties. When a case turns on the facts, then, we should draft the judge's charge on the facts. We draw up the marshaling of the proof as we would like the judge to deliver it, cut that up into a number of requests to charge, and submit them to the judge. It is a perfectly proper thing to do.

Every jurisdiction has a procedural statute on the submission of requests to charge. In the federal courts it is Rule 51 of the Federal Rules of Civil Procedure. The federal rule, and the corresponding rule in most other jurisdictions, has an important but little-noticed provision: if we submit requests to charge, the judge *must* give his rulings before we sum up.[22] There are, in essence, three rulings that the judge can make on each request to charge. He might say, "Granted. I will read this to the jury." He can say "Granted in substance. I don't like this language, but I'll give this idea to the jury." Or it may be, "Denied. I will not give this to the jury." As to the last, the judge will usually be willing to tell us what he does plan to give the jury on the point.

Once we have the rulings, we can use them in our summation — perhaps in much the same words that the judge will use. The judge is locked in and cannot change the rulings. In summation, then, we can pre-echo the judge, much as a recording sometimes pre-echoes the sound in the upcoming groove. The jury has not yet heard the judge's charge. But they remember what we say, and fifteen minutes later, they hear the judge telling them the same thing. "Hey, that's a smart lawyer," they think. "The judge sees things just the same way the lawyer does." We have associated ourselves with the judge's status. Even at that last stage of the trial, we are still doing everything we can to build up our position with the jury.

---

[22]"The court shall inform counsel of its proposed action upon the requests [to charge] prior to their arguments to the jury, but the court shall instruct the jury after the arguments are completed." Fed. R. Civ. P. 51.

## §17.3 Through the Eyes of the Jury

The common law trial has been around for seven or eight centuries, and anything that survives that long must be satisfying its customers. But in this instance, the reasons are not immediately obvious. The common law trial is, after all, something of a Rube Goldberg contraption. We take highly trained professionals, the lawyers. And we put them together with people who are selected precisely because they are not highly trained — the jurors. No other system has anything like it. But somehow, it works.

One possible reason why the common law trial functions so well would, if true, offer some guidance on the kind of arguments we should make to a jury on summation. The speculation rests on the notion that we lawyers and the jurors are complementary. We make a perfect unity — a synergistic combination, with the whole exceeding the sum of its parts.

By reason of training, inclination, and outlook, we lawyers tend to be historians. We look to the past. The first question that we ask every client is, "What happened?" It is on the basis of what happened in the past that we figure out how to handle the trial. We are also professionals. We try this case today, and another case tomorrow. We tend not to pay much attention to the most important fact of all about a trial: When it is over, the litigants go home and back to their places of business, and they try to resume their lives. For them, there is no next day's trial.

Jurors know that when the trial is over, the litigants go home and back to work. Jurors also know that because the past cannot be changed, it is ultimately unimportant. What matters is the future, because we can affect that. Jurors seem to ask not what happened in the past, but what ought to happen from now on. The jurors look ahead to when the people involved must go home, and they try to make that future as satisfactory as possible. This thinking applies even to criminal cases. It appears that jurors are moved most of all by the question whether or not it is best for the future to lock the defendant up. They are less concerned with what happened in the past, except as it provides a reading on the future.

We lawyers and the jury are not doing the same things, and that is precisely why the system works. If there is anything to this idea, it tells us that in summation — delicately, or the jury will sense that we are intruding upon their turf and resist us — we should orient the jury to the future. We speak as an advocate, of course. We suggest the kind of resolution that is best for our client. But at the same time, we direct their attention to the kind of ending that will best help the litigants to leave the lawsuit behind them and go on with the rest of their lives.

# APPENDIX

# Persuading to Acquit:
# A Dialogue

Place: *A court house, anywhere.*
Time: *Immaterial.*

* * *

Lucius: Who is this, complacent in the corridor?

Marcus: Greetings, Lucius.

Lucius: And salutations to you, Marcus.

Marcus: How do you?

Lucius: As well as may be, given my poor wit and weak understanding.

Marcus: Ah, companion of my boyhood, you should have done as I — studied law, inhabited courtrooms, won fame as a defense advocate.

Lucius: I would not have had your success, Marcus, for I lack your piercing eye, fluent tongue, and imposing presence.

Marcus: Certain gifts, I admit, are necessary, and those you mention are among them. But you do yourself less than justice,

---

This "dialogue" first appeared in Litigation magazine (American Bar Association, Litigation Section), vol. 3, no. 4 (Summer 1977).

Lucius. You have acquired the art of putting questions, and putting questions is much the work of defense advocates.

Lucius: True, but defense advocates put questions to some purpose, do they not? To establish some proposition determined in advance?

Marcus: They do.

Lucius: Then there is a difference between an advocate's questioning and mine. I do not ask questions to demonstrate something already decided.

Marcus: Why do you?

Lucius: To learn, Marcus, to learn, for my ignorance is vast.

Marcus: Yet I think you are wise.

Lucius: I know only myself, Marcus. But come, help reduce my ignorance. Give me some answers.

Marcus: At your service.

Lucius: Why do I find you standing in the corridor?

Marcus: Because a few minutes ago I completed a trial.

Lucius: The result?

Marcus: I don't know. The jury is deliberating.

Lucius: Well, I will await its verdict with you. Tell me, is your client innocent?

Marcus: That is not for me to say. My task is to present the defendant's side of the case as persuasively as I can. It is the jury's task to decide, after listening to me and to the prosecutor, whether the defendant is innocent or not.

Lucius: But does your client have a defense?

Marcus: My clients always have a defense.

Lucius: Surely you do not mean that you contrive a defense for every client?

Marcus: No. The law gives each of my clients a defense.

Lucius: What defense is that?

Marcus: The defense of reasonable doubt.

Lucius: Which means?

## Presumed Innocent

Marcus: The prosecutor must prove each element of his case beyond a reasonable doubt. If the jurors, after reflecting on the evidence, are left with a reasonable doubt as to any element of the prosecutor's case, they are obliged to acquit. The reason is something called the presumption of innocence. The defendant is presumed to be innocent and may not be found guilty unless and until the jurors conclude that the prosecutor has proved his guilt beyond a reasonable doubt.

Lucius: How does the presumption of innocence furnish a defense?

Marcus: By permitting me to argue to the jury that there is a reasonable doubt of the defendant's guilt, in consequence of which he should be acquitted.

Lucius: Are you required to make that argument?

Marcus: No.

Lucius: Do you?

Marcus: In every case.

Lucius: Even when your client has another defense?

Marcus: Give me an example of "another defense."

Lucius: May not a defendant argue that he lacked guilty knowledge?

Marcus: Yes.

Lucius: Or that someone else committed the crime?

Marcus: Yes.

Lucius: Those are examples of "another defense."

Marcus: I understand.

Lucius: Well, do you argue reasonable doubt when your client has such a defense?

Marcus: Yes.

Lucius: Why?

Marcus: That is what defense advocates always do.

Lucius: Does that make it right?

Marcus: No, but neither does it make it wrong.

Lucius: Then it is beside the point that defense advocates always do it?

Marcus: I suppose. But since the prosecution's evidence frequently suggests the defendant's guilt, yet not so powerfully as to persuade beyond a reasonable doubt, I shall continue to make the argument in every case.

Lucius: Your task is to persuade?

Marcus: Yes.

Lucius: To persuade whom?

Marcus: The jury.

Lucius: To do what?

Marcus: To acquit.

Lucius: You believe that the argument of reasonable doubt will persuade the jury to acquit?

Marcus: It may.

Lucius: But if it were to your client's advantage not to make the argument?

Marcus: Then it would be my duty not to make the argument.

Lucius: So it follows that we should decide whether to argue reasonable doubt, rather than do it unthinkingly in every case.

Marcus: Yes.

Lucius: Is it not true that in many cases the defendant has some affirmative facts to be argued on his own behalf?

Marcus: Yes.

Lucius: Those are cases in which the defendant says, "I am innocent," are they not?

Marcus: Yes.

Lucius: Let us call them "defense cases."

Marcus: Agreed.

Lucius: Is it not also true that in other cases the defendant has no such defense?

Marcus: Yes.

Lucius: Those are cases in which the defendant says, "They can't prove I'm guilty," are they not?

Marcus: Yes.

## No Defense Cases

Lucius: Let us call them "no-defense cases."

Marcus: Agreed.

Lucius: Then we have separated defense cases from no-defense cases?

Marcus: Yes.

Lucius: But now I will inquire whether the separation signifies that the two kinds of cases must be treated differently.

Marcus: I am ready.

Lucius: Shall we start with defense cases?

Marcus: Agreed.

Lucius: Who presents the other side?

Marcus: The prosecutor.

Lucius: His task?

Marcus: To persuade the jury that the defendant is guilty.

Lucius: Meaning?

Marcus: That the defendant did indeed commit the crime alleged in the indictment.

Lucius: Who presents the defendant's side?

Marcus: I do.

Lucius: Your task?

Marcus: To persuade the jury to acquit.

Lucius: Meaning?

Marcus: That the defendant is innocent.

Lucius: In what respect.

Marcus: That he lacked guilty knowledge, for example, or that someone else committed the crime.

Lucius: In brief, the prosecutor argues guilt and you argue innocence.

Marcus: Yes.

Lucius: Who chooses between the two arguments?

Marcus: The jury.

Lucius: If they choose your argument?

Marcus: Acquittal.

Lucius: Is the jury's only choice between the prosecutor's argument and yours?

Marcus: Assuming that the jury does not deadlock, it is.

Lucius: But is there not a third possibility?

Marcus: No.

Lucius: Consider. If the jury's verdict is guilty, they have been persuaded by the prosecutor?

Marcus: Yes.

Lucius: "We agree with the prosecutor," say the jurors?

Marcus: Yes.

Lucius: "The prosecutor wins," the jurors declare?

Marcus: Yes.

Lucius: And if the jury's verdict is innocent, they have been persuaded by you?

Marcus: Yes.

Lucius: "We agree with Marcus," say the jurors?

Marcus: Yes.

Lucius: "Marcus wins," the jurors declare?

Marcus: Yes.

Lucius: As between the prosecutor and Marcus, the jury has chosen?

Marcus: Yes.

Lucius: The prosecutor over Marcus?

Marcus: Or better, Marcus over the prosecutor.

Lucius: As between two lawyers, each of whom performs well, how is the jury to make a decent choice?

Marcus: I don't know.

Lucius: The jury would not be inclined to favor one?

Marcus: No, because that would dishonor the other.

Lucius: And the jury would not be inclined to favor the other?

Marcus: No, because that would dishonor the one.

Lucius: Were you a juror pressed to decide, what would you do?

Marcus: Choose both.

Lucius: Call each the winner?

Marcus: Yes.

Lucius: Find some middle ground upon which the jurors need not declare a victor and a loser?

Marcus: Yes.

Lucius: Then between the prosecutor and Marcus, the jury will want to choose both?

Marcus: Yes.

Lucius: Call each the winner?

Marcus: Yes.

Lucius: Find some middle ground?

Marcus: Yes.

Lucius: So the question is whether there is such a middle ground?

Marcus: Yes.

Lucius: What of reasonable doubt, the defense you said is given to all your clients by the law?

Marcus: How is it a middle ground?

Lucius: We agree that a verdict of guilty is a finding there is no reasonable doubt?

Marcus: By definition.

Lucius: And a finding of innocence is the other extreme?

Marcus: Of course.

Lucius: But when the jury is not certain of guilt, they must acquit?

Marcus: Yes, because of reasonable doubt.

Lucius: Then reasonable doubt . . .

Marcus: Is neither guilt nor innocence.

Lucius: Might a jury be inclined to take this middle ground?

Marcus: That is what I have been trying to explain to you.

Lucius: And when the jury takes the middle ground of reasonable doubt, what must the verdict be?

Marcus: Not guilty.

Lucius: Neither guilty nor innocent?

Marcus: Exactly. Not guilty.

Lucius: But a verdict quite acceptable to you?

Marcus: Quite.

Lucius: You recall that we have been speaking of defense cases?

Marcus: Yes.

Lucius: You don't still say that you will argue reasonable doubt in every defense case?

Marcus: I do.

Lucius: Should you make the argument, the jurors will perceive that you want them to decide the case on reasonable doubt.

Marcus: Yes.

Lucius: Then for the jury to decide the case on reasonable doubt is to decide in your favor?

Marcus: Yes.

Lucius: To declare you the victor?

Marcus: Yes.

Lucius: Did you not tell me that the jury would rather not choose one lawyer over the other?

Marcus: I did.

Lucius: If you argue reasonable doubt where will the middle ground be?

Marcus: There will be no middle ground.

Lucius: Because you have made it your argument?

Marcus: Yes.

Lucius: Will anyone else argue reasonable doubt for you?

Marcus: Who?


## Judge Will Say So

Lucius: Will the judge in his instruction tell the jury about reasonable doubt?

Marcus: Of course.

Lucius: Hence the jury will know that there is a middle ground between you and the prosecutor?

Marcus: Yes.

Lucius: And the source of the jury's knowledge will be the judge?

Marcus: Yes.

Lucius: Who is a neutral umpire between prosecution and defense?

Marcus: Presumably.

Lucius: Which emphasizes the nature of reasonable doubt as a middle ground?

Marcus: Yes.

Lucius: And which makes it even more appealing as a compromise?

Marcus: Yes.

Lucius: Then in defense cases what will you argue?

Marcus: The defense.

Lucius: And what will you refrain from arguing?

Marcus: Reasonable doubt.

Lucius: In order . . .?

Marcus: To preserve reasonable doubt as a middle ground for the jury.

Lucius: But in a no-defense case?

Marcus: There will be no defense to argue.

Lucius: Your sole argument will be?

Marcus: That the prosecutor cannot prove the defendant's guilt.

Lucius: In short?

Marcus: The argument of reasonable doubt.

## A Summing Up

Lucius: Would you sum up for me?

Marcus: Gladly. In defense cases, an astute defense advocate will argue the defense, not reasonable doubt, hence improving the possibility that the jury will acquit on the ground of reasonable doubt. In no-defense cases, reasonable doubt will need to be argued.

Lucius: Are you an astute defense advocate?

Marcus: Does not this conversation prove that I am?

Lucius: Are you astute enough to be able to find another defense in most of your cases?

Marcus: Assuming scrupulous adherence to the rules of evidence and to proper standards of professional responsibility?

Lucius: Yes.

Marcus: Yes.

Lucius: Then in most of your cases will you argue reasonable doubt?

Marcus: No.

Lucius: Did you argue it in this case?

Marcus: I fear I blundered in this case.

Lucius: Not necessarily. The jury may understand juries better than you or I do.

Marcus: An excellent saying, my interrogative friend. Let us go in to hear the verdict.

Lucius: Why not?

# Table of References to Federal Rules of Evidence

# Index

# O

# S

Scientific evidence
  Expert testimony, 104-05
  Hearsay rule exception for government records, 103-04
  Judicial notice, role of, 95
  Prerequisites to admissibility, 93-94
    Proof of scientific basis, 94, 96-102
Steuer, Max, 163-66
Summation
  Criminal case, 341-50
  Cross-examination, relationship to, 290, 300
  Future, focus on, 338-39
  Preparation, 289-90
  Principles of preparation and delivery, 384-36
  Topics eligible for discussion, 333-34

# T

Theater, trial as, 42, 63, 114-16, 170
Trial, functions of, 4-5
  Model of reality, 4
Trial memorandum, 54-57, 176
Trial notebook, 178-80
Trial, planning for, 289-90
  Ending on affirmative note, 182
  Props, 177-79
  Supporting characters, 180-82
  Theme, 175-77
Trustworthiness, projection of, 7-8
  Opening statement, 75, 77
  Plain English, 67
  Summation, 335
*Voir dire,* 41